Joel Benjamin

American Grandmaster

FOUR DECADES OF CHESS ADVENTURES

EVERYMAN CHESS

Gloucester Publishers plc   www.everymanchess.com

First published in 2007 by Gloucester Publishers plc (formerly Everyman Publishers plc), Northburgh House, 10 Northburgh Street, London EC1V 0AT

British Library Cataloguing-in-Publication Data
A catalogue record for this book is available from the British Library.

ISBN: 978 1 85744 5527

Distributed in North America by The Globe Pequot Press, P.O Box 480, 246 Goose Lane, Guilford, CT 06437-0480.

All other sales enquiries should be directed to Everyman Chess, Northburgh House, 10 Northburgh Street, London EC1V 0AT
tel: 020 7253 7887 fax: 020 7490 3708
email: info@everymanchess.com; website: www.everymanchess.com

EVERYMAN CHESS SERIES (formerly Cadogan Chess)
Chief advisor: Byron Jacobs
Commissioning editor: John Emms
Assistant editor: Richard Palliser

Typeset and edited by First Rank Publishing, Brighton.
Cover design by Horatio Monteverde.
Printed and bound in the UK by Clays, Bungay, Suffolk.

Contents

Acknowledgments

As a personal story, this book has special meaning for me. I have to thank John Emms for not only letting me write it, but actually suggesting it in the first place.

A chess career is nothing without the company of fellow travelers. Thanks for the memories to my grandmaster colleagues, John Fedorowicz, Michael Wilder, Larry Christiansen, Nick DeFirmian, Yasser Seirawan, and Michael Rohde. They made the journey worthwhile.

I wouldn't be in the teaching business now if not for my good friends John MacArthur and Sophia Rohde.

Deborah Quinn Benjamin came into my life very late in my playing career. I can't help feeling some results from the past would have come out differently if I had known her love and support at the time. Thanks to Debbie, I can enjoy the present and future more than a dozen U.S. Championship titles.

My parents, Phyllis and Alan, knew how to support my chess endeavors without trying to control them. My father didn't live to see the recent chapters of my life, but his presence will always be felt. I dedicate this book to his memory.

Introduction

Hi, my name is Joel. I'm a forty-three year-old Pisces. I like sports, crossword puzzles, nature programs, and controlled mating attacks. Welcome to my story.

In the past, when this book was purely hypothetical, I thought a lot about what to include. The games tell much of the story; put in the context of the tournaments, they reveal not only my best accomplishments but also my ups and downs, my dreams fulfilled and my hopes dashed. I have sprinkled in a number of my favorite anecdotes (the ones I can tell in the name of decency) and capsule summaries of several of my colleagues. People and places made the games worth playing. I hope that I have conveyed the excitement, intensity, frustration, disappointment, and joy of being an American chess professional.

It gives me great pleasure (and hopefully some for the readers, too) to recount the "what it was like then", but the "what it is like now" impacts the future of chess in America. In the last section I have described various problems that confront the current American chess scene. I don't claim to have easy solutions, but bringing the issues to the forefront may help us move in the right direction.

Chapter One

In the Beginning

In 1972, Phyllis Benjamin needed an activity for her fifth grade club. All the obvious choices had been taken, so her husband, Alan, suggested chess. Her principal liked the idea, leading to, after many twists and turns, a scholastic chess revolution. It also put P.S. 222 on Bill Goichberg's mailing list. One boy from the club wanted to play in the Greater New York Elementary Championship. More significantly, Phyllis took the flyer home and found her son eager to try his luck in a tournament.

I had learned to play earlier that year, probably from my big brother Steven (that's the family consensus, though I don't remember the moment). My parents were good casual players, and my older sister Rochelle played a little, too (years later she would accidentally play the first six moves of an Alekhine Defense).

I was enthralled by the greatest chess event to date, the Fischer-Spassky match. That summer I watched the match coverage on television and got hooked on chess. I was only a third-grader in the fall, at eight-years-old too young for my school's new chess club. But I wasn't too young for Goichberg's tournament

That event, held in December at the old McAlpin Hotel in Manhattan, marked the beginning of the "Fischer Boom". Parents now viewed chess as a positive activity for their children, and it showed in the attendance. More than 1000 kids, most of them with no tournament experience, produced a zoo-like atmosphere.

I played in the Lower Elementary (third grade and below) section. It was divided into prelims and finals. The rounds of the prelims were unscheduled—you just found someone in your group and played. In my very first game I took advantage of a little girl (heavens no!) who was not prepared for the four-move checkmate. I collected the pieces so fast she wasn't convinced I had won, but a spectator confirmed the mate.

I ended up with a 6-3 score and earned a pocket chess set for my efforts. One year later I was back again to try my luck in the Upper Elementary section. Why the long layoff?

My membership entitled me to receive *Chess Life & Review*, but I don't remember reading it. My uncle, Marty Merado, was a strong tournament player (he holds the record for most consecutive U.S. Open appearances). For some reason we didn't ask him about tournaments. So I managed to stay blissfully unaware of any other competitions.

I did a point better my second time around. My 7-2 score won me my first chess trophy. I was psyched to come back in December 1974.

That probably would have been my next tournament, if not for a chance conversation my mother had with another chess mom. "Is Joel playing at Chess Nuts next month?" the woman asked. My mother had two questions spring to mind: One, "what is 'Chess Nuts'?" (a small club in Queens) and two, "There are other tournaments?" I played in Chess Nuts and took my initial first place trophy with a perfect score. I was off and running.

Chapter Two

Second Coming...of Bobby?

In 1974, school chess programs were virtually non-existent in America (in fact, my mother's program at P.S. 222 was one of the earliest significant ones in the country). Most kids from that era (especially in the Northeast) owe a debt of gratitude to Bill Goichberg's Continental Chess Association (CCA). Over the next few years I nourished my chess cravings on a steady diet of CCA Under-13 and Pre-HS tournaments, as well as the occasional adult open event.

Today Goichberg is known for organizing large open tournaments. But back then he was obsessed with junior chess. He calculated his own rating system and published lists of the top players in each grade. I was thrilled to see my name in the CCA fourth grade list, and stunned to see the rating of the top seventh grader. Lewis Cohen was listed at 2000—it had to be a misprint! Could a rating really start with a two?

Every kid with a decent rating made Goichberg's radar. When he held a competition for the top scholastic players in the metropolitan area, I got an invitation.

There were fewer chess teachers then, and they had a difficult time connecting with potential students. A group called U.S. Chess Masters offered free trial lessons to the kids at the tournament. I had never heard of chess lessons, but when the master showed me how I could have better handled my opponent's Danish Gambit, I was awfully impressed.

Bruce Pandolfini, twenty years from immortality in the film *Searching for Bobby Fischer*, apparently liked what he saw from me. He passed me along with a glowing recommendation to the teacher in the group most adept at working with young children, George Kane. [Years later Pandolfini gave me the note, which praised my parents and stated "Goichberg swears by him".]

Pale and scrawny with long hair, Kane had a spooky appearance but a soothing manner with children. My father, who sat in on the occasional lesson, admired the improvement in my vocabulary (George taught me big words like "motif"). But I learned a whole lot of strategy, too, enough to rise to (USCF) 1600 in the first year and expert level (2000) by the end of 1975. When Kane left for California, I worked with IM Julio Kaplan (former World Junior Champion from Puerto Rico) for a year until he also shipped off to California. A third U.S. Chess Master, IM Sal Matera took me on next...and decided to stay in New York. Matera would take me through the successes of my teen years.

I steadily dominated scholastic and youth events, winning not only Greater New York titles but the inaugural National Elementary Championship in 1976. [Goichberg ran that, too; the USCF did not take possession of the Nationals for several years.] In the spring of 1975 the venerable Manhattan Chess Club began to host a series of events called Young Junior Invitationals. After winning several of these events, I graduated to directing them.

My rating was only among the top players when I won the first Young Junior. I was still pretty much unknown, but club President Moses Mitchell, on the suggestion of club Manager Jeff Kastner, offered me a free membership. That day changed my life, for my long-lasting association with the Manhattan brought me great pleasure and knowledge.

I think it was at the Manhattan C.C. where I first heard people speak of me as the "second Fischer". The label did produce some backlash—one old lady said I was "not worthy of licking Fischer's boots"—but most people were very supportive. But when you think of the prodigious exploits we routinely see from today's chess children, you might wonder why people made so much fuss about me so soon.

First you must consider that we were only a few years removed from Fischer's Championship at the time. More than thirty years later now, we tend to view Fischer's amazing accomplishment as an anomaly we aren't likely to see repeated. But then, anything was possible, if we could just identify the prodigy to replace him. After Fischer forfeited his title and seemed unlikely to return, the search intensified.

Secondly, the world chess community was much smaller and weaker in those days. Many of today's prodigy producing countries like China and India were barely involved in chess then. Azerbaijan and Ukraine were stifled within the Soviet Union, which let few players play abroad. Before databases and the Internet, we knew very little about what was going on in the rest of the world.

Thirdly, Fischer's achievements seemed less daunting thanks to a reachable record he possessed. Fischer set the record for youngest USCF master (2200) at age thirteen. That record had stood for two decades, so people could not foresee that it would be absolutely shattered in the years to come.

The number 2200 is really quite arbitrary for a landmark. Fischer did not truly come into his own until fourteen and fifteen, when he earned the international master and grandmaster titles, respectively. Master to grandmaster in two years is just phenomenal, unlikely to be duplicated by any other American player.

In 1976 Goichberg organized a round-robin international at the Manhattan Chess Club. Such tournaments were few and far between; many players coveted spots in the field. Young players like Michael Rohde, Ron Henley, and Mark Diesen had already established themselves, but the two youngest invitees ignited controversy. Michael Wilder, at thirteen the youngest master since Fischer, and yours truly, age twelve and 2100, took quite a few lumps in the tournament. I managed my first win over an IM (Canadian Bruce Amos) and draws with Rohde and Edmar Mednis. Wilder beat me and finished slightly better.

GM Bill Lombardy publicly criticized our participation in the tournament. I don't know if the search for another Fischer should justify this kind of "affirmative action". But I do know that the experience from my first international helped me to score better the next time around. I scored 50% in a nine-round futurity to earn a 2300 FIDE rating. [Arpad Elo tried to nix that rating as well as the ratings of several other "overrated" Americans.] In my next international, I beat my first GM (Heikki Westerinen) as well as Soltis, Valvo, and Fedorowicz.

So it bugged me when Lombardy claimed that the punishment we received in this tournament would cripple our confidence. No one has ever been ruined by facing strong competition, but plenty of players have failed to develop from not facing strong competition.

The first run towards Fischer's record came in the summer of 1975. I gained about 300 points, 200 coming in the U.S. Open. I scored 6-6 despite being paired up eleven times. Despite still being relatively unknown, I managed to make the front page of the newspaper and play chess with GM Arthur Bisguier on local television (when the Cornhuskers aren't playing, there isn't much going on in Lincoln, Nebraska).

By the end of the year I reached 2000 and broke Fischer's record for youngest USCF expert. The 1975 Atlantic Open provided my first win against a master (Dan Shapiro).

I struggled to make it through the expert class for more than a year. During this time I not only gained valuable experience, but made lifelong friends as well. At the 1976 U.S. Open in Fairfax Virginia I had my first encounters with future GMs John Fedorowicz and Nick DeFirmian. IM Mark Diesen had just returned from a European journey and decided to use me to stir up some trouble. When I was paired with Fedorowicz, Diesen suggested I say something to Fed.

We sat down to play, I looked my older and bigger opponent in the eye and carried out Diesen's instructions. "You're a *wimp*," I said.

Fed was taken aback, but soon got his bearings back. "Well, you're a *wittle kid*."

It was the beginning of a beautiful friendship. Fed crushed me that day, but I retaliated enough subsequently to post a lifetime plus score.

I contested a sharp struggle with DeFirmian in which I dropped a kingside pawn but developed an initiative aimed at his king on the other side. Unable to find a breakthrough, I offered a draw. With his flag hanging, he had no choice but to accept. Our seminal moment of friendship would come two years later (see Chapter 8).

My final push came shortly after my thirteenth birthday. A strong result in the Continental Open in April 1977 brought me to the cusp of 2200. The World Open in July put me over the top. At thirteen and four months, I was the youngest master in USCF history.

Around the time of the World Open I attracted the attention of the producers of an NBC program called "Junior Hall of Fame". I was selected as one of several sports prodigies (the best known by far being tennis star Tracey Austin). The cameras followed me to Philadelphia and filmed the climax of my crucial defeat of veteran Philadelphia player (and future IM) Bruce Rind.

□ **J.Benjamin** ■ **B.Rind**
World Open, Philadelphia 1977

---

1 Nf3 c5 2 e4 Nc6 3 b3 d6 4 Bb5 Bd7 5 0-0 e5 6 c3 Nf6 7 Re1 Be7 8 d4 cxd4 9 cxd4 a6 10 Bxc6 Bxc6 11 Nc3 0-0 12 Bb2 Qa5 13 Qd2 Rfe8 14 Rad1 Rac8 15 h3 h6 16 Nh4 b5?! *(see following diagram)*

After a series of logical developing moves by both sides, the action heats up. Black meets the knight's foray with a counterattack. But objectively, Black should have kept approximate equality with the safer 16...Bd7.

17 Nf5 b4 18 dxe5 dxe5 19 Nd5 Nxd5 20 exd5 Bg5 21 Qd3

I overlooked 21 Qe2! Bb5 (if 21...Bxd5 22 Nd6 wins an exchange comfortably)

22 Qg4 with multiple threats.

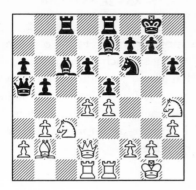

21...Rcd8 22 Qg3 Rxd5 23 h4 Bf6

Not 23...Rxd1 24 Rxd1 Qxa2? 25 hxg5 Qxb2 26 gxh6 g6 27 Qh4 and wins.

24 Nxh6+ Kf8 25 Ng4 Qd8

If 25...Qxa2 26 Rxd5 Bxd5 27 Bxe5 Bxe5 28 Nxe5 Kg8 29 Re3 and Black's unsafe king compensates for his dangerous queenside majority.

26 Rxd5 Qxd5 27 Nxf6 gxf6 28 Qg4 a5 29 Bc1

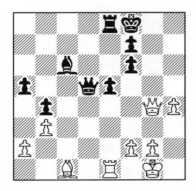

29...Re6??

Short of time, Rind succumbs to an optical illusion. He puts his rook in front of his king to offer protection, but by ceding the back rank, he dooms his king instead. After 29...Rd8 30 Be3 Bd7 I still prefer White slightly. My king is safer, and the h-pawn might become a factor.

30 Bh6+ Ke7 31 Rd1 Qe4 32 Qg8 Bd5 33 f3

The poor black queen is yanked away from the defense of his bishop, leading to a rapid fire finish.

33...Qe2 34 Qf8+ Kd7 35 Rxd5+ Kc6 36 Qc5+ Kb7 37 Rd7+ Ka8 38 Qa7 mate

The crowd drawn by the TV cameras burst into applause, much to the consternation of the masters trying to concentrate on their games. Much to my dismay, the cameraman told Rind that the last few moves happened too quickly for him to follow. Would he mind replaying the finish on camera? I was horrified—imagine asking a basketball player to pretend guarding Michael Jordan while he hits the game winning shot again? To my surprise, Rind agreed—an impressive show of class. I'm not sure I would have managed to do the same.

Chapter Three

Junior Days

Old School

While many of my "civilian" friends had to take on part-time jobs, I jump started my college fund with earnings from scholastic championships. Today the USCF runs very successful National Scholastics, with thousands of kids competing for trophies while their parents shell out big bucks in expenses. In the 70's and early 80's, Goichberg ran these nationals and provided powerful incentives for the best players to participate. By topping a field I outrated by 500 points, I earned $400 in the National Elementary. The Junior High School Title, only slightly more diffi-cult, reeled in $500. That left me with three years to shoot for the National High School title and its $1000 bonanza.

I jumped out to the lead in 1979 with seven wins. When I gave up draws in the last two rounds, Jim Rizzitano caught me and sent the title up for tiebreaks. Hav-ing led the whole way and faced the strongest competition, I expected to come out on top. Unfortunately, one of my defeated rivals decided to drop his last few games on purpose. My tiebreaks were torpedoed and I had to settle for sec-ond...though the money was still split.

Under current rules, two players who tie for first would be considered co-champions. Unfortunately, the USCF does not recognize this as a title for me and has always listed me as a two-time High School Champion.

In the next two years I managed to avoid the dreaded tiebreak, triumphing over worthy rivals in Wilder and Maxim Dlugy. I played on a competitive team for the first time in 1981. With assistance from master Simon Yelsky, my James Madison High team came within a whisker of first, but Boston Latin, led by San-deep Joshi, edged us out. We developed a sudden reputation as a Brooklyn chess school. Two strong Russians, Stan Rosenfeld and future U.S. Junior Champion Jon

Litvinchuk, walked into the school and asked to attend. The faculty chess advisor—my father, Alan Benjamin—was only too happy to facilitate their transfer. Naturally, the year after my graduation Madison won the title.

For an educator, my father was quite a good player, reaching into the 1700s at his peak. The old Madison teams served as a model for the future powerhouses at Edward R. Murrow, profiled in Michael Weinreb's *The Kings of New York*. Their faculty advisor, Eliot Weiss, started as a teacher trainee with my mother at P.S. 222. It's a small world.

Ready for the Big Kids

The rosters of the U.S. Junior Championships of the mid to late 70's boasted historic names, including Larry Christiansen, Fedorowicz, DeFirmian, Diesen, Rohde, Ron Henley, and Jon Tisdall. All these players became GMs except for Diesen, who won the World Junior Championship. But they had all reached their twentieth birthday before my first appearance in 1979.

The most significant holdover was Yasser Seirawan. Despite his heavy favorite status, Seirawan struggled with losses in his first two games. Our own encounter surpassed all my expectations. At 19, Yasser was four years older and more established. His strategical prowess was already well known. If he had one Achilles heel, it was susceptibility to the occasional mating attack. So I knew the best chance to beat Yasser was to throw the kitchen sink at him.

As with many of the old games, this one loses a bit of its luster when *Fritz* is brought in for an analytical consult. Still, I've very proud of this game, which remains my favorite to this day.

□ **J.Benjamin** ■ **Y.Seirawan**
U.S. Junior Championship 1979

---

1 e4 e6 2 d4 d5 3 Nd2 Nf6 4 e5 Nfd7 5 Bd3 c5 6 c3 Nc6 7 Ngf3 cxd4 8 cxd4 Nb6

This is typical of Yasser's inclination to avoid tactical lines in the opening. The standard 8...Qb6 9 0-0 Nxd4 10 Nxd4 Qxd4 11 Nf3 produces a pawn sacrifice that I've enjoyed for much of my career.

9 0-0 Bd7 10 Re1

My move is a bit inaccurate, allowing Black to activate his bad bishop. Theory prefers 10 a3 a5 11 b3.

10...Nb4 11 Bb1 Bb5 12 Nf1 Be7 13 Ng3 a5

This looks like a case of the wrong rook pawn. 13...h5 would keep my knight from reaching a dangerous post.

14 Nh5 Kf8 15 h4!

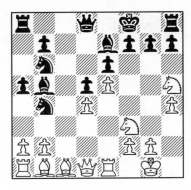

15...h6

Yasser sensibly prevents Ng5 or Bg5. 15...Bxh4? 16 Nxh4 Qxh4 17 g3 Qe7 18 Qg4 leaves the king defenseless.

16 Nh2 g6

16...Bxh4 is still dangerous, for instance 17 Qg4 g6 18 Bxg6 fxg6 19 Qxg6 Bxf2+ 20 Kxf2 Qh4+ 21 Kf3 and White crashes through.

17 Nf4 Ke8!

Clever defense by Yasser. He sees his king is doomed on the kingside, so he makes a run for it to greener pastures.

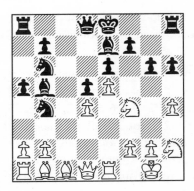

18 Qg4 Kd7 19 Nf3

19 Bxg6 is unconvincing after 19...Rg8! (if memory serves me, Yasser intended to play it safe with 19...Qg8 20 Bb1 Qxg4 21 Nxg4 Bxh4 which also seems reason-

able) 20 h5 Nc6 (or 20...Nc2 21 Bxc2 Rxg4 22 Nxg4) 21 Nf3 Kc8.

19...Qg8 20 Bd2 Rc8 21 a3 Nc6 22 Rc1?

At the time, this seemed like a logical move. I was focused on keeping the black king from escaping to the queenside, and Yasser was just as intent to get it there. *Fritz* points out Black can now go on the offensive with 22...g5! with advantage in all cases.

22...Rc7? 23 Ba2 Kd8

24 Rxc6!?

This exchange sacrifice is a bit speculative, but seems to offer sufficient compensation in all cases. Of course, I wasn't going to pass up this chance to go hacking away.

24...bxc6?

Yasser wanted to close the c-file and support the d5-pawn against possible sacrifices. But he gives White an extra tempo to crack open lines for the attack. The other capture, 24...Rxc6, was obligatory. Then 25 Bxa5 with two main possibilities:

a) 25...g5, and here I turned back *Fritz*'s attempt to ruin my game: 26 Nxd5 (26 Bxd5 exd5 27 Nxd5 might be more forcing) 26...exd5 27 Bxd5 f5 (this is a *Fritz*-like move that Yasser might not have noticed; if 27...Kc7 28 Bxc6 bxc6 29 d5 cxd5 30 Qd4 Qg6 31 e6 wins) 28 exf6! Qxd5 29 fxe7+ Kxe7 (probably Black has to play 29...Kc7 30 Qg3+ Kc8 31 Ne5, but then after grabbing the rook on c6, White will actually be ahead in material) 30 Re1+ Kd8 (30...Kd6 31 Re5 Qc4 32 Qf5 wins) 31 Ne5 Rd6 (if 31...Rf6 32 hxg5, or 31...Re8 32 hxg5! with an overwhelming initiative) 32 Rc1 leaves Black with no adequate defense to the threat of a rook invasion.

b) 25...Ke8 26 Bxb6 Rxb6 27 Bxd5 g5! (not 27...exd5? 28 Qc8+ Bd8 29 Nxd5 Bd7 30 Qa8 Rc6 31 Nf6+ Rxf6 32 exf6 and wins) 28 Nh5 exd5 29 Qc8+ Bd8 30 Nf6+ Rxf6 31 exf6 Bd7 32 Re1+ Be6 33 h5 Rh7 34 Qxb7 Bxf6 35 Qa8+ Bd8 36 g4! and Black is so tied up that White appears to be winning. Unfortunately, 28...gxh4! is a major improvement, and Black seems to defend after 29 Qh3 Qg6.

25 Bxa5 Rb7 26 a4 Ba6

26...Bxa4? 27 Bb1 drops a piece, while on 26...Bc4 I intended 27 b3 Ba6 28 b4 transposing into the game.

27 b4

This crushes Black's hopes, leaving him with no way to keep the position from ripping open.

27...Qe8

27...Ke8 is a better try, but 28 b5 cxb5 29 Bxd5! (not 29 axb5 Bxb5 30 Bxd5 Ra7!) 29...exd5 30 axb5 Bxb5 31 Bxb6 Rxb6 32 Ra8+ Bd8 33 Qc8+ is winning. Now I get to decide the game with a flourish.

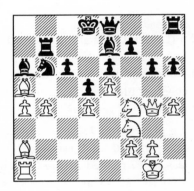

28 b5 cxb5 29 Nxe6+! fxe6 30 Qxe6 Qd7 31 Bxb6+ Kc8 32 Bxd5 Qxe6 33 Bxe6+ Kb8 34 axb5 Bxb5

34...Rxb6 35 Rxa6 wouldn't give Black much chance against the onslaught of White's pawn majority.

35 Bd5 1-0

Yasser Seirawan

More than just a great player, Yasser achieved respect and accolades for his work away from the board. He published (and wrote, for the most part) the excellent magazine Inside Chess; *he attempted to reunite the World Championship and create a more professional chess environment; he found a multi-year sponsor for the U.S. Championship. Yasser's accomplishments — World Championship Candidate, four-time U.S. Champion, and U.S. Chess Hall of Famer — might have been even greater if he had more of an appetite for chess study. He liked to live well, and he tried to make things better for other players.*

Yasser's positional style was rather unique among his colleagues. Yasser rarely played in open tournaments, so our meetings were generally confined to the national championship. Because our games were so infrequent and our styles so different, I enjoyed these confrontations immensely.

I could not keep up the spectacular level. Still, 4-3 and equal second with Sergey Kudrin and Perry Youngworth seemed okay for my first time out. Seirawan stormed back to take first and went on to win the World Junior that year. But he had to survive a losing position against Youngworth, who by all rights should have had that World Junior spot. How history would have changed!

Ready for the World

I had a good consolation prize in the World Cadet (Under-17) Championship. The current World Youth system, with under 8, 10, 12, 14, 16 and 18 sections, would not exist for another decade. In those days the Cadet and the Junior (under 20) were the only international competitions. The USCF could not pay a fee for a coach, but Jeff Kastner agreed to second me for a free trip to France.

Belfort 1979 had no shortage of talent, but young players had far fewer international opportunities back then. Only a handful of players had FIDE ratings, so the pairings were done randomly! Thus it came to pass that I played future GMs Johann Hjartarson and Pia Cramling in the first two rounds. They were already known to be strong juniors; I was proud to beat them both.

□ **J.Benjamin** ■ **P.Cramling**
World Cadet Championship, Belfort 1979

---

1 d4 Nf6 2 Nf3 e6 3 c4 b6 4 Bf4 Bb7 5 e3 Be7 6 h3 0-0 7 Bd3 d5 8 0-0 c5 9 Nc3 Nc6 10 a3 dxc4 11 Bxc4 cxd4 12 exd4 Rc8 13 Ba2 Re8 14 Qd3 Bf8 15 Rad1 Ne7 16 Be5 Ned5 17 Ng5 g6 18 Qf3 *(see following diagram)* **18...Qd7? 19 Bxd5 1-0**

In the fourth round I ran into a stern-looking buzz-saw from the Soviet Union who wiped me off the board. The superior Soviet youth model won all his games with grim determination. Kastner tried to stare him down but could make no impact. He seemed unstoppable...until he started to change midway through the event. He joined our football games and even started to smile. And that opened the door for other players to win the Cadet. So Jaan Ehlvest didn't win, but he did later become a strong grandmaster...and an American!

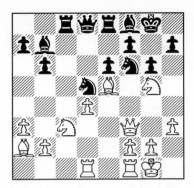

I piled up enough wins to claw my way to the lead with two rounds to go. Alas, I lost to Ivan Morovic (Chile) and Nigel Short in the last two rounds. Short tied for first but lost the tiebreak to an unheralded Argentinian, Marcelo Tempone.

Kastner proved to be an excellent second. While the other players waited every day for the bus to the tournament, we were chauffeured in a private car, thanks to Jeff's friendship with the lovely translator Francoise. Players themselves had few social opportunities; girls championships were played separately from boys in my junior days. Thus Pia Cramling especially stood out in the crowd and brought un-expected pleasure to one opponent. One opponent came out of the hall with a big smile on his face. We were surprised to hear that he had lost. Then why was he smiling? "I got to play footsy with her," he told us.

I was favored in the 1980 U.S. Junior, but I needed good fortune much like Seira-wan the year before. I found myself a half-point behind the rail-thin Californian Doug Root going into the last round. I needed to beat Root to win the title and go to the World Junior. Though I stood better at adjournment, I could find little hope for a breakthrough. I resolved to maneuver about and test my opponent as best as I could. But upon resumption I struck gold right away.

□ **J.Benjamin** ■ **D.Root**
U.S. Junior Championship 1980

1 e4 e6 2 d4 d5 3 Nd2 Nf6 4 e5 Nfd7 5 Bd3 c5 6 c3 b6 7 f4 Ba6 8 Bxa6 Nxa6 9 Ndf3 Nc7 10 Ne2 h5 11 Be3 c4 12 0-0 Be7 13 Qe1 b5 14 g3 Nb6 15 h3 Qd7 16 Ng5 a5 17 g4 hxg4 18 hxg4 f6 19 Nf3 0-0-0 20 Kg2 Qe8 21 Qb1 Qg8 22 Ng3 Qh7 23 Rh1 Qxb1 24 Raxb1 b4 25 Bd2 b3 26 Ra1 Rxh1 27 Kxh1 Rh8+ 28 Kg2 a4 29 a3

29...Nd7 30 Re1 fxe5 31 fxe5 Kd8 32 Rf1 Ke8 33 Nh5 Rg8 34 Kg3 g6 35 Nf4 Kf7 36 Nh3?

36 Ng5+ Bxg5 37 Nxd5+ Kg7 38 Nxc7 Bxd2 39 Nxe6+ and 40 Rh1+ wins.

36...Kg7 37 Bg5 Re8 38 Kh4 Bxg5+ 39 Nfxg5 Re7 40 Rf2 Nf8 41 Rf3 Ne8 42 Nf4 Nc7 43 Rh3 Rd7 44 Kg3 Kg8 45 Rh6 (sealed move)

45...Kg7 46 Rh1 Kg8 47 Nf3 Rh7 48 Nh3 Nb5 49 Nh4 Rd7 50 Ng5 Nc7 51 Rf1 Ne8 52 Rxf8+ Kxf8 53 Nxg6+ Kg8 54 Nxe6 Nc7 55 Nxc7 Rxc7 56 Nf4 Rd7 57 g5 Rh7 58 Nxd5 Kf7 59 Ne3 Rh5 60 Nxc4 Rxg5+ 61 Kf4 Rg2 62 Ke4 Ke6 63 d5+ Kd7 64 Kd4 Rg3 65 Kc5 Kc7 66 e6 Rh3 67 d6+ Kd8 68 Ne5 Rxc3+ 69 bxc3 b2 70 Nc6+ Kc8 71 d7+ Kb7 72 d8Q b1Q 73 Qb8+ Ka6 74 Qa7 mate

I had a busy summer in 1980, with the Cadet in Le Havre, France, and the Junior in Dortmund, Germany, a week later. A few players joined me in double duty. In the Cadet I drew with the Chinese player Rongguang (I was surprised that anyone from China could play that well; things have certainly changed). The next week he was Mr. Ye, such is the confusion with Chinese names.

The contest for first place came down to Valery Salov and Alon Greenfeld. I could not catch them but I decided the winner with my defeat of Greenfeld in the last round. It felt strange beating the Israeli player to give the Soviet the title, but it had to be done. I finished third.

At the U.S. Junior I made a pact with my best friend, Michael Wilder, that the winner would bring the other to the Worlds as his second. Everyone thought I might not be in the best hands with an eighteen-year-old second, and on the way to Dortmund I realized they had a point. When the train rolled over the German border and the border guards came to check passports, Michael could not find his. "You cannot enter Germany without a passport," the guard told him. I thought we were in a bad movie.

So we had to leave the train in Aachen. Or rather Michael did; I just questioned whether I would see him again if I didn't go with him. Michael arranged for temporary papers, but we still had to catch another train. After waiting for hours, we met some nice people in the station. When their train pulled in, we said our good-byes. Only after the train departed did we realize that it was our train, too! We spent the night in the station, mostly playing dozens of games of Scottish chess to kill time.

My games in Dortmund were mostly forgettable. I lost yet again to Short and barely mustered a plus score. But I still had a great time because I had a front row seat for the Kasparov show. We all knew he was the class of the field, but the games really showed him to be a man among boys. I only wish that I could have gotten close enough to be paired with him. I had to be satisfied with facing the great one in blitz. Remember, we're back in the Soviet days. Kasparov was already great but he wasn't rich yet. He didn't mind taking a little hard currency from the other teenagers.

I guess I should be honored that Kasparov refused to give me 5-2 time odds. We played a few games at 5-3. I lost two or three and drew one, as far as I can remember. I've never been so nervous playing blitz!

My junior career continued again in 1982. The 1981 U.S. Junior was smartly scheduled against the U.S. Championship. That not only meant no Junior title for me, it meant I couldn't go to the World Junior that year as well.

Dlugy provided my main competition but I pulled ahead by winning our individual game. I remember South Bend 1982 more for weird vibes than for the games. Animosity developed between Russian-born and American-born players. I remember Vadim Genfan burning a twenty-dollar bill to prove some kind of long-forgotten point.

Midway through I beat a talented master named Bill Adam. Later he lost his will to compete. In the penultimate round he decided to allow the Fool's Mate. The director "excused" him from the last round. Adam was the same player who dumped his last few games in the 1981 National High School. Talented but troubled, he would be found dead under mysterious circumstances while I was at the World Junior.

I didn't know who to get to be my second in Copenhagen. We didn't have lots of grandmasters to choose from like we do now. I eventually tracked down John Fedorowicz in Florida. By the end of the tournament we were the best of friends, and we have worked together a lot since.

The trip got off to a rocky start. No one came to meet us when we landed in Copenhagen, and we didn't know where the tournament was. "I think it's someplace that starts with an H," he said. He walked over to a map and found a place that seemed to qualify. There were about fifteen places that started with an "H". Still, we hopped on a train and went to this mysterious place. The front desk asked us if we were the missing swimmers. "No, we're the missing chessplayers," Fed told them. By some miracle, we were in the right place.

John Fedorowicz

Close friends for more than twenty-five years, Fed and I have shared a lot of experiences over the years. In his youth he was often called "Rocky" for his resemblance to Sylvester Stallone. John's casual dress, Bronx accent, and frank manner of speaking have made him an icon in the chess world.

Now known mostly for coaching and teaching, Fed's successful playing career includes a run through a Soviet gauntlet for first in the 1989 New York Open. He is likely the strongest American-born player never to win the U.S. Championship, missing by an eyelash in 1987.

Years ago, John matriculated at the French Culinary Institute in New York. Lacking the manual dexterity to "tournage" (basically turning a potato into a football), he called it quits after six days. Looking over the manuscript, I notice that Fed makes an appearance in most of the amusing anecdotes. He is like a brother to me, even though he roots for all the wrong sports teams.

In the first round I played a player from Greece I was not familiar with. My opponent handled the Bayonet King's Indian a bit strangely for Black, but somewhere things went wrong for me and I lost. We sat down for the post-mortem and my opponent proclaimed "I am an expert in the King's Indian."

That player, Efstratios Grivas, went on to become a respectable grandmaster. But that game illustrates a hard lesson we learned from these tournaments. Everyone is the best player in their country; even if no one else takes them seriously, they have enough confidence to make themselves dangerous.

We didn't know the Soviet representative either. Andrei Sokolov would make a name for himself later in the decade. He beat me and several other players as well, clinching first place before the last round.

I made a run on the strength of a massive score with Black. One day Fed had to go into town to resolve his plane ticket. So I had to prepare for Alon Greenfeld on my own. In honor of my second, I chose the Polish—1 Nf3 b5!?.

☐ **A.Greenfeld** ■ **J.Benjamin**
World Junior Ch., Copenhagen 1982

---

1 Nf3 b5 2 e4 Bb7 3 Bxb5 Bxe4 4 0-0 Nf6 5 d4 e6 6 Nc3 Bb7 7 Qe2 Be7 8 Re1 0-0 9 Bd3 d6 10 Ng5 Nbd7 11 Bf4 c5 12 Nb5 Qb6 13 Rad1 a6 14 dxc5 Qc6 15 Be4 Nxe4 16 Nd4 Nc3 17 Qg4 Qxg2+ 18 Qxg2 Bxg2 19 bxc3 Bd5 20 cxd6 Bxg5 21 Bxg5 f6 22 Bh4 Kf7

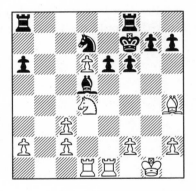

23 Nf5 Bxa2 24 Ra1 Bc4 25 Ne7 e5 26 Bg3 g5 27 h4 g4 28 Re3 Rfb8 29 Ra4 Be6 30 f4 gxf3 31 Rxf3 Rb6 32 Nf5 Bxf5 33 Rxf5 Rxd6 34 Ra5 Ke6 35 Rf3 Rc8 36 Rd3 Rxd3 37 cxd3 Rxc3 38 Rxa6+ Kf5 0-1

In the last round I played too recklessly against Stohl and lost, enabling him to leapfrog me for second. I couldn't catch Sokolov, so I should have played to keep the draw in hand. The impetuousness of youth! My third loss of the tournament with White dropped me into third place. I still finished ahead of future GMs like Short, Morovic, Curt Hansen, and Hjartarson.

I finished my junior career in the 1983 U.S. Junior at the Manhattan Chess Club. I knew Dlugy would be my main competition. The pairings killed the climax as we battled to a draw in the first round. I suffered a shock defeat at the hands of Jonathan Yedidia, but Dlugy dropped games to David Glueck and fourteen-year-old Patrick Wolff. I went into the last round with a half-point lead.

I need a win over David Griego to clinch first, but ran into big trouble. While Dlugy won his game, I adjourned in a losing position. During the dinner break, Griego was approached by Dlugy's coach, Vitaly Zaltsman. Zaltsman, whose coaching fees were paid by the American Chess Foundation, wanted to analyze the adjournment with him!

Now Griego had plenty of motivation for revenge. I had beaten him in the last round of the National High School twice. But to his credit, he felt Zaltsman's advice wasn't proper. On his own, he didn't play well after resumption and I salvaged a draw and a tie for first.

The rules called for a playoff to determine who would go to the World Junior and get the automatic spot in the 1984 U.S. Championship. I was sure to get a Championship spot on rating, and I intended to play first board in the World Student Team Championship instead of going to another World Junior. So I told Dlugy he could have the perks. I didn't realize the USCF would not recognize us as co-champions—another title we disagree on.

Chapter Four

Bright College Years

In the fall of 1981 I matriculated at Yale University. My course load restricted the number of tournaments I could play in, but I did benefit from having a handy practice partner. My best friend, Michael Wilder, started at Yale the same year. The tons of blitz games we played produced a few ideas that I would work into my games over the years. In our freshman year, we occasionally got senior Michael Rohde to join our sessions.

Wilder was not big on school spirit, but we did get him to play for the team in our junior year. We won the Pan-American Intercollegiate easily, concluding with a 4-0 whitewash of Columbia. Noting that his three teammates had all gone down in defeat (future U.S. Women's Champion Inna Izrailov and NM Greg Delia were our other players), my opponent, Mark Ginsburg, asked me if he could transfer. Then he spoiled a good position and lost, too.

While that event was most directly related to my college years, it isn't the most memorable. That distinction goes to a match that came out of the blue and produced a result I could never have anticipated.

In the fall of 1983 Eric Schiller phoned me about a possible match with Nigel Short. The organizers of the Kasparov-Korchnoi and Smyslov-Ribli Candidates matches in London thought a side match might amuse the spectators, especially if the grandmasters decided to make a quick draw. I loved the challenge of taking on Short and watching those terrific matches.

Unfortunately, I was a bit busy at the time. The match would take me away for more than a week during the semester. I couldn't afford to miss all that work and pass my classes. I could only play this match if I could convince my dean to arrange incompletes for my classes and let me make up the work later. Dean Mary Ramsbottom showed an appreciation for life experiences and granted my request.

In 1983 Nigel and I were two of the highest rated young IMs in the world. We were both rated about 2480. He was objectively closer to the grandmaster title and a slight favorite on paper. While I had been looking forward to the match for weeks, Nigel arrived in London tired from another tournament abroad. Worse yet, he said he didn't know about the match. With me already there, he could hardly decline to go through with it.

Thad Rogers flew out from America for the admittedly unchallenging job of match arbiter. A certain young British arbiter seemed to feel she should have had the assignment. I found Sophia Gorman to be a bit pushy then. In a few years she would be married to Michael Rohde, and years after that would become my boss.

On the first day the headliners finished early, or seemed primed to do so, I can't remember which. Ray Keene rushed into our room (nicknamed the "cupboard") and told us we could not draw and had to play on.

□ **J.Benjamin** ■ **N.Short**
London (match) 1983

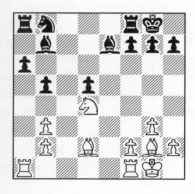

I can't remember if Nigel had offered a draw, but I know I had no intention of taking it. That wasn't what I came across the ocean for! I played **19 Rfc1** and went on to win the game...and three others! The following was the splashiest of them.

□ **J.Benjamin** ■ **N.Short**
London (match) 1983

---

1 e4 e5 2 Nf3 Nc6 3 Bb5 a6 4 Ba4 Nf6 5 0-0 Be7 6 Re1 b5 7 Bb3 d6 8 c3 0-0 9 d4 Bg4 10 d5 Na5 11 Bc2 c6 12 h3

This line was in fashion at the time.

12...Bxf3

12...Bd7 can be met by 13 Nxe5 dxe5 14 d6, but 12...Bc8 13 dxc6 Qc7 is the main alternative.

13 Qxf3 cxd5 14 exd5 Nc4 15 a4

A rarely played move; the main line runs 15 Nd2 Nb6 16 Nf1 Nbxd5 17 Ng3 with compensation for the pawn.

15...g6 16 Bd3 Qd7 17 Qe2 Qb7 18 Rd1 Nb6 19 axb5 axb5 20 Na3 b4 21 cxb4 Rfb8 22 b5 Nbxd5 23 Bg5

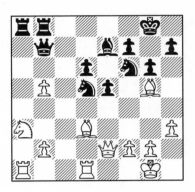

Black will stand well if he can organize his knights and get his center rolling, so I have to work hard to prevent that from happening.

23...Nc7 24 Rac1 Nfd5 25 Bh6 Nb4 26 Bc4 Re8 27 Bxf7+ Kxf7 28 Qc4+ Ncd5 29 Qb3?

29 Bd2 Rec8 30 Qb3 Rxc1 31 Rxc1 Kg7 32 Bxb4 Nf4 33 Rc6 Ne2+ 34 Kh2 Nd4 35 Qc4 Nxc6 36 bxc6 seems to give White good compensation for the exchange. The passed queenside pawns could become quite dangerous. I wanted to threaten 30 Rc6 as well as 30 Bd2, but...

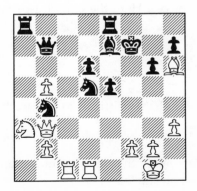

29...g5!

...I totally overlooked this move.

30 h4 Kg6 31 hxg5 Nf4 32 Rc6

There's no choice but to throw another log on the fire.

32...Nxc6 33 Qc2+

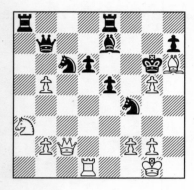

33...Kf7?

The black king is actually safer after 33...Kh5! 34 bxc6 Qc8 35 Qxh7 (or 35 f3 Bxg5 36 Qxh7 Bxh6 37 Rxd6 Re6 38 Qf5+ Bg5 39 Qh7+ Rh6 and Black escapes the checks) 35...Qe6 36 f3 Rh8 and Black will live to enjoy his extra rook.

34 bxc6 Qb4?

The black queen needed to stay in touch with the c6-pawn: 34...Qa6 35 Qxh7+ (35 g3 is quite good except for the strong response 35...Qe2! and Black is fine in the endgame) 35...Ke6 36 g6 Ne2+ 37 Kh1 Qxc6 38 Nc4 puts a complete mess on the board.

35 Qxh7+ Ke6 36 g6

Sometimes pawns can be valuable attacking pieces. Here the c- and g-pawns combine to threaten 37 Qf7 mate.

36...d5

Or 36...Rf8 37 Bxf8 Rxf8 38 g7 and wins.

37 Qf7+ Kd6 38 Bxf4 Qb3

After 38...exf4 39 Qxd5+ Kc7 40 Qd7+ Kb6 41 Rc1 it is difficult to picture the black king surviving for very long.

39 Re1 exf4 40 g7

The pawn advances again with deadly threats. Now the threat to queen and deflect the rook from the defense of the bishop has no suitable answer.

40...Bh4 41 Qxf4+ Kc5 42 Rc1+ Kb6 43 Qxh4

White actually has a material advantage now, so Black has no hope of survival.
43...Ra4 44 Qh6 Ka5 45 c7 Qxb2 46 c8Q Rxc8 47 Rxc8 Rxa3 48 Ra8+ Kb5 49 Rb8+ 1-0

I don't think anyone in either country predicted a 5½-1½ result in my favorite. The British media was a bit taken aback. During the match Leonard Barden phoned my hosts, the King family (as in future GM Daniel King) and asked Mrs. King, "What are you feeding him?"

College probably delayed my grandmaster title for a few years. I came close to a GM norm in an International organized by Goichberg in 1982. I beat two GMs (Shamkovich and Soltis) but I couldn't get the one win I needed in the last two rounds.

The 1981, 1983, and 1984 U.S. Championships were held in the summer and didn't conflict with my studies. When the Championship moved to the fall, I had my B.A. in history in hand and was ready to begin life as a chess professional.

Chapter Five

Iron Man of the U.S. Championship: 1981-1996

Only Walter Browne has played in more U.S. Championships than I have. My total of 23 came consecutively, from 1981-2006. There has certainly been an ebb and flow, but I've produced a lot of good results over this long span of time. Of all my accomplishments in chess, I am most proud of my record in U.S. Championships.

1981 South Bend

I made my first appearance in South Bend 1981. I had to qualify by rating (the Junior Champion was not seeded in zonal years); fortunately DeFirmian and John Grefe declined and opened the door for me. I wanted to make a good showing but worried about being accepted by the older guys. When my parents asked if they could go with me, I told them an emphatic no. "The guys will laugh at me."

I lost a bunch of games and finished ahead of just two players but I took great pride from my wins over Walter Browne, Larry Christiansen, and Boris Kogan.

□ **J.Benjamin** ■ **W.Browne**
U.S. Championship, South Bend 1981

---

1 d4 Nf6 2 Nf3 e6 3 c4 b6 4 a3 c5 5 d5 Ba6

The Benoni treatment of the a3-Queen's Indian was all the rage in the early 80's. A few years later, Browne and I would swap sides in this position.

6 Qc2 exd5 7 cxd5 d6 8 Nc3 g6 9 g3 Bg7 10 Bg2 0-0 11 0-0 Re8 12 Bf4 Nh5 13 Bg5 Qc7 14 Rfe1 Nd7 15 Rac1

This is a bit unusual, but I'm looking towards a future b2-b4 with his queen facing my rook.

15...Rac8 16 a4 Nhf6 17 h3 Ne5 18 Nxe5 Rxe5 19 Qd2 Ree8 20 Bh6

This exchange is not always favorable, as Browne showed me here. After 20...Bh8 I would have been ready to throw my center pawns forward.

20...Bxh6 21 Qxh6 Qe7 22 Qd2 Nd7 23 b3

I'm very careful to keep his knight out—Black threatened ...c5-c4 followed by ...Nc5, but now 23...c4 can be met by 24 b4.

23...Qe5 24 e3 f5 25 f4 Qg7 26 Nd1

26 e4 Qd4+ is unpleasant, but perhaps it was a good moment for 26 g4!? especially since 26...fxg4 27 hxg4 g5 28 Ne4 gxf4 29 exf4 Qxg4 30 Rc3 is too dangerous for Black; while if my pawn gets to g5, it will keep Black's knight out of the game.

26...Nf6 27 Nf2 Rc7 28 e4

I think I saw 28 g4 but it's too late: 28...fxg4 29 hxg4 g5.

28...Rce7!?

Browne displays his usual fearlessness, but 28...fxe4 offers a risk-free edge.

29 e5

This is not bravery; there isn't any choice in the position.

29...dxe5 30 d6 Re6 31 fxe5 Rxe5 32 Rxe5 Rxe5 33 b4

I'm playing "super breakout", trying to penetrate with my rook.

33...Qd7 34 Rd1

The threat of 35 b5 opens the c-file...unfortunately, my rook isn't there any-more.

34...cxb4 35 Qxb4 Re6 36 Qb3!

The pin causes all kinds of problems. Black could hold with the cold-blooded 36...Kf7, but Browne's choice allows White to take over the board.

36...Bc8 37 Rc1 Kf8 38 Rc7 Qd8 39 Qc3 Bd7 40 Rxa7

Not just grabbing a pawn, but forcing Black to open his second rank to avert 41 Ra8.

40...Be8 41 Qc1

41 d7! Nxd7 42 Qh8+ would be a cleaner finish, but I thought the threat of 42 Qh6+ would force resignation; e.g. 41...Kg8 42 Qh6 Bd7 (or 42...Nd7 43 Bd5) 43 Ra8 Bc8 44 Bb7.

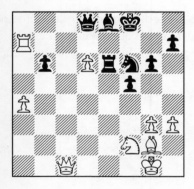

41...g5! 42 Qxg5 Re1+ 43 Bf1

Unfortunately forced, as 43 Kh2?? Ng4+ drops the queen.

43...Bf7 44 Qd2 Re5 45 Bg2

Renewing the massive threat of pinning his queen to his king. Still, Browne fights on.

45...Ra5 46 Rxa5 bxa5 47 Qd4 Bd5 48 Qe5 Bxg2 49 Kxg2 Kg8 50 Qe6+ Kg7 51 Qxf5 Qxd6 52 Qxa5

I thought my immature technical game should be sufficient with a two pawn advantage.

52...Qc6+ 53 Kh2 Kg6 54 Qb4 Qd5 55 Qc3 Kf7 56 Qc7+ Kg6 57 Qc3 Qa2 58 Qd4 h5 59 Kg2 Kf7 60 Kg1 1-0

I've just been dithering for the last few moves to make it to adjournment again. It seems strange that Browne, who had fought so gamely to hang on, would resign here. One has to know the context which doesn't show in the game score. By the time adjournment day rolled around, Browne had another suspended game. He decided to ditch the bad one and concentrate on winning the good one against Shamkovich (he succeeded).

The Kogan game provided much entertainment:

___

□ B.Kogan ■ J.Benjamin
U.S. Championship, South Bend 1981

___

36...Qxe3! 37 Rdd2 Bc6??

Here 37...Bxg2! 38 Rxg2 Qe1 39 g4 Qe5+ 40 Rg3 Qf4! wins.

38 Rde2 Qh6 39 Rf4??

39 Qe6 stops Black's threats, whereas the text allows 39...Qxh3+!.

39...Bd5?? 40 Qe7??

White can still escape with 40 Rxf6 Bxf7 41 Rxh6+.

40...Qxh3+!

Better late than never. Kogan, who would be a consistent "customer" of mine over the years, could only look to the sky.

41 Kxh3 Rh1 mate

Browne recovered from his loss to me, as well as another upset at the hands of Sergey Kudrin, to tie for first with Yasser Seirawan. When Browne notched the last point against Fedorowicz, he stood up and exclaimed, "Thank the gods."

1981 was a last gasp for many players of a bygone generation. Sammy Reshevsky and Leonid Shamkovich would not return to the field again. Robert Byrne, a fine gentleman and friend to me for years since, would make but one more appearance. Anatoly Lein qualified for a few more in the 80's. Larry Evans played in his last U.S. Championship...sort of. Evans lost his first two games to Byrne and Lein. He then claimed to be too ill to continue. Since he had played less than half his games, the games did not count for the standings. Lein was furious, but Byrne philosophical. "Easy come, easy go," he said. [In South Bend, Byrne said something so funny at dinner that everyone spit up their salads...including Bob!]

The old codgers could be pretty amusing. Reshevsky often used an old-style phrase to propose a draw. When he posed the question "Do you play for a win?", Lein responded with a mixture of anger and confusion: "Should I play for a loss?" An argument ensued and voices were raised, particularly Lein's. A few feet away Shamkovich shook his head in frustration. Mild-mannered and often befuddled, Shamkovich was not prone to angry outbursts. But he had reached his limit. Still looking at his position, Shamkovich spoke in a voice barely above a whisper. "Mr. Lein...shut up!"

1983 Greenville

The USCF could not find funding for the Championship in 1982. They held a low-budget tournament at Thiel College in Greenville, Pa. The players had to bunk in dormitories instead of hotel rooms. Since I was a college student at the time, this didn't perturb me. But Seirawan objected, and in a fight with the USCF that would play out many times, declined his invitation.

By 1983, I was already one of the highest rated players and felt ready to make a splash. I jumped out to the lead with three wins over DeFirmian, Kudrin, and Jay Whitehead. Then Roman Dzindzichashvili sent me crashing back down to earth. The assistant arbiter made a crack about me being "crushed like a chicken", which the media naturally seized on in a rare chess report.

With Browne in the last round, I had a chance to impact the title. I was proud of the fighting draw that left Browne tied with Christiansen and Dzindzi for top honors. After this success Browne decided he wanted to be referred to as "Six-Time Champion Walter Browne". It was propitious timing, as Walter never needed to change the appellation, and was nicknamed "Six-time" for years.

In the end I managed +1 and a tie for fifth place. I particularly liked my win over 1981 U.S. Junior Champion Whitehead, because my speculative sacrifice shows the confidence I felt at the time.

___

□ **J.Whitehead** ■ **J.Benjamin**
U.S. Championship, Greenville 1983

___

1 d4 Nf6 2 c4 c5 3 d5 b5 4 Nd2

One of those anti-Benko systems that enjoyed its fifteen minutes of fame.

4...d6 5 e4 bxc4 6 Bxc4 g6 7 b3 Bg7 8 Bb2 0-0 9 Ngf3 e5!? 10 dxe6 fxe6 11 e5?!

This doesn't really make sense because Black can pin. 11 0-0 Nc6 is roughly equal.

11...Nh5?!

11...Ng4 12 h3 Nh6 13 Qc2 d5 gives Black a comfortable edge.

12 Qc2 d5 13 Bd3 Nd7 14 g3 Bb7 15 0-0 Rc8 16 Rac1

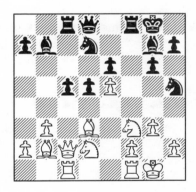

16...Nf4!!?

I can only marvel at the optimism of my past self. Black will get only a pawn for a piece, but White's position is tricky to play.

17 gxf4 Rxf4 18 Rfe1 Qf8! 19 Qd1 Bh6 20 h3

White has no time to reposition his bishop: 20 Bf1 d4 21 Bg2 Rg4 22 h3 Rxg2+ and wins.

20...Rf7

With the bishop uncovered, White still can't reorganize.

21 Qe2 Qe7 22 Rc2

Byrne pointed out an interesting regrouping: 22 Nf1!? Rcf8 23 N1h2, since if now 23...Bxc1 24 Bxc1 White gains control of squares on the kingside.

22...Rcf8 23 Nh2?

Whitehead finally loses his patience. After 23 Rf1 Black's attack is still held at bay.

23...Rxf2 24 Qxf2 Rxf2 25 Kxf2 Qh4+

The white pieces have no footholds. It's just a matter of time before Black picks one off.

26 Ke2 Qxh3 27 Nhf3 d4 28 Rf1

Not 28 Be4? Bxe4 29 Nxe4 d3+.

28...Qg4 29 Nc4 Bf4 30 Rf2 Bg3 31 Rf1 Bxe5 32 Ncd2 Bf4 33 Rg1 Qh5 34 Be4?

But 34 Ne4 Kg7 would win in due time.

34...Bxe4 35 Nxe4 d3+ 0-1

1984 Berkeley

Berkeley 1984 was a giant eighteen-player round-robin zonal. Kamran Shirazi's historic futility—one draw and sixteen losses—certainly stood out. With point money for the lower places, his haul of $37.50 could easily be spent in one place (and he was suspected to have lost lots more than that gambling during the event).

While Shirazi's five-move loss to Peters (1 e4 c5 2 b4 cxb4 3 a3 d5 4 exd5 Qxd5 5 axb4?? Qe5+ 0-1) grabbed attention, the players most appreciated the comedic value of the following game. White stumbles on move six and digs a deeper grave with each move as he tries to hold on to everything.

☐ **K.Shirazi** ■ **J.Benjamin**

U.S. Championship, Berkeley 1984

1 d4 Nf6 2 c4 e6 3 Nf3 b6 4 g3 Ba6 5 b3 Bb4+ 6 Nbd2 Bc3 7 Rb1 Bb7 8 Bb2 Ne4 9 Rg1 Qf6 10 Bc1 Nc6 11 e3 Nb4 12 Rb2

At this point Dzindzi and Christiansen were cackling so hard they had to leave the room. Dzindzi offered a clever prediction: "Next move he will play Rg2, fianchettoing the other rook!"

As pleasant as Shirazi's immobility is, I cash it in for an exchange and two pawns.

12...c5 13 Be2 cxd4 14 exd4 Nxf2 15 Kxf2 Bxd4+ 16 Kg2 Bxb2 17 a3 Bxc1 18 Qxc1 Na6 19 b4 0-0 20 Bd3 Rac8 21 Qb1 h6 22 Bh7+ Kh8 23 Be4 d5 24 cxd5 Bxd5 25 Bxd5 exd5 26 Qd3 Nc7 27 Rf1 Ne6 28 Qxd5 Rfd8 29 Qe4 Ng5 30 Qb1 Qc6 31 Qe1 Rd3 32 h4 Re8 33 Qxe8+ Qxe8 34 hxg5 hxg5 35 Rf2 f6 36 g4 Qe6 37 Nh2 Rxa3 0-1

Lev Alburt scored 12½-4½ to win the first of three titles, while DeFirmian took second with 11-6. Their results turned out to be successful auditions for the Olympic team. I had been higher rated than both of them, but they leapfrogged ahead of me for the Olympic team (see Chapter 17 for more about that).

Maxim Dlugy won a playoff over Tarjan and Fedorowicz for the last Interzonal spot. My score was quite respectable, but seeing a younger player finish ahead of me provided a shock to my system. I was determined to garner a top place in 1985.

1985 Estes Park

The Championship moved to Estes Park, Colorado for the next three years. The inspiration for Stephen King's horror classic *The Shining*, the Stanley Hotel proved especially hospitable for me. Shortly before the 1985 Championship, FIDE changed the rules to permit title norms in national championships (they had not counted before because all the players are from the same federation). I had been close to GM norms while in college. With my studies no longer a distraction, I became obsessed with the title. Getting to the magic +5 score meant more to me than my final standing.

The field contained a few players that I circled as guys I wanted to beat. I took down Vince McCambridge, Shirazi, Kudrin, and Dmitry Gurevich without a loss. In the penultimate round I targeted Junior champ Patrick Wolff for termination, but could only draw.

In other years I might have been on the way to first place, but Lev Alburt was defending his title with great gusto. I had the last chance to catch him, but my priorities as they were, I took a quick draw. Solidly in second place, the norm would be mine if I could defeat six-time champ Walter Browne.

□ W.Browne ■ J.Benjamin
U.S. Championship, Estes Park 1985

---

1 d4 Nf6 2 c4 e6 3 Nf3 b6 4 a3 c5 5 d5 Ba6 6 Qc2 exd5 7 cxd5 g6 8 Nc3 Bg7 9 g3 0-0 10 Bg2 d6 11 0-0 Re8 12 Re1

12 Bf4 was my choice against Browne in South Bend, but 12...Qe7 13 Re1 Nbd7 would transpose to the game.

12...Nbd7 13 Bf4 Qe7 14 h3

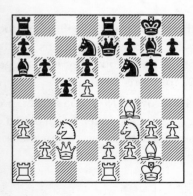

Subsequently White tried 14 e4 in a few games, but after 14...Ng4 Black lands a knight on e5, where it ogles the juicy d3-square.

14...Ne4!

This prepared novelty forced White players to abandon this move order.

15 Nxe4 Qxe4 16 Qd2 Nf6

In two later games Black retreated with 16...Qe7, but it doesn't appear necessary.

17 Rad1

Black is okay after 17 Bxd6 Rad8 18 Ng5 Qd4 19 Qxd4 cxd4 20 Bc7 Rd7 21 d6 h6 22 Nf3 Ne4, and more than okay after 17 Ne5? dxe5 18 Bxe4 Nxe4.

17...Rad8 18 Nh2 Qc4 19 Bg5 Rc8

Not 19...Rxe2? 20 Rxe2 Qxe2 21 Ng4!.

20 Bxf6

Otherwise Black's second knight would jump to e4.

20...Bxf6 21 Ng4 Bg7 22 e4 Qa4 23 Qf4

White would love to swap the dark-squared bishop, but 23 Nh6+ Kf8 24 Qf4 Qd7 does not get the job done.

23...Be2!

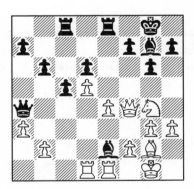

I like this move, trading White's only active piece. Even though 23...f5 24 Nh6+ Bxh6 25 Qxh6 fxe4 26 h4 may be good for Black, it's too messy for my taste.

24 Rd2 Bxg4 25 hxg4 Be5 26 Qe3 c4 27 Rc1 Rc5

White has stopped ...c4-c3, but Black finds a new idea.

28 Rdc2 Qb3! 29 Rxc4?

Retreating the queen was the only option. Browne obviously didn't relish sitting around while the black queenside pawns plow ahead.

29...Qxe3

It may be tempting to take two rooks for the queen with 29...Rxc4 30 Qxb3 Rxc1+, but by exchanging queens and shattering White's pawn structure, Black wins the ending easily.

30 fxe3 Bxb2 31 Rxc5 bxc5 32 Rb1 Bxa3 33 Ra1 Bb2 34 Rxa7 Be5 35 Kf2 c4 36 Bf1 c3 37 Bd3 Rb8 38 Ra2 Rb2+!

Normally it is wrong for the superior side to exchange rooks with opposite-colored bishops, but here it can be worked out to the end.

39 Rxb2 cxb2 0-1

White overstepped while playing 40 g5. The winning plan involves making passed pawns on both wings 40...f6 41 gxf6 Kf7 etc. White would also lose without 40 g5—Black's king march to support the b-pawn would draw White's king out, whereupon Black eats the g3-pawn and pushes his h-pawn.

1986 Estes Park

In 1986, my ultimate goal was not to win, but this time to qualify for the 1987 Interzonals. 1985 had gone almost according to script, but 1986 dealt me stinging losses. I could hardly believe I lost to Shirazi, who had always been a punching bag for me (about twenty-five wins to two losses lifetime). Losing to Lein, already an elder statesman then, hurt a lot, too. But I strung together enough wins to tie for second. I had a nice queenless attack against Kogan, a long endgame win over Rohde, a quick counterattack against Gurevich, and a successful novelty against DeFirmian. I turned the tide against Lev Alburt, who had taken our first six decisions. From this time on, I beat Alburt with consistency.

I could share any of those games, but the luckiest of my wins was in many ways the most interesting. Maxim Dlugy had been my rival since our junior days, and the rivalry stayed strong into our professional careers. Max was an excellent defender and counter puncher. I would typically come out swinging, attack unsoundly, and find myself in a lost position with my flag hanging. Max would then get excited, blitz his moves out wildly and hang things. I lost my share of games to Dlugy, but my own time pressure was a shockingly effective weapon for me.

□ **J.Benjamin** ■ **M.Dlugy**

U.S. Championship, Estes Park 1986

---

1 d4 d5 2 c4 dxc4 3 Nf3 a6 4 e3 Nf6 5 Bxc4 e6 6 0-0 c5 7 a4 Nc6 8 Qe2 Qc7 9 Nc3 Be7 10 Rd1 0-0 11 b3 Rd8 12 Bb2 Nb4 13 dxc5 Bd7 14 e4 Bc6 15 Rd6 Nd7 16 Nd5?!

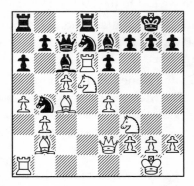

This looked tempting but there's no follow-up.

16...exd5 17 exd5 Bxd6 18 cxd6 Qxd6 19 dxc6 bxc6 20 Nh4 Qf4 21 g3 Qg5 22 f4 Qc5+ 23 Kh1 Nd5 24 Nf5 N7f6 25 Nxg7

More fuel for the fire.

25...Kxg7 26 Qh5 Qe7 27 Qg5+ Kf8 28 Be5

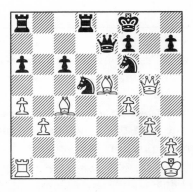

Now 28...Rd6 or 28...Ne8 would preserve a winning advantage.

28...Ne4?? 29 Qh6+ Ke8 30 Qxc6+

White even has a slight material edge now.

30...Qd7 31 Bxd5 Nf2+ 32 Kg2 Rac8 33 Qxd7+ Rxd7 34 Bc4 Ng4 35 Re1 Rd2+ 36 Kh3 f5?? 37 Bc3+ Kf8 38 Bxd2 Nf2+ 39 Kh4 Ne4 40 Bb4+ 1-0

Dlugy's failure to improve on his promising Championship debut may have contributed to his early departure from the game in the next decade.

We found a comfortable place to watch my beloved New York Mets battle the Red Sox in the World Series. With two outs in the bottom of the tenth in game six, I turned to Fed and shook my head. "I can't believe we lost to the Red Sox," I said.

"It ain't over," the wise man replied. Of course, a few batters and one ground ball through Buckner's legs later, the Mets had staved off elimination. [Bronx-born Fed now hates the Mets as much as I despise the Yankees.]

Christiansen refused to join us at Lonnigan's for game seven, preferring the solitude of the "Mountain Man" establishment. "The Mets are going to win, and I can't stand the thought of you guys jumping up and down," he told us.

1987 Estes Park

With the Szirak Interzonal already behind me, I focused on winning the title in 1987. I was as bulletproof as in 1985, but wins were especially hard to come by. Coming down the stretch, I waited in the wings at +1, with only a win over Gurevich. This tournament certainly did not go according to plan. The path to the title went through the top rated tournament leaders, beginning with Yasser.

☐ **Y.Seirawan** ■ **J.Benjamin**
U.S. Championship, Estes Park 1987

---

1 d4 Nf6 2 c4 e6 3 g3 Bb4+ 4 Bd2 Qe7 5 Nc3 Bxc3

"Joel doesn't understand timing in chess," wrote Yasser in his then fledgling magazine, *Inside Chess*. I think the many dozens of times this maneuver has subsequently been carried out in tournament practice suggests my understanding has been underestimated. The reasoning is thus: The b4-bishop is "doomed" to exchanging itself for a knight; if Black waits for White to castle, he will have to play against the bishop pair. My exchanging combination prevents that situation from occurring.

6 Bxc3 Ne4 7 Qc2 Nxc3 8 Qxc3 0-0 9 Bg2 d6 10 Nf3 Re8

10...e5? 11 dxe5 Re8 12 0-0-0! is clearly better for White; but 10...Nc6 would transpose to more common Bogo-Indian positions.

11 Rd1 Nd7 12 0-0 e5

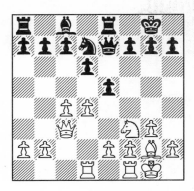

13 Rfe1

Yasser opts for a sophisticated plan, but the more routine 13 e4 Nf6 14 Nh4 gives White a slight edge.

13...e4 14 Nd2 Nf6 15 Nf1 d5! 16 Ne3 Be6 17 f4 Rad8

The text keeps a more complex position; otherwise I could be equal with 17...exf3 18 exf3 Qd7.

18 f5!? Bc8 19 c5 h5 20 Rf1 b6! 21 Rc1 Ba6 22 Qd2 Rb8 23 b3 c6 24 Rc2 bxc5 25 Rxc5 Qd6

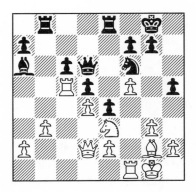

I'm not too concerned about the c6-pawn or the weak c5-square, because his knight is so far away from occupying it. Plus I like my queen on d6, eyeing his king.

26 Rfc1 Rb6 27 Qe1 Nd7 28 R5c2 Qh6 29 Qf2 Bb7 30 Rc3

The knight is not really happy on e3, but its removal is a delicate matter, as the kingside could become vulnerable. Yasser probably didn't want to allow 30 Nd1 e3!?.

30...a5! 31 Nf1 a4 32 e3 Ra8?

I spoil everything with one careless move! I had to exchange on b3 right away, with an excellent position.

33 Nd2

Now White is better, as his knight finally finds green pastures.

33...Qd6 34 Bf1 Nf6 35 h3!? Bc8 36 bxa4 Rxa4 37 Nb3 Ra3

Getting out of the way of Nb3-c5, but also setting a cunning trap.

38 Nc5? Rxc3 39 Rxc3 Bxf5!

40 Qxf5??

In Yasser's terminology, this move is a major "howler". White's passed a-pawn can still offer drawing chances in the endgame. 40 Qf4? Qxf4 41 gxf4 Rb1 and wins is out, but 40 Rb3 would keep the fight going.

40...Qxg3+ 41 Kh1 Rb2! 0-1

Yasser missed that 42 Qf4 does not prevent Rh2 mate.

In the next round I took down the new leader, Gulko, and moved into a tie for first with DeFirmian. In the last round I had to face Christiansen with Black while Nick took on Wilder. They drew rather quickly and both repaired to the bar for an early celebration. Larry was mired in the middle of the pack, but was still determined to win. After a moderate struggle, we agreed to a draw anyway. Fed had a chance to make it a threesome with a win over Browne, but Walter defended in his usual tenacious manner and held a draw.

Nick's victory began a trend that happened with surprising frequency in U.S. Championships. He went from worst in '86 to first in '87. Nick had begun a transition into a more solid, professional style where time pressure no longer crippled his results. He went on to an impressive record in U.S. Championships.

I had broken through for my first U.S. title at age 23. Given my three-year success in Estes Park and age advantage on my rivals, I could be forgiven for thinking future titles would come in bunches. But a lot of changes were brewing. The first was engendered by a night of overly enthusiastic celebration on the last night leading to changes in the status of various relationships. While I am happy to share stories, those events will have to "stay in Estes Park". I'll just report that a guest of one of the players caused damage to the hotel that led to our eviction from the idyllic mountain town.

New contenders from abroad would emerge to challenge my core group of friends for supremacy. We would not play alongside the Women's Championship again until 1995. And I was headed for a slump in this tournament that lasted (excepting '91 and '94) for ten years.

1988 Cambridge Springs

In the midst of one of their recurring financial crises, the USCF reduced the field to ten to cut costs. The scene shifted to historic Cambridge Springs, Pa. Known for the 1904 tournament that produced the eponymous variation in the Queen's Gambit, the old resort town had sunk to depressing standards by 1988. There was nothing to do there, and nobody to watch us play. Conflicts with the German league (Bundesliga) caused Larry Christiansen to miss his first U.S. Championship since I began playing. Larry sure picked the right year to sit out!

I'll never lose the image of Doc Crenshaw operating the demo boards for an empty room. Craig Crenshaw was one of the great friends and fans of the U.S. Championship. For many years he donated prizes for special games in the Championship. After witnessing Diesen drop out in 1980 and Evans in 1981, Dr. Crenshaw proposed switching the order of the pairings to equalize colors should a player have to drop out again (naturally it never happened again). The "Crenshaw System" at least enriched the chess vernacular; dropping out of a tournament became known as "crenshawing".

Early in the tournament, DeFirmian beat Tony Miles with a piece sacrifice in the Pribyl Defense.

☐ **N.De Firmian** ■ **A.Miles**
U.S. Championship, Cambridge Springs 1988

1 e4 d6 2 d4 Nf6 3 Nc3 c6 4 f4 Qa5!? 5 Bd3 e5 6 Nf3 Bg4 7 dxe5 dxe5 8 fxe5 Nfd7 9 Bf4 Bb4 10 0-0 0-0 11 Nd5!? Bc5+? 12 Kh1 Bd4 13 e6! fxe6 14 Bc7 Qa4 15 Ne7+ Kh8

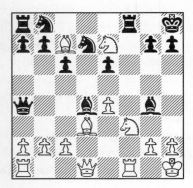

16 Ng5! h5 17 Rxf8+ Nxf8 18 Qf1 Nbd7 19 Qf7 Nf6 20 e5 1-0

Fed, Wilder, and I later made quick draws with each other by imitating the first several moves of that game, sometimes in creative ways:

☐ **J.Benjamin** ■ **M.Wilder**
U.S. Championship, Cambridge Springs 1988

1 f4 c6 2 d4 Qa5+ 3 Nc3 d6 4 e4 Nf6 5 Bd3 e5 6 Nf3 Bg4 7 fxe5 dxe5 8 dxe5 Nfd7 9 Bf4 Bb4 10 0-0 0-0 11 Nd5 cxd5 12 exd5 Be7 ½-½

That may seem silly and unprofessional; I certainly would not repeat the exercise in today's age of live Internet coverage. We were protesting not just the miserable organization but the presence of Miles in the tournament. Frustrated with the British Chess Federation, Miles had decided to switch his nationality for the right conditions. The USCF, prodded by the ACF (American Chess Foundation), invited Miles to the 1988 U.S. Championship. Tony fulfilled his residency requirement with the post office box of the ACF.

What makes a player American enough to play in the U.S. Championship has been a major issue for the last three decades. At times we have had a three-year residency requirement; currently it is one-year. But everyone now agrees genuine residency (citizenship or green card) is essential. What Miles was allowed to do for two years embarrassed our Federation and disrespected our players.

Tony had not gotten his head straight and finished on bottom. Wins proved even tougher to come by than the year before. The winning score shrunk again to +2 for the surprise winner, Michael Wilder. An especially gifted tactician, Mike never had full faith in either his own abilities or the viability of chess as a profession. He closed out a brief three-year Championship stint on top, having already decided to attend law school in the fall of 1989. He never looked back; in the last sixteen years he has played virtually no competitive chess.

Michael Wilder

Mike and I have been buddies since the 1975 Atlantic open where we shared the prize for second in class "A". We both embarked on pro careers after graduating from Yale, but Mike didn't put it all together until his surprise win in the 1988 U.S. Championship. Despite a solid result in the 1989 Haninge International, Mike stuck to his guns and retired from chess in favor of a career in law. He managed to quit cold turkey, too—he has not played a rated game since.

A brilliant combinational player, Mike is also one of the funniest guys I've ever met. Read one of his "Agony" columns and know that he is that entertaining all the time.

1989 Long Beach

Thanks to major sponsorship from Les Crane and his Software Toolworks company, the field was restored to sixteen in another zonal year. Long Beach provided a less depressing backdrop and big city spectators made us feel more at home. Another surprise winner emerged in U.S. Junior Champion Stuart Rachels. A one-time holder of the youngest U.S. master record, Rachels never intended for chess to be a professional career, and this result didn't change his mind. Rachels actually inspired Frank Samford Jr. to endow his annual fellowship for a young outstanding professional.

Seirawan and Dzindzi also tied for first. I had my ups and downs; a horrible blunder against Dlugy nearly wrecked my chances but I managed to finish in a three-way tie for the last two Interzonal spots with Miles and DeFirmian. The next May we got down to settling the tie in a playoff, and I became the odd man out. After losing to Miles in the zonal and the playoff, and watching him take a coveted American slot, you can imagine how bitter I felt. Then the ACF successfully petitioned FIDE for an Interzonal spot for Gata Kamsky, who hadn't even played in the zonal. If the Manila Interzonal had been on TV, I wouldn't have watched.

1990 Jacksonville

Jacksonville 1990 experimented with a sixteen-player knockout. For me it was a relatively short tournament. Christiansen knocked me out in the second round, but I did produce a memorable game from my first round match with Igor Ivanov.

☐ **I.V.Ivanov** ■ **J.Benjamin**

U.S. Championship, Jacksonville 1990

1 c4 g6 2 e4 Bg7 3 d4 d6 4 Nc3 Nf6 5 Be2 0-0 6 Nf3 e5 7 d5 a5 8 0-0 Na6 9 Bg5 h6 10 Bh4 Qe8 11 Ne1

A bit unusual; normally this knight goes to d2.

11...Nc5!? 12 Bxf6!?

On 12 Qc2 Black can employ a common tactic with 12...g5 13 Bg3 Nfxe4 14 Nxe4 Nxe4 15 Qxe4 f5 16 Qc2 f4. Igor was a modern day Chigorin; he liked nothing more than achieving a good knight vs. bad bishop position.

12...Bxf6 13 Bg4 Bxg4 14 Qxg4 Bd8!

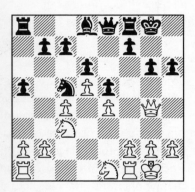

I think this is a rather ingenious solution to the problem of the "bad" bishop. I often use this as a test position for students.

15 Qe2

15 Rd1 Na4! would be awkward for White.

15...c6 16 Rd1 Bc7 17 h4?!

White misses a few chances to block me on the queenside with 17 b3!.

17...Qe7 18 g3 Kg7 19 Nf3?!

White would be better poised for the kingside storm with 19 Ng2.

19...a4 20 h5 Ba5 21 Rc1

Otherwise 21...a3 would sting.

21...Qd7! 22 Rfd1 Rae8 23 Kg2 f5 24 exf5

White has a number of options that are probably preferable to the text:

a) 24 Nh4 Bxc3 25 Rxc3 Nxe4 26 Nxg6 Nxc3 27 Nxf8 Rxf8 28 bxc3 f4 29 Rd3 Kh8 with a slight initiative for Black.

b) 24 hxg6 Bxc3 25 Rxc3 Nxe4 (25...fxe4 26 Nd2 Qf5 27 Re3 cxd5 28 cxd5 Qxg6 29 Nxe4 is nearly equal) 26 Re3 Nf6 with some advantage for Black.

24...Rxf5 25 Ne4 Nxe4 26 Qxe4 Ref8 27 Rd3 Rxh5 28 Nh4

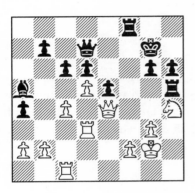

Black cannot rest easily with his extra pawn. White has a pretty good blockade on the light squares.

28...Rxh4! 29 gxh4

Ivanov's recapture is ugly, but the alternative loses by force: 29 Qxh4 Qf5 30 Rdd1 (30 Rcd1 loses a number of ways, one nice method is 30...g5 31 Qh5 Qxf2+ 32 Kh1 Be1) and now:

a) 30...Qxf2+ 31 Kh3 (not 31 Kh1? Qf3+! 32 Kh2 Bd8 33 Qh3 Qe2+ 34 Kh1 Rf5 35 g4 Rf3 and wins) 31...Bd8 32 Qg4 is not completely convincing, as 32...Rf5 is met by 33 Rf1.

b) 30...Bd8! 31 Qh3 Qxf2+ 32 Kh1 Qf3+ 33 Qg2 Qh5+ 34 Qh2 Qg4 35 Rf1 (if 35 dxc6 Rf5 36 cxb7 Qf3+! 37 Qg2 Rh5+ 38 Kg1 Bb6+ 39 c5 Bxc5+ wins) 35...Rxf1+ 36 Rxf1 Qxc4 37 Qh3 (or 37 Qf2 Qxd5+ 38 Kh2 Be7) 37...Qxd5+ 38 Kh2 Qd2+ 39 Kh1 Qg5 40 Qe6 Qe7 and Black wins with his mass of extra pawns.

29...Rf4 30 Qe2 Qf5 31 c5

With a time scramble approaching, Ivanov makes a bid to complicate. 31 Rg3 Bb6 32 Rf1 cxd5 33 cxd5 Rxh4 would mean eventual death.

31...cxd5 32 cxd6 Bb6 33 Rf1 e4 34 Rg3 d4 35 Qd2 e3 36 Qe1 Qd5+ 37 Kh3?

37...Qe6+?

Remember, this game was played in the days of analog clocks and no time delay or increment. When you had a winning position with your flag hanging, you made the time control first and looked for brilliancies later. Still, I took a lot of flak for missing a mate in two: 37...Rxh4+! 38 Kxh4 Qh5 mate was the right way to end the game.

38 Kg2 Qd5+ 39 f3

Not giving me a second chance!

39...Qxd6 0-1

White overstepped in this hopeless position.

Lev Alburt had struggled since his back-to-back titles in '84 and '85, but swept through to a surprising first place finish. Just when the natives had taken measure of his Alekhine's Defense, Alburt mastered his opponents with the totally unexpected Pirc Defense.

GM Alexander Chernin came to Jacksonville to give a well-paid but very poorly attended simul. Somehow, his six or seven opponents stressed him so much that he decided to sit out the U.S. Open. Instead he spent his days teaching Alburt the finer points of Chernin's favorite defense.

Christiansen took an unexpected pounding in the final. Nick DeFirmian, Alburt's victim in the semi-finals, had a string of eight U.S. Championships in a row, but took the next three years off to work in the financial industry. This coincidentally removed another competitor for my consecutive streak.

1991 Los Angeles

The Los Angeles airport area hosted the first U.S. Championship covered by *Chess Chow*. Now sixteen and top-rated, Gata Kamsky fulfilled expectations and cleaned out his side of the bracket.

I won my first match against Dzindzi cleanly and sweated out a marathon against Seirawan. Eventually I just closed him out in the blitz overtime.

☐ **J.Benjamin** ■ **Y.Seirawan**

U.S. Championship, Los Angeles 1991

White is clearly on top, but my clock was very low indeed. After **27...Qb4? 28 Qc1!** only catastrophic material shedding can delay checkmate.

I defeated Gulko's Sicilian to move smoothly into a final match with Kamsky that could have been a classic. Unfortunately, you cannot separate the chess from the atmosphere of paranoia and intimidation created by Gata's father Rustam. A large and threatening individual, Rustam employed strong-arm tactics to aid his son's cause. During the Fedorowicz-Kamsky semi-final match, Rustam noticed Fed brushed past DeFirmian and went ballistic, insisting they had discussed the game.

Rustam's approach could be unorthodox. He would occasionally pay people to follow "suspicious" individuals. Fortunately, the venerable Doc Crenshaw took it in stride when a Kamsky flunky followed him to the bathroom.

In the first of the four-game match, Kamsky surprised me with the Marshall Attack and obtained a crushing position. I battled back to a drawish endgame but saw my position go gradually downhill.

I equalized with a convincing win in game two:

□ **G.Kamsky** ■ **J.Benjamin**

U.S. Championship, Los Angeles 1991

1 d4 Nf6 2 Nf3 g6 3 Bf4 Bg7 4 e3 d6 5 h3 c5 6 c3 cxd4 7 exd4 0-0 8 Be2 Be6

Kamsky had often employed the London System, so I had the opportunity to prepare a good plan against it. Black's plan is based on similar play by Korchnoi with colors reversed.

9 0-0 Qb6 10 Qc1 Nc6 11 Re1 Rac8 12 Na3 Bd5 13 Nc2 Be4 14 Bd1 Rfe8 15 Ng5 Bd5 16 Bf3?

Kamsky didn't want to retreat for nothing, but 16 Nf3 was the lesser evil.

16...e5 17 dxe5 dxe5 18 Be3 Qc7 19 Bxd5 Nxd5 20 Rd1 Rcd8 21 Nf3 e4 22 Nfe1

Or 22 Nfd4 Ne5, heading for the d3-square.

22...Ne5 23 Bh6?

Kamsky tries to ease his cramp by exchanging, but misses a tactical point.

23...Nxc3!

Played with an audible thud.

24 Rxd8

No more hope rested in 24 bxc3 Rxd1 25 Qxd1 Bxh6.

24...Ne2+ 25 Kh1

Kamsky avoids the suicidal 25 Kf1 Rxd8 26 Kxe2? Qc4+.

25...Rxd8 26 Qe3 Bxh6 27 Qxh6 Qb6 28 Ne3

28 Qe3 Qxe3 29 Nxe3 Rd2 leaves Black dominating in the ending.

28...Qxb2

28...Qf6 was also tempting, but I didn't like 29 Rd1, so I opted for greed.

29 N1c2 Nd3 30 Qh4 Rd6! 31 Rf1 Qf6

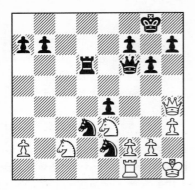

Forcing an endgame with two extra pawns. I don't let up until the end.

32 Qxf6 Rxf6 33 Ng4 Rc6 34 Nge3 f5 35 g3 g5! 36 Na3 f4 37 gxf4 gxf4 38 Nd5 Kf7 39 Nb5 a6 40 Na7 Rh6 41 Kh2 Rh5! 42 Nb6 f3 43 Nc4 Ndf4 0-1

I had to bring myself down from euphoria to prepare for the next game. I didn't want another Marshall Attack (I haven't allowed one since), so I got Ilya Gurevich to teach me the Exchange Variation. The Exchange became a staple weapon for me for the next few years, but I did not receive a proper reward my first time out.

☐ **J.Benjamin** ■ **G.Kamsky**
U.S. Championship, Los Angeles 1991

---

1 e4 e5 2 Nf3 Nc6 3 Bb5 a6 4 Bxc6 dxc6 5 0-0 Qd6 6 d3 Ne7 7 Be3 Ng6 8 Nbd2 c5 9 Nc4 Qe6 10 Ng5 Qf6 11 Qh5 Bd6 12 f4! exf4 13 e5

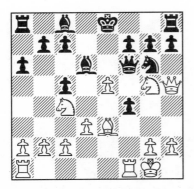

13...Nxe5

This is pretty much forced, since 13...Bxe5 14 Nxe5 Qxe5 15 Bxf4 Nxf4 16 Qxf7+ Kd8 17 Qxf4 is virtually winning for White.

14 Bxf4

I had to wade through some tempting candidates. 14 Nxe5 is also advantageous but Black has a number of options for resistance. 14...g6 15 Qh4 Qxe5 16 Bxf4 Qd4+ 17 Kh1 Be6 18 c3! offers White a big initiative. Black should perhaps settle for 14...Bxe5 15 Nxf7! 0-0 16 Nxe5 g6 17 Nxg6 Qxg6 18 Qxg6+ hxg6 19 Bxf4 Rf7 20 Be3 with some drawing chances for Black.

My move is riskier but objectively correct. As if the stress of making these decisions wasn't enough, I had to deal with a major disturbance created by Rustam Kamsky. Patrick Wolff stood up and approached the demo board to get a better look at the game. Rustam somehow thought Wolff was trying to send me signals and shouted at him to sit down. After I made my move I hustled to the bathroom, only to find the fracas continuing in the hallway.

Blocking out this distraction was easier said than done. I still feel cheated out of this title.

14...Nxc4

Kamsky played this quickly, surmising that 14...Bg4 15 Qh4 Nxc4 16 Qxg4 Qd4+ 17 Kh1 Ne5 18 Rae1 0-0 19 Rxe5 Bxe5 20 Qf5 g6 21 Qxe5 would offer slim hopes for him

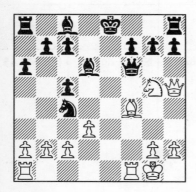

15 Bxd6!!

Nowadays you can be sure that journalists will spot your mistakes when you make them. In the Oct./Nov. 1991 issue of *Chess Chow* that contained the match report, ChessBase advertised "KnightStalker", a forerunner of *Fritz*. Without computer help, annotators often criticized mistakes you *didn't* make.

In *Inside Chess*, GM Lubomir Ftacnik called this "an embarrassing blunder". IM Jack Peters appended "??" in his *Chess Life* article. The text is actually the strongest and most forcing. The alternative 15 Rae1+!? is stronger than I thought at the time; after 15...Be7 16 dxc4 Bf5 I overlooked 17 Be5! with a big advantage for White. Ftacnik suggested 15...Kd7! but missed 16 Bxd6! with a possible transposition to what I missed later.

15...Qd4+ 16 Kh1 Nxd6

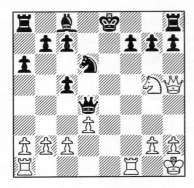

17 Rxf7??

I had no trouble finding the win after 17 Rae1+ Kd8 18 Nxf7+ Nxf7 19 Qxf7 Qd6 (if 19...Qd7 20 Qf8+, or 19...Bd7 20 Qe7+ Kc8 21 Rf8+ wins) 20 Qxg7 Re8 21 Rxe8+ Kxe8 22 Rf7! and mates. [Bizarrely, both Ftacnik and Peters gave Black the win after 17...Kd8.]

But I couldn't crack 17...Kd7 18 Nxf7 Nxf7 19 Qxf7+ Kc6. Only after the game did I learn about the crushing retreat 18 Nf3!!, when Black is busted in all lines, e.g. 18...Qxb2 19 Ne5+ Kd8 20 Qg5+ f6 21 Rxf6+!.

My plan had been 17 Nxf7? Nxf7? 18 Qxf7+ Kd8 19 Rae1 transposing into the main line above. But of course, 17...0-0!! wins easily. So I didn't see what else to do.

17...Qg4!

Even 17...Nxf7 18 Re1+ Kd7 19 Nxf7 Re8! wins for Black, but this move ends the game.

18 Re1+ Kd8 19 Qxg4 Bxg4 20 Rxg7 h6 21 Nh7 Bd7 22 Nf6 Bc6 23 Kg1 Kc8 24 Ree7 Kb8 25 Rxc7 Ne8! 26 Nxe8 Rxe8 27 Kf2 Re6 28 Rce7 Rf6+ 29 Kg3 Ka7 30 Ref7 Rxf7 0-1

I told Gata no one would respect him, no matter how good he got, if his father continued to behave as he did. He didn't seem to understand. In the last game, with Rustam barred from the tournament room (too little, too late), I could muster no offense and agreed a draw in a bad position.

1992 Durango

In 1992 the U.S. Championship abandoned the knockout experiment. The round-robin is an easier format for determining Interzonal qualifiers, but the knockout had been a disappointment to the players anyway. At the time the USCF paid hotel and travel expenses for the players. The USCF didn't have to pay hotel costs for players once they were eliminated. The players had expected the USCF to invest the savings in the prize fund, but somehow an increase never materialized.

The tournament returned to a quiet Colorado mountain town, this time Durango. An autumn blizzard enhanced the lower profile created by the absence of familiar names. Christiansen (Bundesliga responsibilities), DeFirmian (working in finance), Dlugy (embarking on an investment career), and Rohde (law school) joined defending champ Kamsky on the sidelines. In their place a young group consisting of 1989 Champion Rachels, Ilya Gurevich, Wolff, and Alex Sherzer had a shot at the limelight. The best American players to emerge since Wilder, Benjamin and Dlugy, these players accomplished much (only Rachels, who had the shortest career, did not make grandmaster) but did not commit to pro careers.

The battle for first place unexpectedly came down to 23-year-old Wolff and 22-year-old Sherzer. Both players fattened up on the last six players in the cross-table. Going into the last round, Sherzer head a half-point lead but had to face Fedorowicz with White. Fed had some chances for an Interzonal spot; more than that, his pride motivated him to win the game.

I think my colleagues would agree that Wolff was a nice guy, but he had a habit of rubbing people the wrong way. When Dzindzi forgot to hit his clock in the 1989 Championship, Patrick sat on an obvious recapture fifteen minutes. In Durango Patrick offered Ilya a draw in a losing position. So there was a lot of popular sentiment for Alex on that last day.

The Jan-Feb *Chess Chow* cover depicted the position where Sherzer missed his opportunity. Sherzer's loss allowed Wolff to cap off a tremendous result by defeating Boris Men, the tournament enigma. A former Soviet Junior Champion, Men had not played outside of Ohio since his emigration and did not have a FIDE rating. He stunned the crowd by opening with two wins...but lost his last five.

Sherzer's loss dropped him into a tie for second with Gulko. Wolff took his first U.S. Championship with a stellar 10½-4½, a long way from the other end of the tournament. Kamran Shirazi regained his form from 1984. He managed to notch thirteen consecutive goose eggs before drawing his last two (Yermo was fed up while Dmitry clinched an Interzonal spot).

Shirazi created a fair bit of drama on the way to his remarkable score. He lost a completely won position to Wolff in round three. As the tournament wore on he seemed to play with a certain death wish. He achieved inferior but drawable endgames against Sherzer and Gulko. Shirazi mysteriously eschewed threefold repetition and overstepped a few moves later—in both games! One could certainly admire his spirit. Midway through the event Shirazi inquired about the GM norm—though it was already mathematically out of reach for him.

I finished +1 against the field but -4 against the top half. I lost to two kinds of Gurevich. Ilya has always given me fits (and their other "brother" Mikhail for that matter), but Dmitry I would beat sure as the sun would rise in the morning. I had 8-0 (plus draws) against him with wins in the 1984, 1985, 1986, 1987, and 1989 Championships. For that matter, I would lose to him the next year and in 1995 as well.

My game with Alexander Ivanov, which included one of my all-time favorite moves, provided the lone bright spot.

□ A.Ivanov ■ J.Benjamin
U.S. Championship, Durango 1992

---

1 e4 e5 2 Nf3 Nc6 3 Bb5 Nf6 4 Qe2

Ivanov had lost to Sherzer in the Berlin Defense (4 0-0 Nxe4) in the first round, so he protects his center pawn this time.

4...a6 5 Bxc6 dxc6 6 b3 Bd6 7 Bb2 Qe7 8 d3 Bg4 9 Nbd2 Nd7 10 h3 Bh5 11 g4 Bg6 12 d4 0-0-0 13 0-0-0 Rhe8 14 dxe5 Nxe5 15 Ne1 f6 16 Ng2 Bb4 17 Nb1

17...Nf3!!

This just might be my favorite move of my career. The diagram could serve as a kind of Mensa test for chess. This move is hard to find because the knight doesn't take or threaten anything. I found it because the knight going to this square was already on my mind—one move earlier, 17 f3 lost to 17...Bxd2+ 18 Rxd2 Rxd2 19 Kxd2 Nxf3+! 20 Qxf3 Bxe4 21 Qf2 Bxg2 22 Qxg2 Qe3+ 23 Kd1 Rd8+ and mates. The same idea works against 17 f4 as well.

18 a3

Taking the knight is more easily refuted: 18 Qxf3 Bxe4 19 Qg3 Bd6 20 Rxd6 (or 20 f4 Bxg2 21 Qxg2 Bxf4+ 22 Nd2 Rxd2 23 Rxd2 Qe1+ 24 Rxe1 Rxe1 mate) 20...Qxd6 21 f4 Bxg2 22 Qxg2 Qxf4+ 23 Nd2 Re3 with a large advantage for Black. White can hardly move—24 Rf1? Rxd2! 25 Kxd2 Rf3+ 26 Ke1 Qe4+ 27 Qe2 Re3 would conclude the game immediately.

18...Bd6 19 Nc3

Ivanov doesn't find the more testing 19 Rd3, but Black would win anyway: 19...Qxe4 20 Qxf3 Qxf3 21 Rxf3 Re2 22 Ne1 (or 22 Nd2 Be5) 22...Be4 23 Nd2 Bxf3 24 Ndxf3 Bf4+ 25 Kb1 Rd1+ 26 Ka2 Rxf2 with total domination for Black.

19...Bxe4 20 Nxe4 Qxe4 21 Qxe4 Rxe4 22 Rd3 Ng5

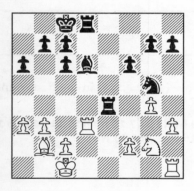

23 h4 Ne6 24 g5 fxg5 25 hxg5 Rg4 26 Ne3 Rxg5 27 Rxh7 Rg1+ 28 Rd1 Rxd1+ 29 Nxd1 Bf4+ 30 Ne3 Bh6 31 Kb1 Ng5 32 Bxg7 Nxh7 33 Bxh6 0-1

White overstepped with seven moves still to go, saving me from exercising my technique.

1993 Long Beach

In 1993 the field was smaller (twelve players) and stronger than ever. Most of the kids were gone, replaced by powerful immigrants. Kamsky returned after a year's absence but could not duplicate his success [Rustam was relatively restrained]. Gregory Kaidanov showed his mettle in his first U.S. Championship, but it was another newcomer, Alexander Shabalov, who tied for first with another dominant entrant of the nineties, Alex Yermolinsky.

Wolff nearly went first to worst, one point out of the cellar. I lost four games and kept Patrick company in the cross-table. Boris Gulko went winless and occupied the cellar.

1994 Key West

Sunny Key West seemed to have a hypnotic effect on the players. Time forfeits came in bunches, with tail-ender Alexander Ivanov the chief offender. My two losses (DeFirmian, Christiansen) came on time, and the clock claimed my first three victims (Seirawan, Finegold, and Ivanov. Though the games were decided anyway—except for Ivanov, who essentially fell asleep—it was still pretty weird. Ironically, my only win on the board came against notorious time pressure addict Walter Browne.

☐ W.Browne ■ J.Benjamin
U.S. Championship, Key West 1994

---

1 d4 d6 2 e4 Nf6 3 Nc3 c6

The Pribyl Defense was a big weapon for me in the mid-nineties.

4 Nf3 Bg4 5 Be2 e6 6 h3 Bh5 7 0-0 Be7 8 Be3 Nbd7

8...0-0 is often played to ensure a retreat square for the f6-knight, but I anticipated White's continuation and felt I might not want to castle at all.

9 g4 Bg6 10 Nd2 d5 11 f3

White doesn't want to waste a tempo, but after 11 e5 Ne4 12 Ncxe4 dxe4 the e4-pawn is difficult to scoop up.

11...Qc7

Black's plan is hard to punctuate. It may be "objectively" best to simply castle, but I saw I could present problems for my opponent that would be difficult to solve, especially with the clock running.

12 e5 h5

The point; the h-file is forced open, because 13 g5 would leave a big hole on f5.

13 f4

Not 13 exf6?? Qg3+ 14 Kh1 Qxh3+ 15 Kg1 Qg3+ 16 Kh1 hxg4+ and mates.

13...hxg4 14 hxg4

Browne consumed some time considering 14 exf6 Rxh3 15 fxe7 Rxe3 16 Bxg4. Here I prepared 16...Bxc2 17 Qxc2 Rg3+ 18 Kh1 Rxg4, which gives Black three pawns for the piece (after the imminent ...Kxe7) as well as the crushing threat of bringing the other rook to the h-line. But in view of 18 Kf2! Rxg4 19 Ne2, the alternate move order 16...Rg3+ 17 Kh2 Bxc2! should be preferred. After 18 Qe2 Bd3 19 Qd1, Black can either take the repetition (19...Bc2) or continue to speculate with 19...Re3 20 Rf3 Rxf3 21 Qxf3 Nf6.

14...Ne4 15 Ncxe4

15 f5 would give Black a dangerous opportunity: 15...Bg5 16 Bxg5 Nxg5 17 fxg6 Nxe5 with an unstoppable attack.

15...dxe4

I rejected 15...Bxe4 because 16 Bf3 looks better for White without danger, though Browne intended 16 Nxe4, which is quite a bit riskier.

16 f5 exf5 17 gxf5 Nxe5 18 Nxe4??

18 fxg6? Ng6 leaves White defenseless (but not 18...Nf3+? 19 Rxf3), while 18 dxe5 Qxe5 19 Bf4 Qd4+ 20 Kg2 Bxf5 gives Black too much for the piece; three connected passed pawns and the white king is not out of the woods yet.

18 Bf4 is of course the critical move. Browne and I both analyzed 18...Bd6 19

Nxe4 (if 19 dxe5 Bxe5 20 fxg6 Bxf4 wins) 19...Nf3+ 20 Rxf3 Bxf4 21 fxg6, but now Walter concluded that 21...Be3+ led to mate, or at least something close to it. The problem for Black is that White's potential discovered checks put a damper on Black's mating threats; e.g. 21...Be3+ 22 Rxe3 Qh2+ 23 Kf1 Qh1+ 24 Kf2 Rh2+ 25 Kg3 Rg2+ 26 Kf4 Qh6+ 27 Kf3 (the simplest) 27...Qh3+ 28 Ng3+ Kd7 29 Qe1 fxg6 30 Bf1 Rf8+ 31 Ke4 and White's king gets away.

Instead 18...Bxf5 turns out to be the best move. After 19 Bxe5 Qd7 20 Nc4 f6 21 Bg3 White's position looks quite defensible, though I don't believe Black's practical chances should be underestimated. As a brilliancy this game is flawed, but nothing ventured, nothing gained.

18...Nd3!

Highly aesthetic, but rather simple for Browne to miss.

19 Rf3 Qh2+ 20 Kf1 Nxb2

The knight won't survive, but it buys time for Black to crash through White's defenses.

21 Qb1 Bxf5 22 Nf2 Bh3+ 23 Rxh3 Rxh3 24 Qxb2 Rxe3 25 Qxb7 Rd8 26 Bc4 Kf8 27 Qxc6 Qf4 28 Rd1 Rf3 0-1

With a minute left on his clock, Browne resigned.

Until Key West Boris Gulko had been a bit of a Championship bust, managing no better than equal second in Durango '92. In 1994 Gulko went from the outhouse to the penthouse. When early leaders Seirawan and Christiansen faltered, Gulko had his first title in America.

As in 1989, I tied for an Interzonal spot with Yermolinsky and Shabalov. Instead of six months of purgatory before a slow playoff, we settled the score with an immediate rapid contest. This time the playoff was held immediately and I won convincingly.

1995 Modesto

When the 1995 Championship came around, I was looking ahead to working with Deep Blue. I was in the midst of a downturn, and Modesto was not the cheeriest site. We experienced an oft overlooked hotel problem; they forgot chess tournaments need quiet, and scheduled a wedding adjacent to the playing hall.

Walter Browne learned from last year and spanked me when I naively repeated the opening. My game with Gulko was the low point—I was lost after my sixth move.

☐ **B.Gulko** ■ **J.Benjamin**

U.S. Championship, Modesto 1995

1 c4 e5 2 Nc3 d6 3 g3 g6 4 d4 exd4 5 Qxd4 Nf6 6 Bg2 Nc6??

7 Bxc6+ bxc6 8 Bg5 Be7

8...Bg7 9 Ne4 is even worse.

9 Ne4 Nxe4 10 Qxh8+ Kd7 11 Qxd8+ Kxd8 12 Bxe7+ Kxe7 13 Nf3

I lasted 62 moves but the game was pretty much over here.

Virtually unable to make the time control the year before, Alexander Ivanov pulled off yet another "worst to first" turnaround. DeFirmian and Wolff also tied for first, with Wolff winning the playoff for the ring. Wolff's effort was aided by a most remarkable swindle.

☐ **P.Wolff** ■ **W.Browne**

U.S. Championship, Modesto 1995

(see following diagram)

Wolff has just secured a draw with **55 h3+,** but Browne found another result:

55...Kf5?? 56 Rh6!

Now Black can only avert mate by parting with his rook.

56...g4 57 hxg4+ 1-0

Modesto would be the last Championship where the USCF paid expenses for the players. The players would be compensated with higher prizes; the larger prize fund would sound more impressive to media and possible sponsors.

The Women's Championship returned alongside the men for the first time since Estes Park. In the convivial atmosphere young stars like Jennie Frenklakh, Anna Hahn and Irina Krush (and Jennifer Shahade the next year) benefited from the wisdom of the men.

1996 Parsippany

The Parsippany (New Jersey) Hilton has always served as a great site for the U.S. Amateur Team East. But what works for a weekender doesn't work for a two-week event. Chessplayers are notorious non-drivers (I didn't get a license until I was 42; Fed still doesn't have one). Anyone without a car suffered; we couldn't even make it to the highway on foot. The restaurant didn't offer a lot of food options either. It didn't take long for us all to go stir crazy.

I don't know if there is a correlation, but the bored natives (Benjamin, Christiansen, DeFirmian) all finished well out of contention. Yermolinsky, in the middle of a great career run, took first place.

For me, the chess was even more miserable. I played hard but could not convert a number of winning opportunities. You could look at the cross-table and conclude from my ten draws that I wasn't trying very hard. In *The United States Championship, 1845-1996*, GM Andy Soltis suggested I was trying to repeat my 1987 strategy of a few wins and a lot of draws. True, I drew ten games, but they were all fights until the last two rounds, when my tank had emptied out. Look at the games instead of the cross-table and you understand I didn't want all those draws. My game with Gulko certainly smacks of manliness.

☐ **B.Gulko** ■ **J.Benjamin**
U.S. Championship, Parsippany 1996

1 d4 d6 2 e4 Nf6 3 f3 e5 4 d5 Nxe4!?

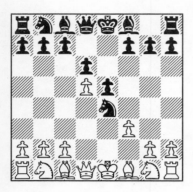

How often do you see a piece sac on move four?

5 fxe4 Qh4+ 6 Kd2 Qxe4 7 Qf3 Qg6 8 Qg3 Be7 9 Nc3 f5 10 Qxg6+ hxg6 11 Nh3 Nd7 12 Ke1 c6 13 a4 Nb6 14 dxc6 bxc6 15 a5 Nd7 16 b4 a6 17 Na4 d5 18 c3 Rb8 19 Be3 d4 20 cxd4 Bxb4+ 21 Bd2 Rh4 22 dxe5 Re4+ 23 Be2 Bxd2+ 24 Kxd2 Rbb4 25 Nc3 Rb2+ 26 Kc1 Rexe2 27 Nxe2 Rxe2 28 Nf4 Rxe5 29 Nxg6 Rc5+ 30 Kd2 Kf7 31 Nf4 g5 32 Nd3 Rd5 33 Rhc1 Ne5 34 Ra3??

34 Rc3 is level.

34...Nxd3??

34...f4! would set up the decisive threat of ...Bf5; while if 35 Rc5 Rxc5 36 Nxc5 Nc4+ wins.

35 Rxd3 Rxa5 36 Rxc6 Ra2+ 37 Rc2 Rxc2+ 38 Kxc2 Ke6 39 Rb3 Ke5 40 Rb6 f4 41 Kd2 Ke4 42 Rc6 Bb7 43 Rc5 Bd5 44 Ra5 Kd4 45 Ke2 g4 46 Kf2 Be6 47 Rxa6 Ke5

White should probably convert this ending, but I managed to "barnacle".

48 Ra5+ Kf6 49 Ke2 Bf5 50 Rc5 Kg6 51 Rc4 Kg5 52 g3 f3+ 53 Ke3 Bd7 54 Rc5+ Kg6 55 Ra5 Kf6 56 Rh5 Kg6 57 Rc5 Kf6 58 h3 Kg6 59 Rc7 Bf5 60 Rc6+ Kg5 61 h4+ Kh5

62 Rf6?

62 Rc5! Kg6 63 h5+ Kf6 64 h6 would have won; e.g. 64...Bh7 65 Rc7 Kg6 66 Rg7+ Kxh6 67 Rxg4 Bg6 68 Rh4+.

62...Bc2 63 Kd4 Bg6 64 Rf4 Be8 65 Ke5 Bb5 66 Rf5+ Kg6 67 Rf6+ Kg7 68 Rf4 Kh6 69 Kf5 Bd7+ 70 Kf6 Bb5 71 Kf7 Kh7 72 Ke6 Bd3 73 Rf6 Bc4+ 74 Ke5 Bb5 75 h5 Kg7 76 h6+ Kh7 77 Ke4 Bc4 78 Ke3 Be2 79 Rf4 Kxh6 80 Rxg4 Bd1 81 Rd4 Be2 82 Rd5 Kg6 83 Kf2 Kf6 84 g4 Kg6 85 Rd6+ Kg5 86 Rd4 Kh4 87 Re4 Kg5 88 Kg3 f2 89 Re5+ Kg6 ½-½

Parsippany did have one redeeming feature—it set the precedent for the all-important "hospitality room". The organizers provided an extra room in the hotel for the players to congregate for conversation, analysis, food and drink. It would be a required condition for the next four years.

In 1996 I set the record with my fifteenth consecutive Championship appearance. The closing ceremony celebrated this mark while mourning the passing of the Championship's biggest fan, Craig Crenshaw. In concluding his Championship history, Soltis saw this era coming to an end: "The generation that dominated U.S. Chess for 15 years was ready to give way to the Tal Shakeds of the future."

Soltis proved premature in burying me and the rest of the older generation. The next six titles would be won by previous champions. I came back rejuvenated after a year with a machine and my U.S. Championship slump melted away.

Chapter Six

Team America

1981 World Student Team Ch., Graz

It might seem strange that I would pass up a shot at the World Junior title to play in the World Student Team Championship. I guess I'm just a team player. I enjoyed my experience in the 1981 World Student Team so much that I wanted to come back for another go.

Back in the pre-laptop and database days of 1981, players had to travel heavy to tournaments. The team tournament started inauspiciously for Kudrin when he failed to get his massive suitcase of books off the train in time. Even today we sometimes smile at the thought of poor Sergey's books chugging off to Istanbul.

Our team captain Eric Schiller managed a bit of sponsorship from Mattel Electronics. In return, we were obliged to wear our Mattel T-shirts whenever possible. Naturally we trotted out our red shirts for the tournament highlight, our showdown with the Soviets.

Ironically, boards two and four provided boyhood reunions of sorts. Kudrin and Psakhis battled to a draw, while our Leonid Bass drew with Vladimirov. That left the match up to two red-blooded Americans, Fedorowicz Black on board one against Kasparov, and me playing Black on four versus Artur Yusupov (Ron Henley and Dmitry Gurevich were sitting out the match). Fed and Garry contested a highly caffeinated game, with a bit of piece banging going back and forth. Eventually Kasparov scored a celebrated victory.

Yusupov generally plays it close to the vest, but he blundered his center and could not recover. I had my biggest scalp to date; Yusupov would go on to bigger and better things, but he was already acknowledged as a strong GM with a World Junior title to his credit.

□ A.Yusupov ■ J.Benjamin
World Student Team Ch., Graz 1981

1 d4 Nf6 2 c4 e6 3 Nf3 b6 4 g3 Ba6 5 Nbd2 Bb4 6 Qb3 c5 7 Bg2 Nc6 8 0-0 0-0 9 Qa4 Bb7 10 e3 d5 11 cxd5 exd5 12 a3 Bxd2 13 Bxd2 Ne4 14 Bc3 c4 15 Nd2 f5 16 Nxe4 fxe4 17 f3 exf3 18 Bxf3 a6 19 e4 b5

I should have played 19...Nxd4! straight off—after 20 Bxd4 dxe4 21 Qxc4+ Bd5 22 Qb4 exf3 23 Qxb6 White is hanging on.

20 Qc2?

20 Qd1 would have avoided Black's combination.

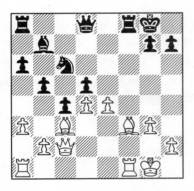

20...Nxd4! 21 Bxd4 dxe4 22 Bxg7 Qb6+ 23 Qf2 Qxf2+ 24 Rxf2 Kxg7 25 Bh5 Kh6 26 Bg4 Kg5 27 Bh3 Rxf2 28 Kxf2 Rd8 29 Ke2 Rd3 30 Rd1 Rb3 31 Rd2 e3 32 Rd7 Be4 33 Ra7 Bd3+ 34 Kxe3 Bf5+ 35 Kd2 Rxb2+ 36 Kc1 Rb1+ 0-1

Despite the tied match, our team didn't finish as high as we hoped. In fact, we lost to France in the last round, despite the fact they forfeited a game. Schiller asked me to offer a draw against Santo Roman to clinch fourth place for the team. I had an excellent position and agreed with reluctance. My opponent did not get to answer because the French captain jumped across the captain to shake my hand.

I didn't mind the draw too much because I had already clinched the board prize for first reserve. It all nearly took a dire turn for me in the middle of the event when I got lost in the middle of Graz. In this era of cell phones and wireless Internet, it seems hard to imagine in 1981 we needed to journey to the post office to make an overseas call. I never even found the post office, and I didn't even remember the address of our dormitory. At some point I even dozed on a park bench for some time, hoping to find some answers when I awoke.

As if by miracle, Fed appeared before me, on his way to some evening refreshment. Which he had to postpone, of course—I insisted he walk me home immediately!

Schiller's facility with the Russian language and some of their players (he was often referred to as "Garry's friend") produced a convivial atmosphere between rivals. After the tournament, Lev Psakhis and Julian Hodgson got into a deep discussion. Fairly inebriated, Julian asked what would have happened if the Russians had not taken first place. "I would have gone to Siberia," Lev replied. Julian expressed shock and dismay, but Lev let the hammer drop. "It's not so bad. I live in Siberia."

1983 World Student Team Ch., Chicago

In 1983 I found that the honor of board one was not all it's cracked up to be. Sure, you get to take on some great players. But then it isn't much fun doing battle with Colombian GM Zapata while your friends are crushing three extras from *Scarface*.

Chicago '83 was largely forgettable for me. The nightly screenings of porno movies did, however, leave an impression. From *Debbie Does Dallas* to *Behind the Green Door*, young chessplayers from around the world received quite an education.

The match against China provided some comic relief. Their board one had caused a stir with a good result underscored by an upset win over Yusupov. Fedorowicz insisted to Leonid Bass, now our captain, that the Chinese guy wasn't so tough and he could take him down. So Bass sat the top two to give Fed a chance to prove his case.

Eventually John received a draw offer and went to Bass to ask for advice.

"I think you should take it," Leonid told him.

"I knew you'd say that," John replied. Then he went back to the board and beat him. [It's best not to insult Fed with an improper draw offer. At the 1989 World Team Championship, John had this to say to Xu Jun: "You must be practicing your English because your position is lost and you should resign."]

I didn't get to team up for years after that. The ACF chose not to select me for the 1984 Team. [I in turn refused the ACF's request to play on the 1985 Student Team, feeling they should have put me on the varsity already. I went to the U.S. Open instead—good move as it turned out!] I chose not to play in Dubai 1986 because Israel was not invited. So I was chomping at the bit when I finally got to play in Thessaloniki 1988.

1988 Thessaloniki Olympiad

The Olympiad is the best tournament in the world—nothing else comes close. You get to see (and hopefully play) the best players in the world. You encounter and re-unite with friends from all over the world. You get to socialize with, for a change, members of the opposite sex. And if you are lucky, you get to represent the USA.

Egypt gave me my welcome to the Olympiad moment. My opponent had a gift for me—a metal plate with a pyramid decoration. [The wealthy Americans of course had nothing for them.] I guessed it to be an ashtray, which seemed a good bet when their team *en masse* whipped out their cigarettes. I could barely see or breathe, but I managed to win. It was the last Olympiad which permitted smoking.

I had an almost entirely satisfying result. Shifting between boards two and three, I was often called upon to "block". I played Black against a murderers' row of Yusupov, Nunn, and Nikolic, and held them all to draws. [In three Olympiads I had now played Yusupov three times. I tried to convince Seirawan and Gulko to take a rest so I could play one of the big Ks, but to no avail.] I converted my Whites to victories consistently, including a cameo on board one vs. veteran Filipino GM Eugenio Torre. I ended up with 7/11.

□ **J.Benjamin** ■ **E.Torre**
Thessaloniki Olympiad 1988

---

1 e4 e5 2 Nf3 Nc6 3 Bb5 Nf6 4 0-0 Nxe4 5 d4 Nd6 6 Bxc6 dxc6 7 dxe5 Nf5 8 Qxd8+ Kxd8 9 b3 h6 10 Bb2 Be6 11 c4!?

This novelty sprang from poor memory. I couldn't remember what teenager Alex Sherzer had shown me two years earlier.

11...a5 12 Nc3 Bb4 13 Ne2 Bc5 14 h3 g5 15 Nc3! Kc8 16 Ne4 Ba7?! 17 Rad1 a4 18 Bc3 Bb6 19 Rd2 axb3 20 axb3 Ra3?

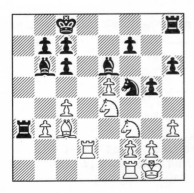

The first, but not the last time Torre forgets about the dangers of the a-file. Black had some chances to resist with 20...Rd8.

21 Bb4! Ra6

If 21...Rxb3 22 Ra1 Kb8 23 Rda2 wins.

22 g4 Nh4 23 Nxh4 gxh4 24 Be7 h5 25 Nf6 hxg4 26 hxg4 Ra5 27 Re1

Black is defenseless against the simple plan of Kh2, f4, f5, but his next move hastens the end.

27...Bc5? 28 Bxc5 Rxc5 29 Ra1! 1-0

If only I could have won one more game. We conducted the last round with Larry Christiansen's wife, Natasha serving as captain. In a surreal cloak and dagger operation the night before, the whole team had accompanied captain John Donaldson to the airport where he eloped with the Soviet player Elena Akhmilovskaya. It seems funny now, but in the Cold War days we were prepared to run interference if the KGB showed up. Unfortunately, the two did not have the happy love marriage we all hoped for.

In my last game against Gyula Sax I had the opportunity to bring us a silver medal with a win. I fought hard, but the draw was only good enough for fourth.

I made a number of friendships that would last many years. My first Olympiad friends were Suzanne Connolly and Mairead O'Siochru, dubbed by a friend who met them in Dubai, the "Irish Chess Babes". Many Olympiads later, Suzanne would introduce me to my wife.

1990 Visa Match, Reykjavik

We had a good Olympic warm-up in March 1990 in cold and snowy Reykjavik. The Visa Match was contested between four teams (Soviet Union, U.S.A., England, and the Nordic countries) over ten boards. I scored three wins (Schussler, Suba, and Azmaiparashvili) against one loss (Eingorn). My victim below is today known more for politics and controversies, but as a player he was a steady 2650+ for many years.

☐ **Z.Azmaiparashvili** ■ **J.Benjamin**
Visa Match, Reykjavik 1990

1 d4 Nf6 2 c4 c5 3 d5 b5 4 cxb5 a6 5 f3 e6 6 dxe6 fxe6 7 e3 d5 8 bxa6 Bd6 9 Bb5+ Nfd7 10 f4 Bxa6 11 Bxa6 Nxa6 12 Nf3 0-0 13 0-0 Nb4 14 Nc3 c4 15 b3 cxb3 16 Qxb3 Qa5 17 a3!? Nd3 18 Bd2 N7c5 19 Qc2 Qa6 20 Nd4 Rab8 21 Rfb1 e5!

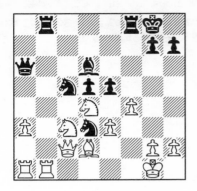

This break hopes to exploit the departure of White's rook from the kingside. It sets a nice trap as well—22 fxe5 Bxe5 23 Nf3? Rxf3! (more accurate than 23...Rxb1+ 24 Qxb1 Rxf3) 24 Rxb8+ (or 24 gxf3 Qg6+ 25 Kf1 Rf8) 24...Bxb8 25 gxf3 Qg6+ 26 Kf1 Qh5 with a winning attack.

22 Nf3 Qc4! 23 Rxb8 Bxb8

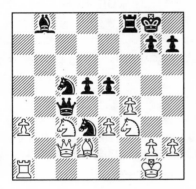

24 Rb1

Interesting tactics abound. 24 Qa2 Nb3 25 Nxd5! Qxd5 26 Rb1 Ndc5 27 Bb4 Ba7 28 Bxc5 Bxc5 29 Qxb3 Qxb3 30 Rxb3 exf4 is equal, but 25...Ba7! puts the pressure on White; for example, 26 Ne7+ Kh8 27 fxe5 Nxd2 28 Qxd2 Qe4 wins for Black, but 26 Nb4 could lead to a long, complicated line: 26...exf4 27 Nxd3 Qxd3 28 Bb4 fxe3 29 Bxf8 e2+ 30 Kh1 Qd1+ 31 Ne1 Kxf8 32 Rb1 Nd2 33 Qd5! Nxb1 34 Qa8+ Ke7 35 Qxa7+ and Black's king march seems to come up a bit short: 35...Ke6 36 Qb6+ Kf5 37 Qc5+ Ke4 38 Qb4+ Ke3 39 Kg1! Qc1 40 g3! g5 41 Qe7+ Kd2 42 Qxg5+ Kd1 43 Qxc1+ Kxc1 44 a4 Kd2 45 Ng2 Nc3 46 a5 with a draw.

24...Ba7

This is fine, though I don't know why I didn't choose the simple 24...exf4.

25 Qa2 Qxa2 26 Nxa2 Ne4 27 Kf1 Nxd2+ 28 Nxd2 Bxe3 29 Ke2 Bxd2 30 Kxd3 Bxf4 31 Nb4 Rd8 32 g3 Bg5 33 Nc6 e4+ 34 Kd4 Bf6+ 35 Kc5 Re8 36 Kxd5 e3

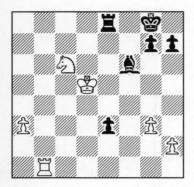

The d-pawn is gone but the e-pawn will cost an exchange.

37 Re1 e2 38 Kc4 Re3 39 a4 Bc3 40 Rxe2 Rxe2 41 Kxc3 Rxh2!

The simplest winning method is to eat quickly and sacrifice the rook when necessary.

42 a5 Rh6! 43 Nb8 Rg6 44 a6 Rxg3+ 45 Kb4

Or 45 Kb2 Rg5 46 Nc6 Rb5+ 47 Ka3 Rb6 48 a7 Ra6+ 49 Kb4 h5 50 Kb5 Rxa7 51 Nxa7 h4 etc.

45...Rg1 46 a7

46 Nc6 Rb1+! 47 Kc5 h5 48 a7 Ra1 changes nothing.

46...Rb1+! 47 Kc5 Ra1 48 Nc6 h5 49 Kb6 Rxa7 50 Kxa7 h4 51 Ne5 h3 52 Nf3 g5 53 Nh2 Kf7 54 Kb6 Ke6 55 Kc5 Ke5 56 Kc4 Kf4 57 Kd3 g4 58 Ke2 g3 59 Nf1 h2 0-1

1990 Novi Sad Olympiad

In many ways 1990 was a watershed Olympiad. The Soviet Union competed for the last time. Yugoslavia was still in one piece and had three teams only because they were the host country. East and West Germany had their last hurrah, even though the Berlin Wall had already come down.

The American team would never again be so...American. Boris Gulko was the sole Russian immigrant, joined by a classic Fischer boom quintet: Seirawan, Christiansen, Fedorowicz, DeFirmian and myself. I've played with a lot of good teammates since, but it's never quite been the same feeling without all my old friends there.

Despite lacking Kasparov and Karpov, the Soviets took the gold comfortably. I didn't get to play in our match. Leonid Yudasin scored the decisive win against Fed. When shaking hands, Yudasin said with his characteristic giggle, "maybe next time I play for your team." Fed was not amused. [Yudasin would later play against us for Israel. He hasn't changed his national status since, though he now lives in Brooklyn.]

I saw my workload greatly reduced, mostly due to a nasty cold during the heart of the event. Eventually I came back to life in time to beat Iceland's Jon Arnason. Then came the critical match against Yugoslavia "C".

Yugoslavia has always had great depth; even the third team could trot out four solid grandmasters. You wouldn't expect to sweep them. Indeed, very rarely has the U.S. been able to sweep an all-GM team. Ever since Dubai, we've referred to resting the top two boards as sending in the "danger squad". The term suggests danger to someone — maybe them, maybe us.

In this case, the danger was to them. Larry beat Cvitan, Nick beat Strikovic, and John beat Djuric. On board two, I completed the sweep.

☐ **J.Benjamin** ■ **G.Cabrilo**
Novi Sad Olympiad 1990

---

1 d4 Nf6 2 c4 c5 3 d5 g6 4 Nc3 Bg7 5 e4 d6 6 h3 0-0 7 Nf3 e6 8 Bd3 Na6 9 Bg5 exd5 10 exd5!? Re8+ 11 Kf1 h6 12 Bf4 Nc7 13 a4 Na6

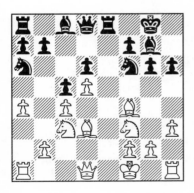

14 Qd2

Objectively I should have stopped for 14 Rc1! Nb4 15 Bb1, but the rook ends up prospering.

14...Nb4! 15 Bb1 g5?!

Black wants to restrict the white pieces, but the kingside is shaky after this.

16 Be3 Qe7?!

16...Nh5 would have avoided the coming tactics.

17 h4! g4?

I thought 17...Ng4 18 hxg5 Nxe3+ 19 Qxe3 Qxe3 20 fxe3 hxg5 21 Nxg5 Rxe3 22 Ra3! would give White a clear edge, but now after 22...Nd3! I'm not sure. But the text just loses.

18 Bxh6! gxf3 19 Bxg7 fxg2+ 20 Kxg2

20...Nfxd5

If 20...Kxg7 21 Qg5+ Kf8 22 Qh6+ Kg8 23 Rg1 Bg4 24 Kh1 Qe5 25 Ne4 leads to mate.

21 Nxd5 Nxd5 22 Ra3! Qe2

Or 22...Kxg7 23 Rg3+ Kf6 24 Qg5+ Ke6 25 Qf5 mate.

23 Qh6! Qg4+ 24 Rg3 Ne3+ 25 fxe3 Qe2+ 26 Kg1 1-0

26...Qe1+ 27 Kh2 Qe2+ 28 Rg2 is the end of the line.

We went into the last round a point behind England and a point ahead of Czechoslovakia (another country about to change). We got Bulgaria, England faced Cuba, and the Czechs took on India. We weren't sure if we were trying to hold on to a medal or catch the Brits for silver.

Cuba helped us by holding England to a 2-2 tie. We showed the great strength of the U.S. team—depth. The Europeans all had good players (and Bulgaria had Kiril Georgiev), but they tended to drop off. Even though Ermenkov was near a board prize, he was no match for Fed. DeFirmian dropped Semkov as well to give us a 3-1 margin. It came down to tiebreaks. Donaldson went running around tabulating last round results. Would our opponents outscore England's opponents? [Let's go Yemen!] The count went our way and we got to celebrate silver.

1992 Cannes

The "all-American" team had one last hurrah courtesy of the GMA. The U.S. team of Seirawan, Christiansen, Benjamin and Fedorowicz battled teams from England, France, and the Netherlands on the French Riviera. Though the team fell short of victory (as my favorite *Chess Chow* headline "Brits Deliver Swift Kick in Cannes" explained), I had a personal success. I went home with two wins over Santo Roman, one over Chandler, draws with Chandler and Sosonko, and the following example of fancy stepping with my king:

☐ **J.Benjamin** ■ **J.Van der Wiel**

Cannes (rapid g/60) 1992

---

1 e4 e5 2 Nf3 Nc6 3 Bb5 a6 4 Bxc6 dxc6 5 0-0 Bg4 6 h3 Bh5?! 7 g4 Bg6 8 Nxe5 f6 9 Nxg6 hxg6 10 Qf3 Qd7 11 Nc3 0-0-0 12 d4 Qxd4 13 Rd1 Qc4 14 Rxd8+ Kxd8 15 Bf4 Kc8 16 Rd1 Bb4 17 Qe3 Qc5 18 Qd3 Qe7 19 Na4 Nh6 20 a3 Bd6 21 Bxd6 cxd6 22 Qxd6 Qxd6 23 Rxd6 Nf7 24 Nb6+ Kb8 25 Rd7 Ng5 26 Rxg7 Nxh3+ 27 Kg2 Nf4+ 28 Kf3 Ne6 29 Re7 Rh3+

30 Ke2 Nd4+ 31 Kd2 Nf3+ 32 Kd1 Rh1+ 33 Ke2 Nd4+ 34 Kd2 Rh2 35 Kd3 Nf3 36 Ke3 Rh3 37 Nd7+ Kc7 38 Nxf6+ Kd6 39 Rxb7 Ke6 40 Ne8 Ng5+ 41 Kf4 Nf7 42 g5 Rh4+ 43 Kg3 Rxe4 44 Ng7+ 1-0

1992 Manila Olympiad

The break-up of the Soviet Union produced a half-dozen new medal contenders and a half-dozen solid teams. Yugoslavia begat strong sides in Bosnia and Croatia. Russia found themselves deprived of major heavies like Ivanchuk, Shirov, and Gelfand. The medal chase would be more exciting than ever.

The face of the U.S. team had changed as well. Our two new players occupied the top two boards. I thought at the time Alex Yermolinsky was placed too high at board two, but he proved to be a solid team member. I remember a conversation where Yermo used the phrase "buzzer-beater". Only in the country two years, Alex's command of American idiom was quite impressive. Of all the immigrants I played with, he fit in the best with the natives.

Gata Kamsky brought obvious talent to the table, but how many points would he have to score to offset the potential turmoil of his father? Hopefully his father wouldn't prove a divisive influence.

On one day off I scanned the following position on the demo board:

☐ **G.Kamsky** ■ **J.Hjartarson**
Manila Olympiad 1992

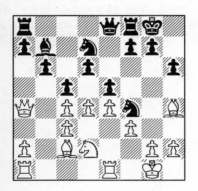

I was surprised to hear the voice of Rustam Kamsky. "Gata, firze, no good." The year of Russian I took at Yale hardly made me fluent, but I could grasp his "Russish". "You think Gata's queen is misplaced?" Rustam shook his head yes. I told him Gata knew what he was doing and he shouldn't worry. In fact, Gata was soon winning, though he went wrong and only drew.

The strained relations with Rustam broke down on the night before the last round. Our FIDE representative, Faneuil Adams, took the team out for a nice meal in the Manila Hotel. Rustam immediately parked himself opposite Adams and asked to talk. Fan hoped to keep the evening light and table the conversation until after the meal. "It's not like I'm going to be hit by a bus," he said. Rustam channeled Ivan Drago from *Rocky IV*: "Anything is possible."

Rustam wanted to know why Gata had not been awarded the Samford Fellowship. He spouted a stream of Russian while Gata translated as fast as he could. I was surprised to hear Rustam say my name—what did I have to do with this?

Rustam had hatched another conspiracy theory: I had convinced Patrick Wolff not to vote for Gata (Wolff was on the Samford Committee). Adams had no choice but to meet Rustam head on. "The reason I voted against Gata," he told him, "is because of unacceptable behavior by you and your son on a number of occasions." He then cited a few examples. The wind taken from their sails, the Kamskys then left, before dinner had even started.

Such unpleasantness did not ruin the tournament for us. Manila in the summertime was hot, hot, hot! A lot of social life revolved around the swimming pools at the various hotels. We had more parties than usual. The players enjoyed an impressive feast hosted by Campomanes as well as the traditional Bermuda party.

We competed for medals throughout...but not gold. Russia compensated for their losses by bringing back Kasparov, who was busy battling Karpov in 1990. He posted seven wins over GMs—Cebalo, Shirov, Loginov, Ivanchuk, Hjartarson, Nikolic, and Kamsky. But even Kasparov was overshadowed by his fourth board, sixteen-year-old Vladimir Kramnik. Two years earlier Lev Alburt had told me about Kramnik, but he was still largely unknown until his amazing 8½/9 in Manila.

Yasser had a bad tournament, but Gulko provided a lot of big wins for us. I was shocked to lose my first game against an unknown Lithuanian, Ruzhele. I recovered to win four games, like the clean job from the Bosnia match:

□ **J.Benjamin** ■ **E.Dizdarevic**
Manila Olympiad 1992

---

1 e4 c5 2 Nf3 e6 3 d4 cxd4 4 Nxd4 a6 5 Bd3 b6 6 0-0 Bb7 7 c4 d6 8 f4 Nd7 9 Nc3 g6
10 f5 Bg7 11 Bc2 Qe7 12 fxe6 fxe6 13 Nf3 Ngf6 14 Bf4 e5 15 Bg5 Rc8 16 Nd2 0-0 17
Qe2 Qd8 18 Rad1 Qc7 19 Be3 Bc6 20 Bb1 Nc5 21 Nd5 Nxd5 22 exd5 Bd7 23 h4 Bf5
24 h5 Qd7 25 Bxf5 gxf5 26 h6 Bf6 27 Qh5 f4 28 Bxc5 Rxc5 29 b3 Rc7 30 Ne4 Be7 31
g3 Qf5 32 Qxf5 Rxf5 33 Kg2 Bf8 34 gxf4 exf4 35 Kf3 b5 36 Rg1+ Kf7

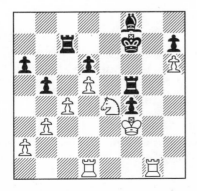

37 Rg7+! Bxg7 38 Nxd6+ Kg6 39 Nxf5 Kxf5 40 d6 1-0

I helped against our rivals winning against Uzbekistan (Yuldachev) and Armenia (Minasian). The latter game featured a serendipitous ending, characteristic of many of my Olympiad games. My opponents seemed to get overconfident often.

☐ **J.Benjamin** ■ **A.Minasian**
Manila Olympiad 1992

White is better after 38...Kf6, but **38...Kxh5?? 39 Kg3!** forced Black to cough up a piece to avert 40 Be2 mate.

In the end we couldn't overtake Armenia or the unheralded Uzbeks, winner of the silver medal in their first attempt.

1993 World Team Championship, Lucerne

Our fourth place finish qualified the U.S. to place a team in the 1993 World Team Championship. Though far less known than the Olympiad, the WTC holds high prestige because it invites only ten premier teams. The USCF decided to invite the same players that had qualified the year before. Not everyone was happy—reigning U.S. Champ Patrick Wolff for one—but I wasn't complaining.

Seirawan declined his spot, replaced by the next man on the rating list, Gregory Kaidanov. Sending teams in consecutive years put a strain on USCF finances. They could only offer $750 fees per player. We were psyched to win and didn't worry about our paychecks.

The Russians sent the same team from Manila, with the slight difference of

Bareev replacing Kasparov. Kramnik moved up to board one, a major hot seat for an eighteen-year-old.

We started to make our move in round three by shellacking the upstarts of Manila, Uzbekistan, 3½-½. The 1993 WTC may be the last major event to utilize the dying institution of adjournments. With sudden death, I would not have an epic story to relate from my game with Zagrebelny.

□ **S.Zagrebelny** ■ **J.Benjamin**
World Team Championship, Lucerne 1993

1 e4 c5 2 Nf3 d6 3 d4 cxd4 4 Nxd4 Nf6 5 Nc3 Nc6 6 Be2 e5 7 Nf3 h6 8 0-0 Be7 9 Re1 0-0 10 h3 Be6 11 Bf1 Nb8 12 a4 Nbd7 13 a5 a6 14 Nd5 Nxd5 15 exd5 Bf5 16 c4 Re8 17 b4 Bf6 18 Be3 e4 19 Nd4 Bg6 20 Qb3 Rc8 21 Red1 Bg5 22 c5!? Bxe3 23 fxe3 dxc5 24 Ne6 Qe7 25 Nxc5 Nxc5 26 bxc5 Qxc5 27 d6 Red8 28 Ra4 Rxd6!

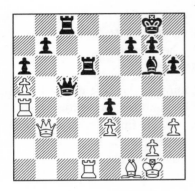

I saw my queen sac would be sufficient for a draw, but I counted on my opponent's optimism to obtain winning chances.

29 Rc4 Rxd1 30 Rxc5 Rxf1+ 31 Kxf1 Rxc5 32 Qb6 Rb5 33 Qd8+ Kh7 34 g4?

After this weakening move I have something to work with.

34...f6 35 Kf2 h5 36 Kg3 hxg4 37 hxg4 Re5 38 Qc7 Rb5 39 Qd8 Rb3 40 Kf4 Rb1 41 Kg3 Rb5 42 Kf4 Re5 43 Qc7 Rg5 44 Qb6 Rb5 45 Qd8 Bf7! 46 Kxe4 Be6 47 Kf3 Rg5 48 Qc7 Bxg4+ 49 Kf4 Bh5 50 Ke4 Re5+ 51 Kf4 Bg6 52 Qd8 Be4 53 Kg3 Kg6 54 Qc7 Rf5 55 Kh2 Rg5 56 Kh3 Bg2+ 57 Kh2 Bc6 58 Qd8 Rd5 59 Qb6 Rb5 60 Qc7 Re5 61 Qb6 Kh5 62 Kg1 Kg4 63 Kf2 Rf5+ 64 Ke2 g5 65 Qc7 Bb5+ 66 Kd2 Rf2+ 67 Kd1 Bc6 68 Ke1 Rg2?

I originally planned 68...Kf3, which could have led to this finish: 69 Qf7 Kg2 70 Qg6 Bf3 71 Qxf6 g4 72 e4 g3 73 e5 Re2+ 74 Kd1 Kf2 75 Qb6+ Kf1 76 Qf6 Rf2+ 77 Kc1 g2 and wins. Unfortunately, during the first adjournment break my teammates had somehow convinced me the text was "simpler".

69 Kf1 f5 70 Qf7 Be4 71 Qe6 Kf3 72 Qh6 Kxe3 73 Qd6 Kf3 74 Qa3+ Kg4 75 Qb3 Bf3 76 Qb4+ f4 77 Qc3 Kg3 78 Qe5 Rf2+ 79 Kg1 Rg2+ 80 Kf1 Be2+ 81 Ke1 g4 82 Qc3+ Bf3 83 Kf1 Rh2 84 Qe1+ Kh3 85 Qc3 Re2 86 Qh8+ Kg3 87 Qc3 Re3 88 Qd2

The game was adjourned for a second time. With my analysis buddy, Yermo, we searched for the increasingly elusive win. Even with late contributions from Boris and Larry, we could not break down White's best defense.

88...Re2

Zagrebelny arrived forty minutes late, complaining that due to the language barrier, he did not know when the game would be resumed. Since this wasn't his first adjournment session, it was hard to sympathize. He finally sat down and the arbiter opened the envelope, causing Zagrebelny to jump back up and claim three-fold repetition. After five more minutes were subtracted from his clock, we soon got answers to our mysteries.

89 Qc3 Re3 90 Qd2 Rb3

91 Qc2!?

We had a plan to regroup after 91 Qe1+ Kh3 92 Kg1 Rb5 93 Qf1+ Kh4 94 Qe1+ g3 95 Qe7+ Kh3 96 Qe6+ Bg4 97 Qh6+ Bh5 98 Qe6+ Kh4 99 Qf6+ Kg4 100 Qe6+ Rf5 101 Qg8+ Kh4 102 Qd8+ Kh3 103 Qd7 Bg4 104 Qh7+ Rh5 and wins. But we found a flaw: 100 Kg2!! Rxa5 101 Qg7+ Rg5 102 Qd7+ Rf5 (not 102...Kh4?? 103 Qh3 mate) 103 Qg7+ Kh4 104 Qe7+ Rg5 105 Qe4 and despite a rook, bishop, and four pawns for the queen, Black is too tied up to have any chance to win.

This move is not easy to crack either.

91...Ra3 92 Qf2+ Kh3

93 Qb2??

93 Qd4! Bc6 94 Qxf4! Rf3+ 95 Kg1! Rxf4 would be one of many stalemates we found. After 93...Re3 the stalemate trap doesn't work: 94 Qxf4? Bg2+ 95 Kf2 Rf3+ 96 Kg1 Rf1+! wins. But 94 Kg1! allows no obvious progress, and the many repetitions floating about make winning even more problematic.

93...Re3!

Now Black is definitely winning.

94 Qd2 Be2+ 95 Kg1

If 95 Kf2 Kh2! wins.

95...Rg3+ 96 Kf2 Bb5 97 Qb4 Rf3+ 98 Ke1 g3 99 Qf8 Kg2 100 Qf7 Rf1+ 101 Kd2 0-1

Zagrebelny sealed the last move but did not resume. Ironically, the future American Gregory Serper scored the only half-point for the Uzbeks in this match.

The Zagrebelny marathon kept me out of another Russia match. Gata rose to the occasion with a huge win over Kramnik which balanced out Larry's only loss of the event at the hands of Dolmatov. With a kindler, gentler Rustam, we could better appreciate Gata's contributions. He scored only fifty percent, but that included 1½-1½ against the power trio of Kramnik, Shirov, and Ivanchuk. I don't think we could have asked for more from any player.

Ill health limited Kamsky to five games. Rustam at first balked when captain Donaldson insisted Gata see a doctor, but relented when he learned it would not cost him anything. The doctor walked in the room and immediately opened the window, which had been shut to block the harmful effects of fresh air. Antibiotics soon had Gata good as new.

We beat China 2½-1½ in the penultimate round, while Armenia dropped the Russians by the same score. Our lead ballooned to two points! It seemed a dream, but four draws with Iceland made it a reality. Our final total of 22½-13½ left us one and a half points up on the Ukraine and two ahead of Russia. Three of our players went undefeated. The U.S. frequently feasts on the lower board, where our superior depth tells. I went 4-0-2 to nab a second gold medal for the best result on board five.

And the best part? The USCF had agreed to give us bonuses for medals. We each added $2500 for our golds. The worst part? Our historic victory went unnoticed in the mainstream media.

1994 Moscow Olympiad

We struggled to keep the momentum going in Moscow. Gulko, Yermolinsky, and I returned, rejoined by Seirawan. Kamsky and Kaidanov declined, the latter reluctantly due to visa problems. Christiansen, for some reason, was not invited in favor of Kudrin, living and working in Moscow at the time. Shabalov had Olympiad experience with Latvia but made his American debut.

The dangers were not just at the chessboard. Law and order suffered with the fall of communism. A number of Olympiad participants were mugged. The Macedonian team was robbed of all their money at the *bank*! Yermolinsky was even kidnapped by thugs hired by his ex-wife! She had apparently become convinced that everyone in America had huge cash reserves. Eventually Yermo got her to accept the cash he brought to Moscow and let him go.

The Hotel Cosmos served as our home and the playing site, with a bar and a few shops to boot. Given the mounting horror stories of life outside, it seemed sensible to hunker down. So I stayed inside for the duration, a good two and a half weeks.

The playing conditions on the stage exceeded those downstairs in the fish tank, where we were soon banished. We sent Captain Donaldson scurrying for cushions to combat the uncomfortable, tacky plastic patio chairs we had to sit on. We had to be careful not to confuse our kings and queens on the weird Russian sets.

Kudrin and Shabalov played poorly. Gulko struggled, and I lost two games in a row. We labored against the likes of Turkey, Moldova, and Kyrgyzstan. But midway through, we caught fire with big wins over Peru, Lithuania, and Romania. Gulko and I started winning again. Yermo had been solid throughout, Seirawan spectacular. He piled up seven wins against no losses *en route* to the gold medal for board four.

Yasser asked to sit out the last round against Yugoslavia to protect his medal...unless we still had a chance for a team medal. Donaldson told him, quite correctly, that our chances were remote. As it turned out, if Yasser had played and won on board four (instead of Shaba, who lost), we would have taken a medal. Instead we finished tied for fifth. Gulko beat Ljubojevic while I saved my best for last.

☐ J.Benjamin ■ P.Popovic
Moscow Olympiad 1994

---

1 d4 Nf6 2 Bg5

My affair with the Trompowsky began in Moscow with 3½/4.

2...Ne4 3 Bf4 d5 4 f3 Nf6 5 e4 e6 6 e5 Nfd7 7 Be3 c5 8 c3 Nc6 9 f4 cxd4 10 cxd4 Nb6

Popovic deviates from a game I had earlier in the Olympiad: 10...Qa5+ 11 Kf2! Nb6 12 b3 Bd7 13 Nf3 Rc8 14 a3 Na8 15 Ra2 Ne7 16 Bd2 Qb6 17 Nc3 Nf5 18 b4! Qd8 19 g4 with a slight edge and an eventual win (J.Benjamin-V.Malisauskas).

11 Nd2 a5 12 a3 a4 13 Bd3 Bd7 14 Ne2 Na5 15 0-0 g6 16 g4 Bc6 17 Ng3 Nbc4 18 Nxc4 Nxc4 19 Qe2 b5 20 f5

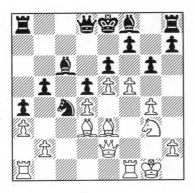

20...Be7 21 Rf3 Bh4 22 fxe6 fxe6 23 Bh6 Qb6 24 Qf2 0-0-0 25 Rf1 Rd7 26 Kg2 Rhd8 27 Kh3 Bxg3 28 Kxg3 b4 29 Bf8 b3! 30 Bc5 Qa5 31 Bb4 Qb6 32 Rf6 Bb5 33 Bc5 Qa6 34 Rc1 Kb7 35 Bf1 Rc8 36 g5 Rc6 37 Bh3 Na5 38 Rc3 Bd3 39 Rf7!

Definitely not 39 Bxe6 Rxe6 40 Rxe6 Qxe6 41 Rxd3 Rf7 with counterplay.

39...Rcc7 40 Rxd7 Rxd7

41 Bb4!!

This might not be the only way to win, but I think it is an excellent human decision. The direct approach begins with 41 Qf8 Bf5 and now:

a) 42 Qe8 Rc7! (not 42...Qc6 43 Bd6 Nc4 44 Rxc4! and wins) 43 Bxf5 gxf5 44 Qxa4 (44 Bb4 might preserve an advantage) 44...Qe2! and White is hard pressed to avoid perpetual check.

b) 42 Bd6 Qa8 43 Qxa8+ Kxa8 44 Bf1 Nc4 45 Bxc4 dxc4 46 Rxc4 Bd3 47 Rxa4+ Ra7 48 Rb4 Rb7 49 d5 Rxb4 50 Bxb4 exd5 51 e6 with good winning chances.

I couldn't be sure where the other lines would lead, but I could calculate the text move to a clearly winning position. Trading off Black's potentially troublesome knight simplifies the process.

41...Bf5

42 Bxa5! Qxa5

On 42...Bxh3 43 Qf8 wins.

43 Rc5 Qd8

Both 43...Qb6 and 43...Qa6 would be effectively met by 44 Bf1.

44 Qd2 Rc7 45 Bxf5 gxf5

Black also loses after 45...Rxc5 46 Qb4+ Ka8 47 dxc5 Qxg5+ 48 Bg4 Qxe5+ (if 48...h5 49 Qxa4+ Kb7 50 Qd7+ Kb8 51 Qe8+ Kc7 52 Qf7+ Kb8 53 Qf4 wins) 49 Kh3 Qe3+ 50 Kg2.

46 Qb4+ Kc8 47 h4

47...Qe8

Or 47...Rxc5 48 Qxc5+ Kb7 49 Qb5+ etc.

48 Qa5! Rxc5 49 Qa8+ Kd7 50 Qxe8+ Kxe8 51 dxc5 1-0

The FIDE Congress generated more interest than usual. Florencio Campomanes had reigned for years as President without much opposition. But Bachar Kouatly ran a serious campaign and seemed to have support to win. Campomanes wasn't even on the ballot.

The USCF had intended to vote for Kouatly, with an eye towards a professional FIDE free of corruption. Despite years of feuding with Campomanes, Kasparov suddenly decided that Campo should stay in office. Campo needed a special vote just to get on the ballot. After the Russian delegate Makarov spoke in a threatening manner to his colleagues, the votes came through. Campo was back on the ballot. Kasparov told the USCF Policy Board to switch their vote, and promised to make significant public appearances in the U.S. if they did so.

Fan Adams, still serving as FIDE representative, balked when he was told to vote for Campo. He tried to argue Kouatly would better serve our interests. He told them it was wrong to let Kasparov essentially buy the U.S. vote, but to no avail. So he cast his vote as directed and promptly resigned.

1996 Yerevan Olympiad

The next Olympiad came in the midst of my IBM stint, but I had worked out time off. After months of inactivity, I was raring to go. Several federations banded together to arrange two charters to fly to Yerevan. The chess plane had the mood of an airborne party, bringing us there in festive spirits.

Armenia is a former Soviet Republic, but don't confuse it with Russia. In Moscow, danger lurked everywhere; in Yerevan, the locals would always try to help you. Despite serious governmental upheaval during the tournament, we always felt free and comfortable.

The players were provided with copious quantities of delicious fresh fruits and vegetables. Unfortunately, these foods weren't the safest things to eat (imagine Mexico). Lots of players fell ill during the event, and Armenian medicine was a bit below our standard. Though the tournament doctor seemed conscientious enough, he didn't seem to have the right medications to alleviate our stomach woes.

I caught the bug the morning of our match with Israel. Unfortunately, I was in the lineup. I would have loved to draw quickly and go back to bed, but GM Huzman would likely try to press me with White. The toilet facilities at the tournament hall were, at least in my view, unacceptable. There was no way I was going to do my business in a hole in the ground. The hall did have a conventional toilet, but it was reserved for Kasparov. If the urge to evacuate had taken me over, I was prepared to bust that lock. Fortunately I maintained cohesion in my game (a solid draw) and otherwise.

Luckily for us we were quartered in the same hotel as the Swiss delegation. They had a doctor on the team who had brought enough medicine to treat our whole team. On a healthy stomach I scored pretty well—four wins against one loss with a few draws. The win over Greece contained one of my favorite moves.

□ **J.Benjamin** ■ **I.Miladinovic**
Yerevan Olympiad 1996

1 e4 c5 2 Nf3 Nc6 3 c3 d5 4 exd5 Qxd5 5 d4 e5!?

This move had escaped my Deep Blue preparations.

6 Nbd2!?

The text is the sharpest try for White, worked out over the board.

6...exd4 7 Bc4 Qf5 8 0-0 Be6 9 Bxe6 fxe6 10 cxd4 0-0-0 11 dxc5 Bxc5

12 Qe1!!

This may not be objectively stronger than 12 Qe2, but I'm proud of the deep idea that comes to fruition in three moves.

12...Nf6 13 Nb3 Bb6 14 Be3 Bxe3 15 fxe3!

Opening the f-file and the queen's route to g3 gives White a decisive tactical boost.

15...Qd5 16 Rc1 Kb8 17 Qg3+ Ka8 18 Nc5 Rhg8 19 Ng5 Qd6 20 Qf3! Qd5 21 Ngxe6 Qxf3 22 gxf3 Rc8 23 Kf2

After only 23 moves we are in the technical phase, but with 17 moves to get to the time control! There were plenty of opportunities to misstep in time pressure.

23...b6 24 Nd3 Kb7 25 Rc4 Nd5 26 Rfc1 g6 27 e4 Nf6

If 27...Ndb4 28 Nxb4 Nxb4 29 Rxc8 Rxc8 30 Rxc8 Kxc8 31 Ke3 Nxa2 32 Nf8 maintains the extra pawn in the endgame.

28 h4 Rge8 29 Ndf4 h6 30 a3 Nd7 31 b4 Nde5 32 R4c3 a6 33 Ke3 b5 34 Nc5+ Ka7 35 Rd1 g5 36 hxg5 hxg5 37 Nfe6 Re7 38 Nxg5 Rg8 39 f4 Nf7 40 Rd7+ Rxd7 41 Nxd7 Nxg5 42 Rxc6 Kb7 43 Rf6 Nh3 1-0

It all came down to the last round match with Georgia. We unleashed the "danger squad", resting Gulko and Yermo. Nick made the move look good in grinding down Azmai with help from a cute tactic in the endgame.

___

☐ **N.DeFirmian** ■ **Z.Azmaiparashvili**
Yerevan Olympiad 1996

___

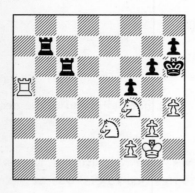

45...Rcb6? 46 Rxf5! Rb5

46...gxf5 47 Nxf5 is mate, but it's mate in three anyway.

47 Ng4+ 1-0

Kaidanov lost to Giorgadze, but Christiansen won on fourth board. It looked like I would need to win my game for a medal. I was playing Gennady Zaichik, a frequent visitor and future émigré to the U.S. I handled him most of the time, but this game the win looked elusive. I knew I needed to press hard, but for all I knew, a draw might be good enough for bronze. Donaldson feverishly calculated tie-breaks, but in the end I couldn't avoid a draw anyway. J.D. came to my board when it was over. "We just missed," he told me.

Our team spent some glum moments before we found out that John had miscalculated! He forgot that England's last round opponent, Hungary, had fewer points than Georgia. So we nipped them out and took the bronze, behind Russia and the Ukraine. The magic feeling from Novi Sad returned, but if anything, this was sweeter. The world was a lot tougher than in 1990.

There were long-term effects away from the chessboard, as romance abounded. Nick got together with Dane Christine Jensen (they would have a child), while Yermo met and eventually married a tall Lithuanian, Camilla Baginskaite. Camilla would later become a welcome addition to the American team as well.

1997 World Team Championship, Lucerne

Our bronze finish qualified us for the 1997 World Team Championship. The six returnees brought talent and chemistry to defend our title from 1993. My U.S. Championship win catapulted me to board two, behind only Yermo. The extra challenge of a high board took an early toll on me. I lost my first game to Zdenko Kozul of Croatia and didn't expect to play against England. Board two meant a date with powerhouse Michael Adams, a tough opponent to play when you haven't scored yet. But when the game was offered to Gulko in the team meeting, Boris didn't feel he matched up well with Black.

"Maybe Joel," he suggested. Thanks Boris. That game put me 0-2.

I got back on my feet against Switzerland. Before the match, Yermo balked at the prospect of playing Korchnoi. "He's going to insult me after the game, and I just don't feel like dealing with that." Korchnoi, I must say, has always been very kind to me. But he is notorious for post-game verbal barrages on his opponent. Yermo changed his mind and made a strong draw with Black. And Korchnoi insulted him.

I slid down to board two with White and defeated British émigré Joe Gallagher. That boosted my confidence for the Russia match and a difficult assignment against Peter Svidler.

☐ **P.Svidler** ■ **J.Benjamin**

World Team Championship, Lucerne 1997

---

1 e4 e5 2 Nf3 Nc6 3 Bb5 a6 4 Ba4 Nf6 5 0-0 Bc5 6 c3 b5 7 Bc2 d6 8 a4 Bg4 9 h3 Bh5 10 b4 Bb6 11 axb5 axb5 12 Rxa8 Qxa8 13 Na3 Nd8!?

I had become an expert on this opening preparing for Kasparov on behalf of Deep Blue. The text attempts to place the knight more actively than 13...Na7.

14 Nxb5 Nxe4 15 d4 0-0 16 dxe5 dxe5 17 Qe2 f5 18 Kh2 c6 19 Na3 Bc7 20 g4!?

20...Bf7

I was afraid of 20...Nxc3 21 Qc4+ Nd5 (not 21...Bf7? 22 Qxc3 e4+ 23 Kh1 exf3? 24 Bb2 and wins) 22 gxh5 e4+ 23 Kh1 exf3 24 h6, though White's threats on the long diagonal are not as powerful as I thought. In the game Black gets sufficient compensation for a pawn.

21 Bxe4 fxe4 22 Ng5 Bg6 23 Qc4+ Kh8 24 Nxe4 Ne6 25 f3 Nf4 26 Bxf4 Rxf4 27 Nb1 Bb6 28 Nbd2 Rf8 29 Kg2 Be3 30 Qe2 Bf4 31 Nb3 Bxe4 32 fxe4 Qa3 33 Qc2 Qa6 34 Nc5 Qc4 35 Qd3 Qg8 36 Qd7 Rd8 37 Qe6 Rd2+ 38 Rf2 Qd8 39 Nb3??

Black's counterplay was sufficient to draw, but after this blunder Black will obliterate White's pawn chain.

39...Rd3! 40 Rf3

40 Rxf4 exf4 41 Qxc6 was actually a better try, though I don't trust it in the long run.

40...Rxf3 41 Kxf3 Qd3+ 42 Kf2 Qe3+ 43 Kf1 Qf3+ 44 Ke1 Qxc3+ 45 Kf2 Qe3+ 46 Kf1 Qf3+ 47 Ke1 Qg3+ 48 Ke2 Qe3+ 49 Kf1 Qxh3+ 50 Kf2 Qg3+ 51 Kf1 Qd3+ 52 Kf2 Qe3+ 53 Kf1 Qf3+ 54 Ke1 Qxe4+ 55 Kf1 Qf3+ 56 Ke1 Qe3+ 57 Kf1 Qd3+ 58 Kf2 Be3+ 59 Ke1 h6

By throwing in a few extra checks I've earned a little extra thinking time. White must trade queens but the ending is hopeless.

60 Qc8+ Kh7 61 Qf5+ Qxf5 62 gxf5 Kg8 63 Na5 Kf7 64 Ke2 Bb6 65 Kd3 Kf6 66 Ke4 c5! 67 Nc6

If 67 Nc4 cxb4 68 Nxb6 b3 69 Nd5+ Kg5 wins easily.

67...c4 68 b5 c3 69 Nb4 Ba5 70 Nd5+ Kg5 71 Kd3 e4+ 72 Kc2 Kxf5 73 b6 Bxb6 74 Nxb6 h5 75 Nd5 h4 76 Kxc3 h3 77 Ne3+ Kf4 78 Nf1 g5 0-1

The final position is a curious twin to the Azmai game from Reykjavik 1990.

We went into the last round with a half-point margin and the tiebreak edge. We faced a beatable opponent in Kazakhstan, but Russia had the even more beatable Georgian women's team. We wanted to win as big as possible to control our own destiny.

I played board one against Pavel Kotsur in a most unusual game.

□ P.Kotsur ■ J.Benjamin
World Team Championship, Lucerne 1997

1 e4 e5 2 Nf3 Nc6 3 d4 exd4 4 Nxd4 Bc5 5 Be3 Qf6 6 c3 Nge7 7 Bc4 Ne5 8 Be2 Qg6 9 0-0 d6 10 Bh5!? Qxe4 11 Nd2

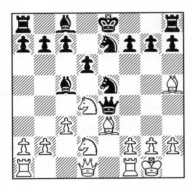

11...Qd3

This move leaves Black with no real options. 11...Qh4 is the safest way to avoid the repetition, but 12 Nb5 0-0 13 Bxc5 dxc5 14 Nxc7 Rb8 15 Qe2 is pretty equal anyway. 11...Qd5 is more combative but may favor White after 12 f4 Nc4 (or 12...Nf5 13 Bf2 Bxd4 14 cxd4 Ng6 15 Re1+ Nfe7 16 Rc1) 13 Nxc4 Qxc4 14 Re1.

12 Be2 Qg6 13 Bh5 Qd3 14 Be2 Qg6 15 Bh5 Qd3 ½-½

But why would Kotsur play for a draw with White? And why did Rublevsky bear hug him like a long lost brother??

Kaidanov drew on board two but Nick and Larry pulled out wins. You wouldn't think a 3-1 last round win could be a tragedy, but the Russians beat Georgia 4-0! We finished half a point behind in second place. We would have celebrated such a result from the beginning, but under the circumstances we were bitter. The Georgians were "outmanned" (pun intended), but not to score even one draw? It felt all too familiar. In the 1986 Olympiad, the U.S. went into the last round with the lead, only to see the Soviets take the gold by thumping Poland 4-0 (England went 4-0 as well against Brazil, dropping the U.S. to third). Over the years our suspicions were confirmed by confessions from some of the Polish players. They were compelled to throw the games for political reasons. [Ironically, the Bulgarians were waiting the night before for the Americans to approach them with an offer.]

Yermo, Larry, and I were stumbling around in anger after the last round. We started to shout "F***ing Postovsky", referring to the metal-mouthed captain of the Russian squad [under the theory that he had arranged the last match]. As we passed by Gulko's room, the door opened and Gulko stepped outside. We peered inside and saw Gulko's guest, Boris Postovsky.

Yermolinsky wrote an extremely controversial article in *New In Chess* accusing the Russians of buying the last round from the Georgians. He admitted he could not prove his case, but didn't care. "I don't care about evidence, I know what happened." It took a lot of guts to write that article, and I heard that Yermo lost a few friendships over his comments.

The evidence is highly circumstantial. Rublevsky hugging Kotsur is weird, but it doesn't mean he knew they had won the gold. Khalifman sitting out the last round (the theory is he would refuse to participate in a scam) doesn't really prove anything. And Russia certainly could beat Georgia 4-0. Unlike the Soviet days, Georgia couldn't be compelled to dump the match. It's hard to see Maia Chiburdanidze, a deeply religious woman, dumping a game.

I don't doubt that the Russians meddled in the Kazakhstan match (Bareev said as much at the time), which you can label improper, but it isn't illegal. So while the events look not quite kosher, I can't conclude we were victims of anything more than bad luck. It wasn't the first time, and wouldn't be the last that our team would experience heartbreak in the last round.

We would have to wait almost ten years for the Kazakhs to face the music. Did you guys enjoy "Borat"? Very nice!

Alex Yermolinsky

Yermolinsky cheered when the U.S. Hockey team pulled off its miracle win over the Soviets in the 1980 Olympics. Yermo was destined to come to America, and he fit in well with the natives from the beginning. In addition to the aforementioned article, he also wrote the no-holds-barred website Yermo's Diary *(1997-98, 2000-01). While one has to admire his brutally outspoken nature, there is a fine line between muckraking and nasty attacks.*

Alex's best run from 1996-97 took him to #1 in the U.S. rankings, when his mastery of technical positions brought him fame as the "Yerminator". Since then his play has declined as family obligations and a job at the Mechanics Institute have placed demands on his time.

Purgatory and Consolation

How does one go from board two to off the team in one year? Although I was defending U.S. Champion, and nearly successfully defended my title in '98 (second to DeFirmian), I had to watch the Olympiad on the Internet. I suppose I had some bad results over the course of the year to fall out of the top six, but I felt I belonged on the team.

I missed some excitement in Elista, the capital of FIDE President Ilyumzhinov's Kalmykia. The "City of Chess" was not built in time for the first round, so players had time to sit around and wait. As legend has it, vodka proved invaluable in creating team unity. The U.S. went into the last round with the lead but couldn't hold it, an unfortunate repeat of the previous year's experience.

I didn't get invited to the party in 2000 either, though I was actually U.S. Champion at the time of the Olympiad. I had a wonderful consolation prize. The Cap d'Agde rapid tournament wanted to invite two Americans and the scheduling conflict opened the door for me to get in (Serper got the other spot).

I never heard of Cap d'Agde, but when I googled it I found it was known for its nudist colony. I didn't find the colony, but I did find fine French food and more wine than I could possibly drink. I also found the type of event I would love to see in America. Two eight-player grandmaster round-robins met in an auditorium with digital boards screening the games for the audience to see.

I was pretty excited to play Karpov. I had met him before in a simul at fourteen (draw) and a blitz tournament (loss), but this would be a more serious game. I won a pawn and should have been in a position of strength, but I was relieved by the time the draw was concluded.

I qualified to the match portion with wins over Bologan, Zhang Pengxiang and rising star Etienne Bacrot. Since he has since surpassed the 2700 barrier, I will have to share how I annihilated his queenside.

☐ **J.Benjamin** ◼ **E.Bacrot**
Cap d'Agde (rapid) 2000

1 e4 c5 2 Nf3 Nc6 3 Bb5 e6 4 0-0 Nge7 5 Re1 a6 6 Bf1 d6 7 c3 e5 8 h3 g6 9 d4 Qc7 10 dxc5 dxc5 11 Be3 b6 12 Nbd2 Bg7 13 Nc4 0-0 14 Qd6 Qb8 15 Qxb8 Rxb8 16 Nd6 a5 17 Bc4 h6 18 Rad1 Be6 19 Bxe6 fxe6 20 Nc4 a4 21 Rd7 Rfd8 22 Red1 Rxd7 23 Rxd7

Kf8 24 Nd6

24...Na5 25 Nd2 g5 26 Kf1 Bf6 27 Ke2 Nac6 28 f3 Nd8 29 Ra7 Ndc6 30 Rxa4 Rd8 31 N2c4 Rb8 32 Ra6 b5 33 Nb6 Kg7 34 Bxc5 1-0

Mikhail Gurevich ejected me from the tournament and went on to win first place. I was glad to be away from the stink of the U.S. team's poor finish in Turkey, not to mention miss the torture of watching my beloved Mets lose the World Series to the evildoers from the Bronx.

China Summit Match, Seattle 2001

During my Olympic purgatory I got my team fix from an event organized by the AF4C, the U.S. Championship sponsors. Seattle hosted the first U.S.-China Summit in March 2001. The match, my first major event after my father died, was good therapy. As an alternate, I popped into the lineup in different places, playing three different players. Along with draws with Xie Jun and Zhang Zhong I executed a nice squeeze and combination against a strong veteran.

☐ **J.Benjamin** ■ **Xu Jun**
U.S.-China Summit match, Seattle 2001

---

1 e4 c5 2 Nf3 d6 3 d4 cxd4 4 Nxd4 Nf6 5 Nc3 a6 6 a4 g6 7 Be2 Bg7 8 0-0 0-0 9 f4 Nc6 10 Be3 Qb6? 11 a5! Qc7

11...Qxb2? 12 Na4 Qb4 13 c3 Qxa5 14 Nxc6 bxc6 15 Bb6 is clearly out of the question. 11...Nxa5 12 e5 looks too dangerous as well, e.g. 12...Ne8 13 Nf5 Qd8 14 Nxe7+ Qxe7 15 Nd5 Qd8 16 Bb6 with a clear advantage, or 12...dxe5 13 fxe5 Nd7 14 Nf5! Qd8 (if 14...Qxb2 15 Nxe7+ Kh8 16 Ned5 Nc6 17 Ra2) 15 Nxg7 Kxg7 16 e6! fxe6 17 Rxf8 Kxf8 18 Qd4 e5 (or 18...Kg8 19 Bg4) 19 Qd5 and wins.

12 Nb3 Be6 13 Nd5 Bxd5 14 exd5 Nb8 15 c4 Nbd7 16 Nd4 Rfe8 17 f5! Ne5 18 b3 Rac8 19 Kh1 Qd8 20 g4!

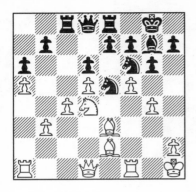

20...Nfd7? 21 g5

I missed 21 fxg6 hxg6 22 Rxf7 with the idea of Ne6 trapping the queen. This was good on the next move as well.

21...b6 22 Qd2 bxa5 23 Rxa5 Nc5 24 b4 Ncd7

The alternative 24...Nb7 25 Rxa6 Nxc4 26 Bxc4 Rxc4 27 Rc6! Rxc6 28 dxc6 loses immediately.

25 fxg6 hxg6 26 Rxa6 Nxc4 27 Bxc4 Rxc4 28 Qf2! Rf8

Or 28...f5 29 gxf6 Nxf6 30 Qg2 Qc8 31 Qxg6 with a winning attack.

29 Nc6 Qe8

30 Ra8!!

The combination is not difficult to calculate, but the sacrificial entrée is highly aesthetic.

30...Qxa8 31 Nxe7+ Kh7 32 Qg3 Nf6

33 Rxf6

Not 33 gxf6? Bxf6 34 Rxf6 Qa1+ turning the tables.

33...Qa1+ 34 Bg1 Qd1

White wins after 34...Qc3 35 Rf3 Qxb4 36 Bf2.

35 Rf3 Bh6 36 gxh6

The hasty 36 Qh3? Rh4! would spoil everything.

36...Qb1 37 Nf5! Rxb4 38 Nxd6 Qd1

39 Rd3

Short of time, I couldn't quite work out 39 Nxf7! Qxd5 40 Ng5+ Kxh6 (if 40...Kg8 41 Qc7 Rb7 42 h7+ Kh8 43 Bd4+ or 40...Kh8 41 Qe5+ mates) 41 Qh3+ Kxg5 42 Be3+ Rbf4 43 Qg2+! (the move I missed; instead 43 Qg3+ Kh5 44 Bxf4 g5 draws) and White wins. I didn't want to take a risk in a team event and so had to grind for another twenty moves.

39...Qe2 40 Re3 Qh5 41 Qf3 Qxf3+ 42 Rxf3 f5 43 Bc5 Rb1+ 44 Kg2 Rd1 45 Ne4 Ra8
46 Nf6+ Kxh6 47 Be7 Kg7 48 d6 Kf7 49 Nh7 Ra2+ 50 Rf2 Raa1 51 Ng5+ Ke8 52 Nf3
Ra4 53 h3 Re4 54 Ra2 Kd7 55 Ra7+ Kc6 56 Rc7+ Kb6 57 Rc2 Kb5 58 Kf2 Rd5 59 Rd2
Rxd2+ 60 Nxd2 Rd4 61 Nf3 1-0

We outscored them on the main boards but the Chinese pulled out the match on
the women's and junior boards (it should be noted that two women, Xie Jun and
Zhu Chen, played against our men).

China Summit Match, Shanghai 2002

We got a rematch next year in Shanghai, following an open tournament in Tsing-
tao (nice town, nice beer). We had a great and rare opportunity to see China and
learn about its culture. Shopping in China was a bizarre experience. Everything is
negotiable, and shopkeepers typically start with a price that is at least double
what you should pay.

One day Dmitry Schneider and I went out to buy pearls for our mothers. Alex
Goldin came along with us and proved to be a skilled bargainer. When the pro-
prietor offered a price that seemed reasonable to us, Goldin said "no" emphati-
cally and beckoned us to leave the store. Within seconds the price came down
considerably!

This time I played four games against one opponent—young talent Ni Hua. I
helped our team with opportunistic wins in the first two games.

□ **J.Benjamin** ■ **Ni Hua**
U.S.-China Summit match, Shanghai 2002

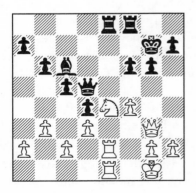

23 f5 Qe5? 24 Nd6! Qxe2 25 Nxe8+ Qxe8 26 Rxe8 Bxe8 27 Qb8 gxf5 28 Qxa7+ Bf7

29 Qxb6 Re8 30 a4 Bd5 31 Qa7+ Bf7 32 a5 1-0

In the second game Ni Hua pressed too hard in an equal endgame and lost a piece.

□ Ni Hua ■ J.Benjamin
U.S.-China Summit match, Shanghai 2002

42 Rc8?? Rb3 0-1

2002 Bled Olympiad

I made the team again in 2002, thanks partly to attrition (Nick and Yermo fell off considerably). Nestled in a picturesque lake, Bled, Slovenia, presented one of the nicest settings for an Olympiad. The lake provided the backdrop for humor involving a physical challenge of grandmasters. Ivan Sokolov (Yugoslavian born but now representing the Netherlands), confident of his fitness, taunted our Larry C about his conditioning. Somehow they agreed on a bet. They would contest a foot-race around Lake Bled. A heavy set lifelong smoker, Christiansen would get a head start. Sokolov overcame the spot and chugged to the finish line (where a crowd of Olympians had gathered). Larry had actually hatched a failed plan; somewhere up the trail Ilya Gurevich (U.S. Women's Captain) waited for Larry with a bicycle. It would have been glorious to see Ivan's face as he found Larry waiting for him at the finish. But Larry couldn't find Ilya and the joke was ruined.

The pleasant time away from the board contrasted the struggles over it. We were weakened by the loss of Shabalov, pulled out over money issues. [Unfortunately, it seems that every year we have protracted negotiations with the USCF over fees.] Only Seirawan found good form, challenging for a medal until a late loss to Kazimdzhanov. The rest of us varied from mediocre to awful, and the team finished wedged in the middle of the pack.

FIDE had introduced a new time control: ninety minutes for the game, with thirty seconds increment (time added for each move played). It takes a lot of practice to master this control. You need to play at a crisp pace and avoid time pressure altogether. I've always been used to making a time control with little to spare and moving on to the next hour. But here once you get into time pressure, you never get out of it; there is no next hour. You are glued to the board with no time to relax, no time to survey the position, and no time to even go to the bathroom.

I couldn't handle it at all. Although things started well (my first opponent inexplicably let his time run out), I was plagued by the clock the whole way. I lost four games, two to players I had previously conquered in team competition (Malisauskas and Zagrebelny). An unknown 2350 from Turkmenistan dealt me the most ignominious defeat. I had a comfortable position out of the opening and into the middlegame, but whittled away my time getting there. I was forced to play blitz the rest of the way, and my opponent, playing the first aggressive moves of the game, blew me away.

I could find my only escape from despair in Pub Bled, the favorite tournament hotspot. Some may be surprised to hear how much drinking goes on at tournaments, while others may look down on such practice. Chess is so stressful that players need to unwind, and I badly needed to unwind that night.

Over a few mojitos, I got to know Deborah Quinn from the Irish team. Fifteen months later we were married. Out of a tragedy came a blessing! Debbie had been playing in the Olympiad since 1990. Though I knew most of her teammates, somehow we had not met before. Could we have had many more years together, or would the wrong timing have ruined everything? Just another mystery of life to ponder.

After a second straight failure, we heard murmurs about an aging U.S. team no longer able to compete (age hadn't been a problem when we were winning). I also heard talk that some members of the team didn't care about the tournament. Nobody values the Olympiad more than I do. After many years of success, I hate to think that I may have ended my Olympic career on such a down note.

2004 Mallorca Olympiad

With relationship issues dominating my time and consciousness, my rating skidded and I didn't compete for a spot on the 2004 team. The standards are a bit lower for Irish women; hundreds of points lower than me, Debbie got to play. I joined her in the middle to offer moral support (she was having a terrible tournament) and catch up with some old friends. It was fun to watch so many great games, but it gets old after a while.

I soon got a lot more to do. The Irish captain, Eamon Keogh suffered a fall and broke his collar bone. He needed to return to Ireland for surgery and the lads needed a new captain. With access to the floor I could see a lot more action, so I agreed to do it.

You can't be captain without being drawn into the drama of the team. The top priority during my tenure in Mallorca was aiding Sam Collins' quest for the IM title. I fed him some extra Whites and he responded. The night before the last round we couldn't figure out if he had made the norm. During the round, one of the tournament staff punched it up on the computer and confirmed that Sam had his title. I thought he should know, but I didn't want the arbiters to freak out if they saw us talking. So I handed him a coffee and said, "Here's your coffee, International master." [He won easily anyway.]

That was not the only happy ending; Ireland came first in Category C, a kind of Olympiad class prize. Brian Kelly and I were the only team members on stage at the closing ceremony. Most of the team had taken early plane flights and missed out on the medals. They also missed the Spanish security takedown of Zurab Azmaiparashvili, who had approached the stage in a threatening manner. I, however, had a ringside seat, about twenty feet away.

2006 Turin Olympiad

In 2006 I came back as the official Irish team captain. We were all excited to stay in the Olympic Village until we realized that most of the amenities—phones, televisions, fridges, washing machines—had been stripped from the dorms.

The realm of possible results makes coaching a mid-major country an exciting proposition. In the end, though, a group of talented amateurs is bound to struggle against the heavyweight teams. We were pumped for our battle with Poland. I finally convinced Alex Baburin, Sam, and Mark Quinn (no relation to my wife) to let me bring them coffee (Irish captains had not done that in the past). Unfortunately, they all lost. Only Brian Kelly, who doesn't even drink water during his games, managed a draw. We battled back only to suffer another 3½-½ beatdown from Latvia. Our final tally placed us in the middle of the pack, about where our seeding was.

It's weird when people ask me how my team did and I have to ask them which one. Having seen me at Olympiads for years with the U.S. team, people don't think of me as "Irish". Of course, it's not unusual for a grandmaster to coach another country, though most of my colleagues get paid to do it. Qatar had GM Kuzmin; Luxembourg veteran Czech GM Vlastimil Jansa. Jansa was taken aback to see me in the adjacent coaches chair. I told him that if our teams should tie, we could have a playoff for the match.

* * * * *

The Olympiad is one tournament that I still want to play in, but it doesn't look like I'm going to make it back. I'm not likely to gain enough points to make it to the top six. There is an outside possibility I could switch nationalities and play for Ireland. That would be a drastic step, especially for a guy English IM Ali Mortazavi once dubbed "Stars and Stripes".

Chapter Seven

The Circuit

Americans feed on a steady diet of Swiss system events. From my early days through my professional career, open tournaments have accounted for many of my successes, as well as much of my frustrations.

World Open

Bill Goichberg has organized most of the major open tournaments in the U.S. for as long as I can remember. The World Open has been the flagship through the years, and my favorite as well. Early on it offered the best competition for my development; later it offered the best bang for the buck of a professional. Other tournaments require an equal monetary investment but do not match the World Open's prize fund.

The World Open was born in my childhood and will surely continue for a good time longer. I started in the second World Open in 1974 and followed the event from New York to Philadelphia. But the only World Open held outside of these cities—New Paltz 1981—provided the backdrop for my first World Open victory.

□ **J.Benjamin** ■ **K.Regan**
World Open, New Paltz 1981

---

1 d4 Nf6 2 c4 e6 3 Nf3 b6 4 a3 c5 5 d5 Ba6 6 Qc2 exd5 7 cxd5 Bb7

Though hotly debated at the time, this pawn grab soon fell out of favor.

8 e4

Weaker is 8 Nc3? Nxd5 9 Qe4+ Qe7!.

8...Qe7 9 Bd3 Nxd5 10 0-0 Nc7 11 Bg5 f6 12 Bh4 Nc6 13 Nc3 0-0-0 14 b4 g5 15 Bg3

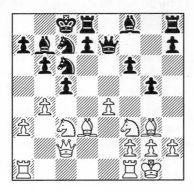

15...Ne5?

Black is anxious to block the h2-b8 diagonal, but keeping the c-file closed with 15...d6 should have been the first priority.

16 Nxe5 fxe5 17 bxc5 Qxc5 18 Rfc1 Kb8 19 Qb1 Qa5? 20 Nd5!?

White could win material immediately with 20 Nb5, but then 20...Nxb5 21 Bxe5+ Bd6 22 Bxh8 Rxh8 leaves White with technical problems.

20...Bd6 21 Ne3!

This leaves Black with no satisfactory defense to the threat of 22 Nc4.

21...Rhe8 22 Nc4 Qc5 23 Nxe5

Once again, White has a choice of powerful knight jumps. I missed a cleaner execution with 23 Nd2! Qa5 24 Nb3 Qa4 25 Rc4 winning at least a piece.

23...Qxc1+ 24 Qxc1 Bxe5 25 a4!

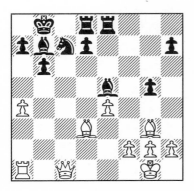

White will accentuate the powers of the queen by breaking down the pawn cover for Black's king.

25...Bxg3 26 hxg3 Ne6 27 a5 Nc5 28 Qa3 Re6 29 f3 h6 30 Bc4 Re5 31 axb6 axb6 32 Qa7+ Kc7 33 Rb1 d6 34 Bd5 b5 35 Rxb5 1-0

I blew the last round in New York '83, but fared better the next year in Valley Forge. I tied for first and topped it off by winning the newly instituted playoff for the title. In the next few years the World Open settled into a permanent home at the Adams Mark Hotel on the outskirts of Philadelphia. Consistently high entries produced record high prizes. I could not capitalize on this "golden age". When DeFirmian pocketed $26,000 in 1986, I could have tied him with a win in the last round. Unfortunately, Seirawan, in a rare open tournament appearance, did not comply and knocked me off the prize list.

Sometime in the 90's I soured on the grind of the American open tournaments in general and the World Open in particular. If you didn't manage a share of first place, you weren't going to turn a profit. A beefier middle of the prize fund could help a lot. Goichberg augmented it by extending the prize list down to thirtieth place. This was quite a savvy move. It was in Goichberg's interest for every grandmaster to win a prize because they only paid an entry fee if they earned a prize. So the bulk of these $300 prizes never get paid out.

In the late nineties I came back with a more Zen approach. Somehow, after twenty-five years of World Opens I found the formula for winning in 1999.

□ **R.Ziatdinov** ■ **J.Benjamin**
World Open, Philadelphia 1999

---

1 e4 g6 2 d4 Bg7 3 Nf3 d6 4 Be2 Nf6 5 Nc3 0-0 6 0-0 e6!?

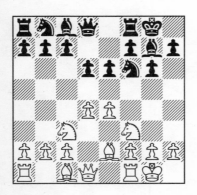

This was a personal specialty I developed in 1998 and used successfully in several games. A.Yermolinsky-J.Benjamin, U.S. Championship, Denver 1998, was a dramatic example: 7 e5 dxe5 8 dxe5 Qxd1 9 Rxd1 Nfd7! 10 Nb5?? a6! and White had to cough up the e5-pawn for nothing, since 11 Nxc7 Ra7 would put his knight in mortal danger.

At the 2002 World Youth, a teenage girl from the Ukraine asked me to pose for a photo with her. This sort of thing does occasionally happen; a 2600 rating does offer a fair degree of animal magnetism. But in this case the nice young lady was a fan of my ideas in the Pirc Defense. I was quite taken aback—I had never published any articles on my "Classical Hippopotamus" variation. Though I noticed Ponomariov repeated my opening, I was still surprised my invention made an impact upon the youth in faraway Ukraine. The chess world has become quite small. [Katerina Rohonyan, who finished third in the Under-18 section, eventually succeeded in coming to America to study.]

7 Bg5?! h6 8 Bh4

After 8 Be3 the move ...h7-h6 is quite useful for Black, preventing the plan of Qd2 and Bh6 trading the pivotal fianchettoed bishop. I had won a nice game against New Zealander Paul Garbett in the 1998 U.S. Masters: 8...Nc6 9 h3 b6 10 Qd2 Kh7 11 Rad1 Ne7 12 Nh2 Bb7 13 f3 Nh5 14 Qe1 f5 15 g4 Nf6 16 Bd3 a6 17 Qh4 Qd7 18 a4 Rf7 19 Rde1 Raf8 20 gxf5 gxf5 21 e5? Ng6 22 Qf2 dxe5 23 Rd1 exd4 24 Bxd4 Ng4! 25 Nxg4 Bxd4 26 Ne3 Qe7 27 Kh2 Qc5 28 Rde1 Rg7 29 Rg1 Rfg8 30 Ncd1 Ne5 0-1. But now Black gains dark-square control.

8...g5 9 Bg3 Nh5 10 Bc4 Nc6 11 d5 Nxg3 12 hxg3 Ne7 13 dxe6 fxe6 14 Qd3 Nc6 15 Rae1 g4 16 Nd2 Qg5 17 Bb3 Bd7 18 Nc4 b5 19 Ne3 Ne5 20 Qd1 Kh8 21 Ne2 Rf6 22 c4 h5 23 Nd4 a6 24 a4 bxa4 25 Bxa4 Bxa4 26 Qxa4 h4

27 Nc6 Rh6 28 Nxe5 Bxe5 29 Qd1 Rg8 30 f4 gxf3 31 g4 Qf4 32 Rxf3 Qh2+ 33 Kf1 Bg3 34 Ke2 Bxe1 35 Qxe1 Qe5 36 Qb1 Rf6 37 Rh3 Rgf8 38 Kd3 Rf4 39 Qh1 Qxe4+ 40 Kd2 Rf2+ 41 Kc1 Kg8 0-1

I beat Fishbein in the seventh round to grab a share of the lead. Ehlvest showed up in the morning expecting to play me, surprised to learn I was not playing him...or anyone else. I had put in earlier for an irrevocable half-point bye for round eight. I had found that the morning of the last round—an early game after a late game the night before—is extremely difficult for my body to adjust to. So I arrived rested and refreshed for the last round, still tied for the lead. This time we really did play, clinching a tie for first with a draw.

[I took the strategic bye approach one step further in the Chicago Open. I made the trip to give some simuls arranged by my good friend Ken Marshall. I wanted to spend a minimum of time at the tournament, so I requested byes in the last two rounds and played the fast schedule. On Sunday I played four G/60s (three wins and a draw), one slow game (beat GM Gildardo Garcia), and retired to a Memorial Day barbecue in the suburbs. 5½-1½ proved good enough for equal first. Thus I began the legend of the "one-day schedule".]

In 2000 I stumbled in the first round of the World Open, losing to the Mongolian woman Battsetseg. Humbling as it was, the loss did not affect my ultimate chances. I won the next four games and extended my streak with a cute combination against Walter Browne, who seemed less intimidating without his trademark mustache.

□ **J.Benjamin** ■ **W.Browne**
World Open, Philadelphia 2000

20 Rxe5! Bxe5 21 c4 Bxc4

If 21...Qd4 22 Nf3 Qxb2 23 Bxe5, or 21...Qd6 22 Ng4 f6 23 Qxh6+ Kg8 24 Qxg6+ Kh8 25 d4 wins..

22 Bxe5 Qxe5 23 dxc4 and White won.

By 2000 one could expect a GM opponent with 5-1 in the World Open. Instead I played FM Emory Tate, a colorful personality with a go-for-broke attacking style. Tate has acquired a kind of cult following, but I've always believed anyone can produce an occasional brilliancy if you sacrifice pieces in every game. Here Tate could only watch his opponent sacrifice for fun and profit.

□ **J.Benjamin** ■ **E.Tate**
World Open, Philadelphia 2000

---

1 e4 e6 2 d3 c5 3 Nf3 d5 4 Qe2 dxe4?! 5 dxe4 Ne7 6 Na3! Nec6 7 c3 Be7 8 Bf4 0-0 9 Qc2 Nd7 10 Bb5 g5?

This is the kind of optimistic lunge that few other players would dare to consider. But sometimes principles do matter.

11 Be3 f5 12 exf5 exf5 13 0-0-0 f4 14 h4! gxh4

If 14...fxe3 15 hxg5 Rf7 16 Bc4, or 14...g4 15 Ng5 Bxg5 16 hxg5 Qe7 17 Bd3 wins.

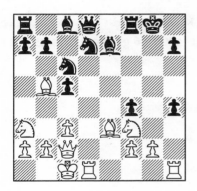

15 Bxc5!! Bxc5 16 Rxh4 Qe7

If 16...Rf7 17 Bc4 Qf6 18 Qxh7+ Kf8 19 Bxf7 Qxf7 20 Qh8+ Ke7 (or 20...Qg8 21 Rxf4+) 21 Rh7 wins.

17 Bc4+ Kh8 18 Rdh1 Nf6 19 Ng5 Be3+ 20 Kb1 h5 21 Rxh5+ Nxh5 22 Rxh5+ Kg7 23 Qh7+ Kf6 24 Rh6+ Ke5

Or 24...Kxg5 25 Qg6 mate. Now I decided a knight mate was a bit sweeter than 25 Qe4 mate.

25 Nf3 mate

In 2001 I joined the leaders with a rather instructive endgame win in round eight.

☐ **J.Benjamin** ■ **G.Zaichik**
World Open, Philadelphia 2001

42 Bf5 Be6 43 Bxe6+! Kxe6 44 a4 Kd7 45 f4! gxf4 46 Bxf4 Ke6 47 Bb8 Ke7 48 Kd5 Kd7 49 h4 Ne7+ 50 Ke4 Nc8

Or 50...Kc8 51 Bd6 Kd7 52 Bxe7 Kxe7 53 Kd5 Kd7 54 h5 etc.

51 h5 Ke6 52 g4 Ke7 53 Kf4 Ke6 54 Ke4 Ke7 55 Kf5 Kf7 56 g5 fxg5 57 Kxg5 Kf8 58 Kf5 Kf7 59 Ke5 Ke7 60 Kd5 1-0

If 60...Kd7 61 Be5 wins.

In the last round I survived an extended grilling from Alex Onischuk to maintain a share of first place. As soon as the draw was agreed, Leonid Yudasin rushed over to stick his two cents in. "Great Defense!" he exclaimed. "It was such losing position." Both players shot him an angry look.

I got back to the winners' circle in 2006 with nice wins over A.Ivanov and Stripun-sky. If I had finished off a winning position against Kamsky, I could have won clear first. But the main story was not of the winners, but a ghost of World Opens past.

In 1993, a dreadlocked man entered the open section under the name John von Neumann. He pulled off some surprising results (including a draw with GM Helgi Olafsson) but lost in strange ways. He let his clock run out in the middle of games, as if incapable of making more moves. He moved the pieces as if they were totally unfamiliar objects.

It was obvious to all that moves were somehow transmitted to this player. In choosing an obviously phony name (that of a pioneer of computer science) this individual made little attempt to get away with his crime.

In 2006 we saw improved tactics and technology. An unaccomplished amateur named Eugene Varshavsky defeated several players way beyond his 2100 rating. A spectacular win over GM Smirin could have easily been played by a computer. The biggest evidence against Varshavsky was how badly he played on the stage, when his technology failed him. The way he lost pieces in the opening of two games betrayed the fact that his genuine strength is far, far below master.

Another player in a class section was actually caught red-handed with a receiver on his person. Two incidents in one tournament indicate a possible future epidemic. With computers even stronger than grandmasters, a wired-in player can do more damage than ever. Escaping detection may be another matter.

U.S. Open

The U.S. Open is my other favorite tournament, but for quite different reasons. Its prize fund is not high enough to balance the high expenses of a longer event. But it's the rare American tournament with one game per day. As I've aged, I've also realized that I play much better when rested. The leisurely pace allows the U.S. Open to actually feel like a vacation.

The Open has an extra friendly feel with all the players in one section. It has traditionally provided great opportunities to juniors, something I appreciated a lot in my youth, but not so much now. I broke through as a contender in Hollywood 1985. Drawing with Seirawan and Boris Spassky, I managed to tie for first with the two heavyweights. I closed it out with a crushing defeat of Boris Kogan.

☐ **J.Benjamin** ■ **B.Kogan**
U.S. Open, Hollywood 1985

---

1 e4 e6 2 d4 d5 3 Nc3 Bb4 4 e5 Ne7 5 a3 Bxc3+ 6 bxc3 b6 7 Qg4 0-0 8 Bg5 Nd7 9 Bd3

f5 10 Qg3 Qe8 11 h4 Kh8 12 Nh3 Rg8 13 h5 h6 14 Bh4 c5 15 Nf4 Nf8 16 Qe3 c4 17 Be2 b5 18 Kd2 a5 19 f3 Kh7 20 g4 fxg4 21 fxg4 Rh8 22 Rhf1 Bd7 23 Rf3 Nc6 24 Rg1 Ra7

25 g5 hxg5 26 Bxg5 Ne7 27 Bxe7 Qxe7 28 h6 1-0

I didn't make it back to the winners' circle in 1986, but I have other memories from Somerset. The annual meeting of the USCF delegates takes place during the Open. I've attended all or parts of many of these conferences, though I find them too frustrating to do so today.

One day I was relaxing in my room watching the Mets on TV. I got a frantic call from my roommate, Fedorowicz. "You better get down here, they just put Gulko in the U.S. Championship!"

The delegates thought they were simply making a nice gesture to a man who had unquestionably suffered in the past. But at the time, Gulko was still resident in Israel and had never even been to America before the Open. He didn't even have a USCF rating. After Fed's call, I stormed into the meeting and grabbed the mike. I explained why the invitation process needed to be respected. I reminded the delegates that this was a zonal year; if Gulko qualified for the Interzonal, another American would lose his place.

Lev Alburt bizarrely offered to give up his spot in the Championship to Gulko (I should have agreed since he went on to win that year!). I suggested that I might just as well offer my spot to my garbage man. Lev could offer his spot to the next guy in line, Eugene Meyer, but he could not choose his successor. The delegates rescinded their vote.

It was the last U.S. Open for Sammy Reshevsky. For years he used the Sabbath to engineer easier pairings—strong players rarely wanted to be inconvenienced by playing at unusual hours. In Somerset, his proper last round pairing was against

Fedorowicz. When Fed was so informed the night before the last round, we implored him to agree to the 9:00 a.m. start.

Reshevsky came down bright and early to find Fed in the hotel lobby.

"What are you doing up so early?" Reshevsky inquired.

"I'm here to play you Sammy."

"You can go back to bed, they'll find someone else for me to play."

Fed looked him straight in the eye. "No Sammy. I *want* to play you!"

And Fed won the game before I even woke up.

In '85 and '86 the organizers offered me a free hotel room (provided I shared with another player), but in Boston '88 I could not get the same perk. With more and more GMs flooding into the community, organizers didn't see the need to offer incentives to draw strong players. The Open lost a lot of its attraction for me, and thus I sat out most of the 90's.

In 1998 my old friend and co-author Eric Schiller (*Unorthodox Openings*, 1987) invited me to play in the Open in Kona, Hawaii. Schiller ran a wonderful Open with good conditions for GMs and low class prizes. It was a financial disaster for the USCF, but a great time for me.

I competed for first until Judit Polgar took me down in the last round. But my defeat of Eduard Gufeld gave me continuing sustenance. Gufeld, who died in 2002, was the worst person I ever met in chess. In our last game in the National Open, he asked the arbiter to tell me he would not shake my hand. There was not much chance of that anyway. In the 1999 Open in Reno, he called me a "Jew" during an argument. I was as puzzled as I was offended that he would use that term pejoratively. Gufeld was Jewish himself, and frequently claimed to be a victim of anti-Semitism.

In the Hawaii International that preceded Kona, I was prosecuting an extra pawn in a queen ending when disaster struck.

□ **J.Benjamin** ■ **E.Gufeld**
U.S. Masters, Hawaii 1998

(see following diagram)
80 Ke5?? Qe6 mate

Ouch! I was much relieved to obtain redemption with a flashy finish in our Open game.

□ J.Benjamin ■ E.Gufeld
U.S. Open, Kona 1998

1 e4 c5 2 Nf3 d6 3 d4 cxd4 4 Qxd4 a6 5 c4 Nf6 6 Nc3 Nc6 7 Qd2 e6 8 Be2 Be7 9 0-0 0-0 10 b3 Qa5 11 Bb2 Rd8 12 Rfd1 b5 13 cxb5 axb5 14 a3 Bb7 15 b4 Qb6 16 Qe1 Ba6 17 Qf1 Rab8 18 Rac1 d5 19 exd5 exd5 20 Na4 bxa4 21 Bxa6 Ne4 22 Bd3 Bd6 23 Rc2 Bf4 24 g3 Bh6 25 Re2 f5 26 Qh3 Rf8 27 Bb1 Rbe8 28 Ba2 Ne7 29 Ne5 Qb5

30 Rxe4! fxe4 31 Qe6+ Kh8 32 Qxh6!! Nf5

32...gxh6 33 Nf7+ Kg8 34 Nxh6 is mate.

33 Ng6+ Kg8 34 Rxd5 1-0

For the rest of the tournament I held regular "screenings" of the game for the juniors in the hospitality room. "Come children," I would say. "It's time to see the 'Mona Lisa'."

In the twenty-first century I made it back to the winners' circle in Framingham 2001 and again in Phoenix 2005. I can picture playing in the U.S. Open long after I've retired from competitive play.

New York Open

Jose Cuchi's New York Open was never a commercial success and has disappeared from the tournament circuit. On several occasions the top section was run as a one game per day international and attracted even more elite grandmasters. I played a lot of interesting chess there over the years, and made a lot of memories. As the one tournament played on my home turf, it had a different dynamic from the others.

The 1984 New York Open provided my debut as a member of the world top 100 (Elo 2520). I went into the last round with a shot at first until the leader, Kevin Spraggett, beat Dzindzi to finish clear first at 7½/9. Still, a share of second would be mine if I could finish off my gangly, shaggy Yugoslavian opponent.

☐ **B.Abramovic** ■ **J.Benjamin**
New York Open 1984

Despite my extra queen, I couldn't find a clear continuation for the longest time. Finally I found an inspired move.

1...Bxg2!!

I was proud enough of this move to send it to the *Informant* for the combination section (a fortunate step, because I can't find it anywhere else). *Fritz* spoils everything these days, so I'm not surprised that it offered 1...Bg7 2 b6 Qe8 3 Nc6 Qa8 4 Ra7 Qf8 with an inevitable decisive penetration. But it still confirms the correctness of my continuation.

2 Kxg2 e4 3 d6 Qf3+ 4 Kh2 Bg7 5 Nc6 Qe2+ 6 Kh1 e3 7 Re7 Qd1+ 8 Kg2 Qd5+ 9 Kf1 Qxb5+ 10 Ke1 Qxc6 0-1

Alas, I could not enjoy this game for long. When the game ended my father told me that my Grandpa Ted died that day.

In the 1989 New York Open Fedorowicz ran a gauntlet of Russian grandmasters to take first place. One of the greatest American results ever was (unfairly, I believe) overshadowed by the defection of fourteen-year-old Gata Kamsky.

I spoiled too many good positions to keep pace with Fed, but I took pride in a win over a young player soon to join the world elite.

□ **B.Gelfand** ■ **J.Benjamin**
New York Open 1989

1 d4 Nf6 2 Nf3 e6 3 c4 b6 4 Nc3 Bb4 5 Qc2 Bb7 6 Bg5 h6 7 Bh4 Bxc3+ 8 Qxc3!? g5 9 Bg3 Ne4 10 Qc2 d6 11 e3 Nd7 12 Bd3 Ndf6 13 0-0-0 Qe7 14 d5 Nc5 15 e4 e5 16 Nd2 Nh5 17 Bf1 a5 18 f3 Bc8 19 Bf2 0-0 20 g4 Nf4 21 h4 Kg7 22 Nb1 Bd7 23 Nc3 Qf6 24 Ne2 Rh8 25 Ng3

We would likely have had a boring draw after 25 h5, but now Black livens it up with a pawn sac.

25...h5! 26 Nf5+ Bxf5 27 gxf5 g4! 28 Rg1 Rag8 29 fxg4 hxg4 30 Rxg4+ Kf8

My computer gives White a two-point edge here, but even with two knights against two bishops Black's dark square control offers good practical chances.

31 Rxg8+ Rxg8 32 b3!? Qh6 33 Kb2 Qh5 34 Re1 Qf3 35 Re3 Qh1 36 Re1 Qh2!

Going for the win in the time scramble!

37 Kb1 Rg4!

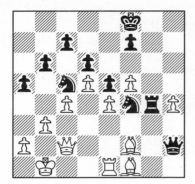

38 a3?

White is a bit pressed for a move, but this one allows 38...Nxb3.

38...Nfd3?! 39 Bxd3 Nxd3 40 Qxd3 Qxf2 41 Qe2 Qxh4 42 Ka2 Rg3 43 Qc2?

After 43 a4! White's defenses would be much harder to breach.

43...Qh3 44 Re2 Rc3 45 Qb2 a4! 46 bxa4 Qd3! 0-1

1990 left me with many memories. After I beat Bisguier in the first round, I barely made the cut and played the lowest first round winner, Robert Feldstein. The International section had a hefty entry fee for lower-rated players, so there were few easy points. But Feldstein, easily the lowest rated player in the section, got a first round bye.

It was the first night of Passover, and I wanted to wrap up quickly to join my family in Long Island. The game went quite smoothly, but I had to play very quickly to catch my train in time. Feldstein used all his time and didn't resign, despite losing all his pieces. It ended with a ladder mate—with a queen and *two* rooks. I declined his request to analyze the game.

Leonid Yudasin stopped my momentum in round four most painfully.

☐ **J.Benjamin** ■ **L.Yudasin**
New York Open 1990

(see following diagram)

Yudasin has just played **23...Rc5-b5??**. Suspecting nothing, I played **24 Qc2??** and went on to lose. Better would have been 24 Qa3+! Qxa3 25 Rd8+ Nxd8 26

Rxd8 mate. I'm still looking for my first win over Yudasin!

Two rounds later, I played another nemesis, Jaan Ehlvest. Jaan had come from a party where he enjoyed himself a bit too much. He was clearly inebriated when he sat down to play. But I still wasn't prepared when Ehlvest tried to make two moves in a row.

"What are you doing?" I exclaimed. He mumbled something unintelligible; I believe I had been thinking too long and he assumed I must have moved somewhere. I looked at the next board to Wolff. He was equally incredulous, but had no idea what to do either. Perhaps I should claimed the right to make two moves as well. After he took back his second move, he gradually regained his wits. I found my position becoming unpleasant. I thought I better offer a draw before he sobered up fully and realized how good his position was!

This was my first New York Open in the massive Manhattan apartment I shared with IM Mark Ginsburg. Mark had invited Hellers to stay with us for the tournament, and we got on quite well. One night we were sitting around discussing openings over a bottle of Absolut Citron.

Ferd told me about a strange and random gambit invented by a fairly obscure Swedish player named Sjodin. He pronounced the name like he was pointing his mouth in several directions at the same time. He would just shake his head when I would try to pronounce the name. Finally I contorted my mouth in a horrible scowl and tried to say it one last time. "Now you're not even trying," he said.

By this time the bottle was empty and the stupid gambit looked pretty good. And it actually worked the next day.

☐ **J.Benjamin** ■ **A.Machulsky**
New York Open 1990

1 d4 e6 2 Nf3 f5 3 e4 fxe4 4 Ng5 Nf6 5 f3 c5 6 fxe4 cxd4 7 Bd3 Nc6 8 0-0 d6 9 c3 h6 10 Nf3 Be7 11 cxd4 0-0 12 Nc3 e5 13 Bc4+ Kh7 14 Kh1 Bg4 15 Be3 Rc8 16 dxe5 dxe5 17 Bd5 Bb4 18 h3 Bxf3 19 Rxf3 Qe7 20 Rc1 Bc5 21 Bxc5 Qxc5 22 Be6 Rcd8 23 Nd5 Qd6 24 Nxf6+ Rxf6 25 Qxd6 Rxd6 26 Rxf6 gxf6 27 Bc8 b6 28 Bb7 Nb4 29 Rc7+ Kg6 30 Bc8 Kg5 31 g3 f5 32 Bxf5 Rd2 33 Rf7 Nc2

34 h4+ Kh5 35 Rg7 Ne3 36 Be6 Rf2 37 Bf7+ Rxf7 38 Rxf7 Kg4 39 Kh2 a5 40 Rf6 b5 41 Rg6+ Kf3 42 h5 Kxe4 43 Kh3 Kf5 44 g4+ Kf4 45 Rf6+ Kg5 46 Rf3 1-0

I found complete success in the 1993 New York Open. I tied for first at 7-2, with three of my wins—up-and-coming Hungarian GM Zoltan Almasi, DeFirmian, and Alburt—coming against grandmasters. Alburt dominated me early on; I think he took the first six decisions. Beginning with the 1986 U.S. Championship, I started to turn things around. Taking measure of his Benko and Alekhine, I had won five times before the following game. It has a bit of a twist—the Grünfeld appeared in my repertoire for only about a year.

☐ **L.Alburt** ■ **J.Benjamin**
New York Open 1993

1 d4 Nf6 2 c4 g6 3 Nc3 d5 4 cxd5 Nxd5 5 Bd2 Bg7 6 e4 Nb6 7 Be3 0-0 8 a4?! a5 9 Be2 Nc6 10 d5 Nb4 11 Rc1 f5
(see following diagram)
12 Nb5? c6 13 dxc6 Qxd1+ 14 Kxd1 Nxa4 15 Bc4+ Kh8 16 Nc7 f4! 17 Nxa8 fxe3 18 Nf3 Bxb2 19 Bb3 Nc3+ 20 Rxc3 Bxc3 21 c7 b5 22 Ke2 a4 23 Bd5 exf2 24 Nb6 e6 25 Rc1 exd5 26 exd5 Bb2 27 Rd1 a3 28 d6 Nc6 29 d7 Bxd7 30 Rxd7 a2 31 Rd1 Ne7 0-1

The 1995 New York Open (held, ironically enough, in Newark) granted a unique opportunity. Though I didn't do much to get there, I reached 6/7. In the seventh round Lembit Oll forced a suicidal transition into a lost pawn ending (tragically, the talented Estonian committed suicide for real a few years later). With high profile GMs bogged down in draws, only Pavel Blatny matched my score and I would have White against him in the eighth round.

I've played Blatny a few times and usually beaten him. I could see $$ before my eyes. Sadly, when I needed to beat him, I came up with a zero. I got a cool headline for my *New In Chess article*—"Discovered Czech in New York Open"—for what it's worth.

I still had a chance for a share of second, and I got there with a long and highly flawed game with DeFirmian. Though Nick and I have long been the best of friends, we have had a number of barn-burners over the years. He has won some big games against me, but somehow I had his number in the New York Open—I beat him in '93, '94' and '95, the last two in the final round.

I've never been fond of the other major open through the years, the National Open. Though enormously popular, the tournament was slow in beefing up its prize fund while quick in increasing its grandmaster content. To their credit, chief organizer Fred Gruenberg, and later Al Losoff, have cut down the expense of the trip by providing free hotel rooms to GMs. But the value of the tournament hinges on how you feel about Las Vegas.

Vegas is a soulless, artificial environment based on gambling. There are shows and concerts to see, but during the tournament you don't have time for anything but chess and gambling. In an early National Open, Fred Gruenberg gave a few of his favorite players some money to gamble with. I sat down at a blackjack table and played for a while, accepting a few complimentary bar drinks along the way.

Soon my money was gone. I had some money, and then I didn't. I just felt stupid. And I've rarely sat at a gaming table since. [For the same reason, I've only attended the Foxwoods Open sporadically.]

Of course, I would enjoy the tournament much more if I played better there. I think I tied for first once in the eighties, but subsequent visits have produced last-round losses and draws any time I had a chance for the winners' circle.

New York State Championship

Most state championships are held over the Labor Day weekend. More often than not I've been in Saratoga Springs, or Albany, Rye, Kerhonksen, Rochester, or wherever New York held its state championship. I've been credited with ten titles. I think I tied for some that didn't get counted, but they are balanced by years that out-of-state players finished ahead of me. I may not get to add to this title now that I have moved to New Jersey, but I still like playing in New York.

The prize fund is always just big enough. The competition is sufficient to get my interest, but not strong enough to chase me away. Most of all, the N.Y. State Championship appeals to me because my parents had a deep commitment to the state association. My late father served as President for many years, while my mother continues to serve as Secretary.

One of my more memorable games comes from a year I didn't even win. I've shown the finish to a number of classes.

□ **T.Rowland** ■ **J.Benjamin**
New York State Championship 1993

1 e4 c5 2 Nf3 e6 3 c3 d5 4 exd5 exd5 5 d4 Nf6 6 Be2 Be7 7 0-0 0-0 8 Be3 Qb6 9 Qc2 Nc6 10 Nbd2 Re8 11 dxc5 Bxc5 12 Bxc5 Qxc5 13 Nb3 Qd6 14 Rfe1 Bg4 15 h3 Bh5 16 Nbd4 Rac8 17 Qa4 Re4 18 Qb5 Rce8 19 g4? Bxg4 20 hxg4 Rxg4+ 21 Kf1 Ne4 22 Nf5

22...Qh2!! 0-1

Manhattan Chess Club Championship

Because the MCC helped me when I was young and unknown, I always had a sense of loyalty towards the club. I played in many of their championships in four decades, until they closed shop in 2002. I won seven titles, but the one I remember the most fondly is the first title, back in 1978. In the final group (the format was later changed to a Swiss), I defeated Sergey Kudrin, Larry D. Evans, and veteran master George Kramer.

□ **J.Benjamin** ■ **G.Kramer**
Manhattan CC Championship 1978

---

1 c4 e5 2 Nc3 Nf6 3 g3 d5 4 cxd5 Nxd5 5 Bg2 Ne7 6 Nf3 Nbc6 7 b4!

I knew Kramer liked this system against the English, so I was well prepared.

7...a6 8 a3 g6 9 Bb2 Bg7 10 d3 0-0 11 0-0 Nf5 12 Rc1 Ncd4

Black's play is inconsistent. If he wanted to drop this knight to d4, then 11...Nf5 was unnecessary.

13 Nd2 c6 14 Nc4 Nd6 15 Nxd6 Qxd6 16 Ne4 Qe7 17 e3 Ne6 18 Qb3 Kh8 19 Nd2

The knight maneuvers to probe the weaknesses in Black's position.

19...f5 20 Nc4 Nc7 21 Qa2 Bd7 22 Qa1 Rae8

23 Rce1 Nb5 24 f4 e4

This loses routinely, but 24...exf4 25 exf4 Bxb2 (or 25...Qf7 26 a4 Nc7 27 Nd6) 26 Rxe7 Bxa1 27 Rxd7 also costs material.

25 a4 Nc7 26 dxe4 fxe4 27 Nd6 Rb8 28 Nxe4 Nd5 29 Nc5 Rf7 30 Bxg7+ Rxg7 31 Qd4 Be8 32 e4 Nf6 33 f5 Rd8 34 Qb2 Rf7 35 e5 1-0

Lone Pine

The greatest tournament of my childhood was contested in a tiny California town nestled between Mt. Whitney and Death Valley. Sponsored by Louis Statham, Lone Pine offered enough prize money to entice high class European players. They provided rare competition for Americans, particularly a large contingent of hungry youngsters.

Lone Pine had quirky rules which added to its lore. Every player—no matter how famous—was expected to wear a name tag. You didn't dare ask for a complimentary sandwich without your badge. [Thus the classic Lone Pine riddle: A man is on the ground with a bullet hole in his head and a half-eaten tuna sandwich in his hand. What happened? Answer: He tried to get a sandwich without his badge and (head director Isaac) Kashdan shot him.]

In those days, Lone Pine provided the only opportunity for American juniors to see foreign stars in action. Each day Wilder and I would confer deity status on a new grandmaster. While we marveled at their play, we took in the interesting lifestyle choices of many colorful characters. One year Argentine GM Miguel Quinteros contested a marathon blitz session with the recent immigrant Roman Dzindzichashvili. The players took advantage of the free day to plant themselves for a good twenty-four hours straight. The physically fit Quinteros looked remarkably fresh, but Dzindzi looked like something a really large and powerful cat dragged in. Spectators would suggest Roman call it quits and go to sleep. "Sleep?" Roman queried. "I slept last Wednesday!" After all those games the differential remained very minimal.

Roman Dzindzichashvili

This bear of a man (think Fred Flintstone) can best be described as a lovable rogue. He had his best run in the eighties with two U.S. Championship titles and a strong result on board one in the 1984 Olympiad.

It may not be well known that Dzindzi always got on well with the natives, generally preferring their company to his fellow "Russians" (Roman came from Georgia). He was full of fruitful ideas and liberal with chess advice, though occasionally he forgot to mention some important detail in his analysis (I once got badly burned by blindly following a Dzindzi suggestion).

His gambling caused him trouble from time to time, most humorously in 1984 when Shirazi didn't earn enough prize money to pay off his debt.

Lone Pine required a minimum rating which I was only able to meet for the last three years—when Statham died, the historic event died with him. None of my results were spectacular, but some of the games were.

☐ **J.Benjamin** ■ **J.Silman**

Lone Pine 1979

1 e4 c5 2 Nf3 Nc6 3 b3 e5 4 c3 Nf6 5 Bb5 Be7 6 0-0 0-0 7 d4 exd4 8 e5 Nd5 9 cxd4 cxd4 10 Bb2 Nc7 11 Bxc6 dxc6 12 Nxd4 c5 13 Nc2 Qxd1 14 Rxd1 Be6 15 Nc3 Rfd8 16 Ne3 f6 17 Ne4 fxe5 18 Bxe5 Nb5 19 f4 Nd4 20 Kf2 Nf5 21 Nxf5 Bxf5 22 Kf3 Rd7 23 Nd6 Bg6?

24 Nc8!

This is not an obvious square for the knight, but it came to me when I saw 24 Nf5 Bxf5 doesn't work. I heard Silman mutter "cheap bastard". I'll assume he meant this in a gracious way—Jeremy and I have since been good friends for years.

24...Rxd1 25 Nxe7+ Kf7 26 Rxd1 Kxe7 27 g4!

I want to win a pawn in the best possible way. After 27 Bd6+ Kf6 28 Bxc5 Be8! Black suffers no further damage. With only a one-pawn majority, White will be hard pressed to win. In opposite bishop endings, the stronger side needs two passed pawns or a two-pawn majority. So I want to take the g-pawn—but 27 Bxg7 Bh5+! (not 27...Rg8 28 Re1+!) 28 g4 Bxg4+ 29 Kxg4 Rg8 wins back the pawn.

After the text, Black can't save the g-pawn: 27...Rg8 28 Bd6+ Kf6 29 Bxc5 gives White a decisive initiative. So Silman trades rooks, to enhance the drawing power of the opposite bishops.

27...Rd8 28 Rxd8 Kxd8 29 f5 Bf7 30 Bxg7 c4 31 bxc4 Bxc4 32 a3 Ke7 33 h4 Bb3 34 h5 Bd1+ 35 Kf4 Kf7 36 h6 a5 37 Bc3 a4 38 g5 Bc2 39 g6+ Kg8 40 Kg5 Bb1 41 Kf6 Bc2 42 Bd2 Bd3 43 gxh7+ Kxh7 44 Ke6 Kg8 45 f6 Bc4+ 46 Ke7 Bb3 47 f7+ Bxf7 48 h7+

Kxh7 49 Kxf7

I had foreseen I would have the wrong bishop and rook pawn combination here. If I waltz my king to his pawns, he will park his king on a8 and laugh. But the typical stalemating technique converts my a-pawn into a winner.

49...Kh8 50 Bc3+ Kh7 51 Bg7! b6 52 Bf8 Kh8 53 Bh6 Kh7 54 Bg7 b5 55 Bf8 1-0

The writing is on the wall. 55...Kh8 56 Bh6 Kh7 57 Bg7 compels the suicidal 57...b4.

I first played Walter Browne in the 1979 World Open. He surprised me with a move in the Queen's Indian I had never seen before: 1 d4 Nf6 2 c4 e6 3 Nf3 b6 4 g3 Ba6!?

I lost, but something he said increased my motivation for the next time: "I thought I played you before, but it was that other kid Root."

Browne was a bit of a litmus test for juniors, a way to "make your bones". He actually lost a lot to youngsters because his uncompromising style often left him vulnerable. Though I had success early and often against him, I always respected his accomplishments and determination. In Lone Pine 1980 I won the prize for the best game of the first round.

□ **W.Browne** ■ **J.Benjamin**
World Open, Philadelphia 1977

---

1 d4 Nf6 2 Nf3 g6 3 c4 c5 4 Nc3 cxd4 5 Nxd4 Bg7 6 e4 0-0 7 Be2 Nc6 8 Be3 b6 9 0-0 Bb7 10 f3

There were a few grandmaster games at the time where White incorrectly believed he could omit this move: 10 Rc1? Nxd4 11 Bxd4 Bh6 and 10 Qd2 Nxd4 11

Bxd4 e5 12 Bxe5 Nxe4. But now I was more or less making things up

10...Rc8 11 Rc1 Nxd4 12 Bxd4 Bh6 13 Rc2 Nh5 14 g3 Ng7 15 f4 f5 16 Rd2 Bc6 17 e5 Ne6 18 Be3 g5 19 Bf3 Qe8 20 Bh5 Qd8 21 Bf3 Qe8

I'm okay with a draw with the then four-time U.S. Champion.

22 Bh5 Qd8

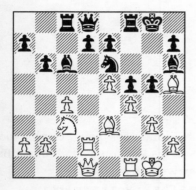

23 Nb5!?

Walter's fighting spirit leads him into danger. A few years later, against Grandmaster Benjamin, he might have settled for a draw here.

23...gxf4 24 gxf4 Kh8!

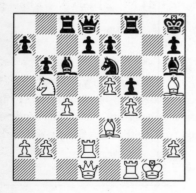

25 Rff2

This looks like a sensible precaution, but it was actually possible to grab here: 25 Nxa7 Rg8+ 26 Kf2 Nxf4 27 Nxc6! (the bishop is too strong to let live; the greedy 27 Nxc8 is refuted by 27...e6! 28 Bxf4 Bxf4 29 Ke2 Rg2+ 30 Rf2 Rxf2+ 31 Kxf2 Qh4+ 32 Kf1 Bxd2 33 Qxd2 Qxh5 34 Qe2 Qh3+ 35 Ke1 Qh4+ with a clear edge for Black) 27...Rxc6 28 Rxd7 Qf8 29 Bxf4 Bxf4 30 Qd4 Bxh2 31 e6+ Qg7 32 Qxg7+ Rxg7 33 Bf7

Rg4 with an unclear ending.

25...Rg8+ 26 Kf1 Rg7!

The organization of heavies on the g-file works out perfectly for Black!

27 Nxa7 Qg8 28 Ke2?

Browne misses the other point of my queen maneuver. Better defense is offered by 28 Qb3 Nxf4 29 Bxf4 Rg1+ 30 Ke2 Bxf4 31 Rxf4 Qg5 with extremely murky complications.

28...Nxf4+ 29 Bxf4 Qxc4+ 30 Rd3 Bxf4 31 Nxc6

Or 31 Nxc8 Qe4+ 32 Kf1 Rg1+! 33 Kxg1 Qh1 mate.

31...Qe4+ 32 Kf1 Rcg8 33 Rg3 Rxg3 34 hxg3 Qh1+ 35 Ke2 Qxh5+ 36 Rf3 Rxg3 37 Nd4 Rg2+ 38 Kd3 Rd2+ 39 Qxd2 Bxd2 40 Kxd2 e6 0-1

I didn't do anything memorable in the 1981 tournament, but I had a front row seat to one of the more amusing chess incidents. In the midst of a tense struggle, Sammy Reshevsky offered Fedorowicz a draw. Fed thought for a bit and accepted, only to find a bemused Reshevsky claiming he hadn't offered one. After arguing and looking around for an arbiter, Fed finally stopped the clock. Reshevsky started it again. After this happened a few times, Fed's tablemate Helmut Pfleger suggested he put the clock in his pocket.

Outside the hall, both players gave their versions of events. Reshevsky claimed he had offered a draw on an earlier move. Fed's testimony, backed up by two witnesses (Karl Burger and myself), was not enough to sway Sammy's old friend, Kashdan. "Both players are so sure what happened, I'm going to have to let the game continue."

He turned to Fed and asked him, over Reshevsky's objections, how much time he lost waiting for an arbiter. Upon resumption, Fed found himself right back in terrible time pressure because he couldn't remember what move he was going to play! Somehow he navigated the complications and reached a winning position. Fed made the time control and went for a victory walk. When he returned, he noticed Reshevsky had overstepped. "You're down!" he chuckled, and looked for an arbiter again. Kashdan was about to award a forfeit when Reshevsky pointed out he had made his 45th move, the last of the time control.

"That's true," Kashdan admitted. With eyes bulging, Fed explained that the flag needed to stay up after the move. Other arbiters came by and enlightened the chief TD. "Sorry Sammy," he told his buddy. "You lose!"

* * * * *

Since the nineties I've played in far fewer open events. The competition has gotten increasingly difficult, while the sites are still as boring. As I've aged the grind and stress of these two games a day events appeals to me less and less. During the school year I have little energy for weekend trips and not much time for preparation. So I only play in the big opens when the mood strikes me. They have been a lot of fun though.

Chapter Eight

International Adventures

Skien, Gausdal, Lloyds Bank 1978

I made my first European trek in the summer of '78. My parents were cool and trusting enough to send me off with adult players for chaperons. With fewer options for European events, American players tended to have common itineraries. I had many friends to look after me.

Skien, Norway was mostly unmemorable, though I did defeat a 2400 player. I do remember how carefully Goichberg's opponents approached him, intimidated by a lofty Elo of 2535.

Gausdal is a picturesque ski resort in the Norwegian mountains. I don't think my parents would have approved of the group trip the Americans took into the mountains...especially the return in the icy darkness of night!

In Gausdal Goichberg decided he didn't want to be bothered by having a kid around, so I roomed with Nick DeFirmian. One day Nick returned to the room and I asked him how he did. He told me he lost to "Siggy" (Icelandic GM Gudmundur Sigurjonsson). "Siggy played guitar," I told him.

Nick's eyes lit up. "Oh, you know your Bowie." It was the beginning of a beautiful friendship.

Nick DeFirmian

Soft-spoken, extremely polite, and overly generous (especially when it's time for another round), Nick has earned a reputation as the "epitome of laid-back California cool". Quietly as his demeanor, Nick has amassed a superstar career with three U.S. Championship titles and eight Olympic team appearances.

Nick likes his sports but doesn't follow his teams like a New Yorker. When his beloved Warriors made their recent playoff run he had to admit he only knew a few players on the team. But he knows a lot more about wine than I do.

My parents decided on a vacation in London and joined me for Lloyds Bank. I threatened the IM norm but was eliminated before the last round. My final opponent, veteran player and writer Michael Basman, could garner the title with a win. The organizers decided to bump us up to board two so the spectators could view the game on the demonstration board. This provided me extra motivation. Basman chose an unorthodox line I was prepared to refute, and had to wait longer to get his title.

☐ **J.Benjamin** ■ **M.Basman**
Lloyds Bank, London 1978

1 e4 c6 2 d4 d5 3 Nc3 g6 4 h3 Bg7 5 Nf3 Nh6 6 Bf4 f6 7 exd5 cxd5 8 Nb5 Na6 9 c4 Nf7 10 cxd5 g5 11 Bg3 h5 12 Nc3 h4 13 Bh2 Kf8 14 Qb3 Nc7 15 Be2 b6 16 0-0 Rh6 17 Rfe1 Bb7 18 Bd3 Qd7 19 Rac1 Rd8 20 Qa3

20...g4 21 Bxc7 gxf3 22 Bxd8 Qxd8 23 Qxa7 Nd6 24 Nb5 Nxb5 25 Qxb7 Nd6 26 Qc7 Qe8 27 Rc6 f5 28 Rxb6 Rg6 29 Rb8 Rxg2+ 30 Kh1 Qxb8 31 Qxb8+ Kf7 32 Qc7 Bf6 33 Qd7 Rxf2 34 Qe6+ Kf8 35 Rg1 Bg7 36 Qg6 Rg2 37 Rxg2 fxg2+ 38 Kxg2 Bxd4 39 Qh6+ Ke8 40 Qh5+ Kd8 41 Bxf5 Bxb2 42 Bd3 Bf6 43 a4 1-0

A year and a half younger than me, Nigel Short had a disappointing result. I learned how brutal the chess press can be when I read reports describing Nigel's "groveling among the tail-enders".

Traveling on my own provided the occasional pitfall. People often overlook the effects of long flights and jetlags on American chess performance. The 1984 Berlin Summer Open got off to a rocky start for me when my flight to Frankfurt was delayed eight hours. I missed my connection and didn't make it to Berlin until late in the night before the first round. Nearly delirious, I sank into a deep sleep. Eric Schiller woke me up with a phone call. "Get down here," he said. "Your clock is running." I had slept for thirteen hours straight. [I returned for the same tournament five years later, one of the last before the Wall came down.]

Hastings 1984/85

The Hastings tournament is steeped in folklore, iconic enough to appear in the classic song from the musical *Chess*, "One Night in Bangkok". That song came out around the time of my first appearance in Hastings. Although the 1987 GM-laden edition was much stronger and more prestigious, I appreciate the memories more from 1984.

As we walked from the train station, my travel partner, Fedorowicz, regaled me with stories of Hastings past—something about a pantomime below the Yelton Hotel. We lugged our bags there only to find out the tournament had moved to a new site; fortunately signs in the town pointed us to the Queens Hotel.

Hastings proved as cold, windy, rainy and nasty as advertised. Unfortunately, the climate inside the hotel was not much better. While Fed huddled under the covers reading the *Informant* in his room, I bought masking tape to plug the numerous holes in my bathroom.

I came a solid second behind Sveshnikov (the guy with the opening). I drove home a nice attack against future GM and lawyer, Willie Watson.

□ **J.Benjamin** ■ **W.Watson**
Hastings 1984/85

---

1 Nf3 Nf6 2 c4 g6 3 g3 Bg7 4 Bg2 0-0 5 0-0 d6 6 Nc3 Nc6 7 Rb1 a5 8 a3 e5 9 d3 Nd4 10 Bg5 h6 11 Bxf6 Bxf6 12 b4 axb4 13 axb4 Bg4 14 e3 Ra3 15 Nd5 Nxf3+ 16 Bxf3 Bh3 17 Qc1 Rxd3 18 Be4 Bf5 19 Bxf5 gxf5 20 b5 e4 21 Qc2 c6 22 bxc6 bxc6 23 Rb8 Qxb8 24 Nxf6+ Kg7 25 Nh5+ Kh7 26 Rb1 Qa7 27 Qb2 f6 28 Ra1 Qc7?

White's vigorous play might have come to naught after 28...Qf7! 29 Nf4 Qxc4.

29 Nf4 d5 30 Ne6 Qe7 31 Nxf8+ Qxf8 32 Ra7+ Kg6 33 Qb7 Qg8 34 Ra8 Qf7 35 Qb8 dxc4 36 Qh8 *(see following diagram)* **36...c3 37 Rg8+ Kh5 38 h3! 1-0**

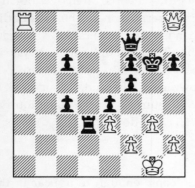

Jerusalem 1986

I made my first (and to this point only) *aliyah* to Israel in 1986 for a protest tournament to the Dubai Olympiad. I was joined by players from boycotting nations (Agdestein of Norway and Curt Hansen from Denmark), my countryman Dmitry Gurevich, and several Israeli players. A nasty attack of strep throat and mononucleosis torpedoed my final result.

My game with Yakov Murei featured a most unusual situation. When the game started, we were both IMs. When the game was adjourned, we were both GMs (it was during the FIDE Congress). When the game ended, I was still a GM but my opponent was back to being an IM (the report of his GM application's acceptance proved to be erroneous).

I was welcomed to the GM fraternity by a children's lesson from the great Viktor Korchnoi. I felt I was lost in the adjourned position, but I didn't see the winning maneuver.

☐ **J.Benjamin** ■ **V.Korchnoi**
Jerusalem 1986

(see following diagram)

As I sealed 57 Kd1, Korchnoi stood up and said, "I know something about triangles." With a feeling of dread, I looked to Gurevich to enlighten me with his Soviet endgame education. After his explanation, I sheepishly resigned. "It is the ABCs of chess," he quite correctly stated.

The finish would have been: 57...Kd5! (not 57...Kd3?? 58 Ke1 e2 59 g5 fxg5 60 g4 with a draw) 58 Ke1 Ke5! 59 Kd1 Kd4 (zugzwang) 57 Ke1 Kd3 58 Kd1 e2+ 59 Ke1 Ke3 60 g5 fxg5 61 g4 Kf3 and Black wins.

Moscow 1987

In those days, European travel challenged the finances of young American players. To save money at the Reykjavik Open, Fedorowicz, Wilder, and I bunked together in a tiny room. In pricey Iceland, we subsisted on the one menu item we
could afford—the egg sandwich with shrimps.

The dynamic changed next year as a grandmaster supported by the Samford
Fellowship. Wilder and I moved to Barcelona to set up training camp in the
apartment Fedorowicz shared with his girlfriend. We holed up indoors most of
the time, but the rare occasions when the three marginal Spanish speakers went
out on the town produced comic results. We produced a most unusual dessert
order in our favorite Chinese restaurant, Restarante Los Pandos. I ordered "he-
lado" (ice cream), Mike ordered "rollos primaveras" (spring rolls), and John opted
for "cerveza" (beer).

We ordered a bunch of *New In Chess* Yearbooks and got down to business.
"Pasajeron the handboeken," Fed would say, in a weird mixture of three lan-
guages. I would make them play training games with me in various openings.
Mike complained bitterly when I made him play the Dutch! Some of the preparation is ironic in hindsight. I decided to learn an old, offbeat line against the
Nimzo-Indian. At the time only a handful of GMs played the Qc2 variation, but
now it is the main line!

The marathon analysis sessions left me better prepared than I had ever been
before. I was raring to go for my Interzonal warm-up in Moscow.

I found circumstances behind the Iron Curtain as advertised—Spartan conditions, creepy surroundings, and mysterious phone calls in the middle of the night.
I didn't much care—I was in full "kill a Commie for mommy" mode. I wanted
scalps, and I didn't care about losses...which mounted until I ended up -1.

I took down Romanishin, Lputian, Vasiukov, Hodgson, and Petursson. See if you can spot the oddity in the following game:

☐ **J.Benjamin** ■ **S.Lputian**

Moscow 1987

---

1 Nf3 Nf6 2 c4 g6 3 Nc3 d5 4 cxd5 Nxd5 5 Qa4+ Bd7 6 Qc2 Nb4 7 Qb3 N8c6 8 a3 Be6 9 Qa4 Nd5 10 Ne5 Nxc3 11 dxc3 Qd5 12 Nxc6 Qxc6 13 Qxc6+ bxc6 14 Be3 Bb3 15 g3 e5 16 Bg2 Kd7 17 Rc1 a5 18 c4 a4 19 Rc3 Ra6 20 g4 Bg7 21 Be4 Ke6 22 Rg1 Rd8 23 Rc1 Ba2 24 f3 Bf8 25 Bd3 Bg7 26 Bf5+ Ke7 27 Be4 Rb8 28 Bc5+ Ke6 29 Bb4 Bf6 30 g5 Be7 31 c5

31...Rh8 32 Bd2 Bd5 33 Bd3 Raa8 34 Rg4 Bf8 35 Rb4 h6 36 e4 Bb3 37 Rb7 Rc8 38 Ba6 Ra8 39 Bf1 hxg5 40 Rxc7 Rxh2 41 Rxc6+ Kd7 42 Rb6 g4 43 c6+ Kc7 44 Rb7+ Kc8 45 Be3

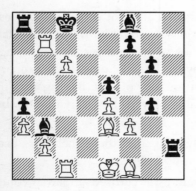

45...Rxb2 46 Ba7 Be6 47 Ba6 Rxa7 48 Rxa7+ Kb8 49 Rxf7 Bd6 50 c7+ Bxc7 51 Rfxc7 gxf3 52 R7c2 Rb3 53 Bc4 1-0

In fifty-five moves the white king never moved!

Unfortunately, the losses mounted up—Gurevich, Malaniuk, Dolmatov, Geller, Hjartarson. I was shocked to lose two games to the Dutch Defense. I had always considered the Dutch to be incorrect (and Wilder too, obviously), mainly because most of my games in it were against weaker opponents. I now learned that strong players in other countries effectively used different strategies than I was used to.

Szirak Interzonal 1987

The American contingent—I, Fed, Wilder, Christiansen and his second DeFirmian—arrived in Hungary with confidence quickly dampened by the depressing surroundings. Christiansen and I snagged rooms at the site hotel in Szirak, but our seconds were housed miles away in the village of Acsa. We were in the middle of nowhere, with a month to kill. FIDE did not easily find takers for the traditional round-robin Interzonals. They sweetened the deal by stretching the tournament (adjournment days on top of free days) so the hotel could make as much money as possible. While "chess rates" in the U.S. suggests a discount, the chess rate in Szirak greatly inflated the standard cost of the rooms.

Other rates would unexpectedly rise. Perpetually on a tight budget, Wilder checked the phone rates before calling his girlfriend. When the charges turned out to be orders of magnitude higher, he complained to the hotel clerk. She thought for a moment and answered in her best Ivan Drago (from *Rocky IV*), "You must pay!" [He didn't pay.]

We struggled to keep our sanity throughout the ordeal. One night Nick, Fed, and Mike danced around maniacally as they cranked up a Tom Jones special on television. Nick greeted Romanian GM Mihai Marin at the door. "Come on in, it's Tom Jones," Nick told him. "Yes, it's very pleasant," Marin answered in his high-pitched voice. "But I need to sleep now."

We were so bored, we found amusement at the expense of each other. One day Larry dropped a lit cigarette down his shorts. "No, get out of there," he told the butt, which chose not to burn him. My boys descended to practical jokes. One day Mike showed up alone for pre-game preparation, shaking his head. "John got into Elvar's vodka." As I started to fume, John stepped in the room laughing his head off. [I got my revenge by sending John into Budapest to reconfirm our flights...which we had already reconfirmed.]

Hungary endured a major heat wave during the tournament. Without the air conditioning we are accustomed to in America, I wilted in the heat. I felt unfairly disadvantaged against Brazilian GM Milos, who surely felt at home in the muggy conditions. The tournament staff showed no sympathy. One day I wore shorts to combat the heat. An arbiter stopped to admonish me. "You are a man, not a boy.

Do not wear short pants." I was disappointed to finish on fifty per cent, but not sorry for the experience. Today many highly rated players are largely anonymous, but then the premier players were larger than life figures. In Szirak I had my first encounters with the likes of Ljubojevic, Andersson, Beliavsky, and Portisch. The finish to my game with the legendary Hungarian was quite noteworthy.

□ **L.Portisch** ■ **J.Benjamin**
Szirak Interzonal 1987

---

1 d4 Nf6 2 c4 e6 3 Nf3 c5 4 d5 exd5 5 cxd5 Bd6?!

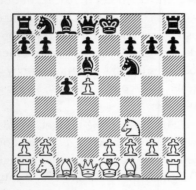

The Snake had some moments in the eighties, but 6 g3 Bc7 7 d6! put the line out of business, as Fed found to his chagrin against Stuart Conquest. Portisch did not have the same success, though. I did well until I dawdled too much.

6 Nc3 Bc7 7 Nd2 d6 8 Nc4 a6 9 a4 Nbd7 10 Bg5 0-0 11 e4 Re8 12 Bd3 Rb8 13 Ne3 h6 14 Bh4 Ne5 15 0-0 Bd7 16 Bc2 Ng6 17 Bg3 b5 18 axb5 axb5 19 f3 c4 20 Ne2 Nh5 21 Bf2 Bb6 22 g3 Ne5 23 Kg2 b4 24 Re1 Rc8 25 Ng1 Nf6 26 Rc1 Bc5 27 Nf1 Bxf2 28 Kxf2 Qb6+ 29 Kg2

29...Ra8 30 Bb1 Rec8?! 31 Ne3 c3 32 b3 Ra3?! 33 h3 Bb5? 34 f4 Ned7 35 Nf3 Re8 36 Nf5 Nc5 37 e5! dxe5 38 fxe5 Nxd5!?

Black is in danger of being overrun, e.g. 38...Nh7 39 N3d4 or 38...Nfd7 39 e6! fxe6 40 Qd4. So I make a stand for counterplay while I can.

39 Qxd5 Bc6 40 Qd4 Rxb3 41 e6 f6 42 e7?

42 Bc2! Rb2 43 e7 would have killed my combination.

42...Bxf3+ 43 Kxf3 c2+ 44 Kg4!

44...Qc6

For years I believed this move was forced, but *Fritz* now reveals 44...cxb1Q is good enough for a draw! 45 Qd5+ Ne6! 46 Rxb1 Rxb1 47 Rxe6 Rd1! surprisingly holds. 48 Qe4 (or 48 Qc4 Rc1!) 48...Qc7 49 Nxh6+ (if 49 Rxf6 Qd7! defends, though 50 Re6 still looks like a draw) 49...Kh8 and perpetual check seems to be the best White can do.

45 Kh5! cxb1Q 46 Rxb1

46...Qf3+??

137

This is the move that doomed me to defeat. Now my king is boxed in and the a2-g8 diagonal to my king is completely undefended. Instead I could have turned the tables with 46...Kh7!!—for example, 47 Rxb3 g6+! 48 Kh4 Nxb3 49 Qd3 Nd2! and Black has a winning position (if 50 Qxd2? g5+). I probably rejected 46...Kh7 because of 47 Qg4 Qf3 48 Qxf3, overlooking the shocking mating net after 48...g6+! 49 Kh4 (49 Kg4? h5+ just costs White a tempo because 50 Kf4 g5 is mate) 49...Rxf3 50 Nd6 h5!. The rook on e8 is now immune because 51...Kh6 forces mate, and otherwise White is in big trouble with his king stuck on the side, e.g. 51 Rxb4 Nd3 52 Rbb1 Nxe1 53 Rxe1 Kh6! 54 Nf7+ Kg7 55 Nd6 Rh8 56 e8N+ Kf8 57 Nxf6 Rxf6 and Black enjoys an extra exchange.

47 Kg6 Rd3

If 47...Rxb1 48 Qc4+ and Qf7 wins.

48 Qxc5 Rd5 49 Rf1!

Unfortunately, great players don't fall for traps like 49 Qc8?? Qxg3+! 50 Nxg3 Rg5 mate.

49...Rxf5 50 Qxf5 Qxg3+ 51 Kh5 Rxe7 52 Rg1 Qc3

I had to try 52...Qb8 but the extra rook should win eventually.

53 Rbc1 Re5 54 Rxc3 Rxf5+ 55 Kg6 1-0

I concluded my European summer in Lloyds Bank. I finished tied for second, part of an American invasion that brought first place to Wilder. I avenged my loss to John Nunn in Szirak. Unsure how to tackle his King's Indian, I opened with 1 Nc3!? and managed to win a long endgame. I encountered Nigel Short while pacing during the game. "Don't worry, he's not making faces at you," Nigel told me. "He always does that."

World Chess Festival, St. John 1988

The U.S. Championship title put me in a great career position. I wrote to the organizer of Lugano and requested a starting fee of 3000 Swiss francs to participate in the 1988 open. My request was granted. Times would never be better for a Western grandmaster. After the collapse of the Soviet Union, the glut of grandmasters would bring an end to appearance fees in opens for all but elite grandmasters.

1988 started with a bang at the World Chess Festival in St. John, New Brunswick in Canada. I started with three quick wins and faced an unlikely co-leader, eighteen-year-old Patrick Wolff. He offered an early draw. Sorry, rook, you have to earn that kind of respect. 4-0. After that I sprinkled in draws with Rohde, Chernin, and Gulko around one more win.

□ J.Benjamin ■ V.Eingorn

St. John 1988

1 e4 e6 2 d3 c5 3 Nf3 Nc6 4 g3 d5 5 Nbd2 g6 6 Bg2 Bg7 7 0-0 Nge7 8 Re1 h6 9 h4 b6 10 c3 a5 11 a4 Ba6 12 exd5 exd5 13 Nb3 0-0 14 d4 c4 15 Nbd2 Bc8 16 Nf1 Be6 17 Bf4 Qd7 18 b3 cxb3 19 Qxb3 f6!? 20 Qxb6 g5 21 hxg5 hxg5 22 Bc1 Rfc8 23 Qb5 Rab8 24 Qe2 Nd8

25 Bxg5

I didn't need to speculate here—White keeps a nice edge with 25 Ne3. But I had guts, didn't I?

25...fxg5 26 Nxg5 Rb6 27 Qd3 Qe8 28 Ne3 Qh5 29 f4 Bf7 30 Bf3 Qg6 31 Qxg6 Rxg6 32 Ra3 Rd6 33 Nxf7 Kxf7 34 Rb3 Ne6 35 Kg2 Rcc6 36 Rb7 Nc7 37 Bh5+ Kg8 38 Rb8+ Bf8?

White has gradually gained ground, but 38...Kh7 would keep it unclear.

39 Ng4 Nf5 40 Re5 Ng7 41 Rg5

41...Nce6

It's too late too save the game. Failing defenses include 41...Rxc3 42 Ne5 Rf6 43 Nd7 and 41...Na6 42 Ra8 Nc7 43 Rc8 Na6 (or 43...Nce6 44 Nf6+ Kh8 45 Rg6) 44 Bf7+! etc.

42 Nf6+ Kh8 43 Rg6 Nxf4+

Black has no choice but to enter a hopeless ending.

44 gxf4 Rxf6 45 Rxf8+ Rxf8 46 Rxc6 Nxh5 47 Rh6+ Kg7 48 Rxh5 Rc8 49 Rxd5 Rxc3 50 Rxa5 Rc4 51 Kf3 Rxd4 52 Kg4 1-0

In the last round I just needed a draw to clinch first. I met Mihai Suba's Hedgehog cautiously, then eagerly found a combination to trade two sets of minors. When he offered me a draw, I paused to consider my windfall—10,000 dollars, even when they're Canadian, is pretty awesome! When I accepted, Suba asked me incredulously, "What were you thinking about?"

The second international drew some extra heavies, including some losers from the Candidates Matches. I scored a solid 6-3, including a win over living legend Svetozar Gligoric. I finished my dream month by losing to my roommate (awkward pairing there) Wilder in the World Blitz Championship. I started to think I was worth the money the Swiss were about to pay me.

Lugano 1988

Lugano was paired under the Bucholz system, which used ongoing tiebreaks instead of ratings to make pairings. When my Bucholz points slid into the bottom half, I faced GMs like Gulko (loss), Reshevsky (a win; wish I had the game score), and an East German at his career peak (2575):

□ **U.Bönsch** ■ **J.Benjamin**
Lugano 1988

---

1 d4 Nf6 2 c4 e6 3 Nf3 b6 4 g3 Ba6 5 b3 Bb4+ 6 Bd2 c5!?

Just a little something that popped into my head while walking on the frozen boardwalk of Hastings in 1984, though I didn't get a meaningful test until 1988. The novelty is provoking b2-b3 in conjunction with ...c7-c5. This means an exchange on b4 will leave a hole on c3.

7 Bg2 Bb7 8 0-0 0-0 9 dxc5

My opening held up one month earlier: 9 Bxb4 cxb4 10 a3 Na6 11 axb4 Nxb4 12 Nc3 Ne4 13 Qc1 Nxc3 14 Qxc3 a5 15 Ne5 ½-½ (A.Yusupov-J.Benjamin, St. John 1988). Another point of my variation is the opening of the long diagonal for tactics in the line 9 d5 exd5 10 Bxb4 cxb4 11 Nh4 Ne4 12 cxd5 Qf6 with complications.

Probably the critical reply is 9 Bc3. A few months before this game I showed my idea to Korchnoi, who suggested the continuation 9...Na6 10 Bb2 d5 11 a3 Ba5. He also played the line a few times himself.

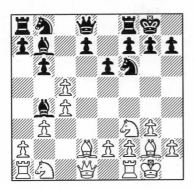

9...Bxc5 10 Nc3 Ne4 11 Qc2 Nxd2 12 Nxd2 Bxg2 13 Kxg2 f5

The white knights won't have an easy time finding active squares.

14 Rad1 Nc6 15 Nf3 Qe7 16 Nb5 a6 17 Nbd4 Nd8!

Black needs to keep a knight on the board for potential attacking chances.

18 e4 fxe4 19 Qxe4 Nf7 20 h4?!

White forgets about the queenside. 20 a4 keeps things level.

20...b5! 21 cxb5 axb5 22 Rd2 b4

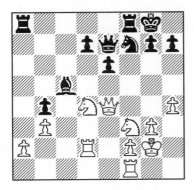

Sometimes pawn islands lie. Black's pawn structure gives him dynamic play. The b-pawn holds White's pawn majority, while the center pawns will provide outposts for Black's pieces.

23 Re1 Qf6 24 Ree2 Ra5 25 Nh2 Nd6 26 Qd3 Qd8!

My cool queen maneuver is a prelude to interesting rook use.

27 f4 Qa8+ 28 Ndf3 Rf5! 29 Kh3 Rd5 30 Qc2 Rxd2 31 Qxd2 Ra7! 32 Qc2 Rc7 33 Qd3 Nf5 34 Ng4? Bf8?

I missed a big chance here: 34...Bd6! causes a catastrophe on the third rank.

35 Nge5 d6 36 Nc4 d5 37 Nce5

I thought that 37 Nb6 Qc6 38 Ng5 was stronger, but instead of 38...Qxb6 39 Rxe6 Qg1 40 Qxf5 Qh1+ 41 Kg4 Qd1+ with a draw, 38...Qc3! is crushing.

37...Rc3 38 Qb5 Qc8 39 Rd2 h6 40 Kh2 Nd6 41 Qf1 Ne4 42 Rg2 Bd6 43 Nd4 Rc1 44 Qf3 Bxe5 45 fxe5

45...Re1?

Giving up the c-file prematurely should have cost me the win. 45...Qc3! forces simplification into a winning endgame: 46 Qxc3 bxc3 47 Rg1 (otherwise Black breaks the blockade on his passers) 47...Rxg1 48 Kxg1 Nxg3. Black has time to gobble more pawns and run back to stop White's connected outsiders.

46...Nc3 47 Qh5?

The calm 47 a3! should equalize the game once and for all.

47...Re4 48 Ne2 Qf8 49 Nxc3?

49 Nf4 offered the last chance to resist.

49...bxc3 50 Kg2 d4 51 Rf2 Qa8 52 Qf7+ Kh7 53 Kh3 Rxe5 54 h5 Qh1+ 55 Rh2 Qe4 56 Re2 Qf5+ 0-1

From the sublime to the ridiculous. I played an unrated German on my birthday and lost. He told me it would be a great pleasure to analyze the game with me, but I confessed it would not be my ideal birthday celebration. I went to join Fed who was hanging out with a crazy member of the Rothschild family.

Cannes 1989

In early 1989 I finished my Samford term with a stint in Paris, staying with Mike Wilder and his future wife Elizabeth. I managed my first tournament victory in Europe in the Cannes Open. I couldn't wait to bring home my first European trophy, which I gave to Angela Day (then working for the GMA, which held a concurrent event) to store while we all went out to celebrate. The next day I asked for the trophy back. She looked at me quizzically. "Oh, you wanted that thing? I gave it to Spassky; he's giving it to his son to play with." The decisive encounter was with a former trainer of Kasparov, GM Josif Dorfman. I was booked up in those days, so I prepared a novelty on move thirty. I don't often engage in theoretical duels, but this day I did.

□ **J.Benjamin** ■ **J.Dorfman**

Cannes 1989

1 e4 e5 2 Nf3 Nc6 3 Bb5 a6 4 Ba4 Nf6 5 0-0 Be7 6 Re1 b5 7 Bb3 d6 8 c3 0-0 9 h3 Nb8 10 d4 Nbd7 11 Nbd2 Bb7 12 Bc2 Re8 13 Nf1 Bf8 14 Ng3 g6 15 a4 c5 16 d5 c4 17 Bg5 h6 18 Be3 Nc5 19 Qd2 h5 20 Bg5 Be7 21 Bh6 Nfd7 22 Qe3 Bf8 23 Bxf8 Rxf8 24 Rf1 Rb8 25 Nd2 Bc8 26 f4 exf4 27 Qxf4 Ne5 28 Nf3 Qe7 29 axb5 Rxb5?!

Dorfman is the first to diverge! The position after 29...axb5 had occurred before, in L.Ljubojevic-A.Beliavsky, Belgrade 1987. I had prepared a new move for the game...but after all these years, I haven't the faintest idea what it was!

Dorfman's move gains a tempo by hitting b2, but he has to be careful about his now isolated c-pawn.

30 Rab1 Nxf3+ 31 Rxf3 Qe5 32 Qh6 Rb7 33 Re3!

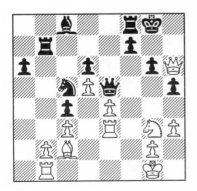

White creates an incidental threat of 34 Nf5, but the main idea is Ng3-f1-d2 where the knight will strain Black's defenses.

33...Re8?

This casual move costs a critical tempo. The queen looks nice on e5, but it cannot stay there. Black needs his knight on e5 to consolidate. Thus Dorfman's suggestion 33...Nd7 was absolutely necessary. In that case I like 34 Ba4 with two possibilities: 34...Qg7 35 Qxg7+ Kxg7 36 Bxd7 Bxd7 37 Nf1, or 34...Nc5 35 Bd1 with ideas of Bxh5 and Be2.

34 Nf1

Now Black gets thrown back in confusion.

34...Nd7 35 Nd2 Rc7 36 Ba4 Rc5 37 Nf3 Qf6

On 37...Qg7 38 Qf4 hits d6 most unpleasantly.

38 Rf1 Rf8

Unpinning the knight and threatening to jump to e5, but White is ready.

39 e5!

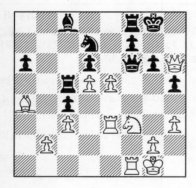

39...dxe5

If 39...Qg7 40 Qxg7+ Kxg7 41 e6 Nb6 42 e7 Nxa4 43 exf8Q+ Kxf8 44 Ng5 wins.

40 Nxe5 Qxe5

Black must cough up his queen. 40...Qd6 41 Nxf7! (winning more convincingly than 41 Nc6 Rxc6) 41...Rxf7 42 Rxf7 Kxf7 43 Qh7+ Kf8 44 Qh8+ Kf7 45 Qe8+ Kg7 46 Re7+ Kh6 47 Re6! Qg3 48 Qh8+ Kg5 49 Rxg6+ snares the queen.

41 Rxe5 Nxe5 42 Rd1 Rd8 43 Rd4?

I rejected 43 d6 because of 43...Nd3, but I missed 44 Qe3 Rd5 45 Bb3! with a winning position.

43...Rcxd5 44 Qe3 Be6 45 Bc2 Rxd4?!

After 45...Re8 White might not be able to break down the defense.

46 cxd4 Nd3 47 b3!

Black would have a fortress after 47 Bxd3? cxd3 48 Qxd3 a5, whereas now Black loses coordination.

47...Nb4 48 Bxg6 cxb3 49 Qh6! Rd6

49...Re8 50. Bh7+ Kh8 51 Be4+ Kg8 52. Qg5+ Kh8 53 d5 is just as conclusive.

50 Bh7+ Kh8 51 Bf5+ Kg8 52 Bh7+ Kh8 53 Be4+ Kg8 54 Qg5+ Kf8 55 Qc5 1-0

A few months later I had the opportunity to train with Mr. Dorfman. One moment stands out in my mind: He showed me a position and announced, "Here I understood it was necessary to trade queens." For the next five moves, his queen chases the other guy's queen around until he has to trade. I can't remember what game it was, but I really enjoyed it.

Wijk aan Zee 1989

Today Wijk aan Zee is a top shelf invitational, and I'm proud to have made an appearance there. In 1989 it was a high class international, but still accessible for regular GMs like me. I started off against the lowest rated player with a great game that ended with a sickening thud.

□ **J.Benjamin** ■ **R.Douven**
Wijk aan Zee 1989

---

1 e4 c6 2 d4 d5 3 exd5 cxd5 4 c4 Nf6 5 Nc3 e6 6 Nf3 Bb4 7 cxd5 exd5 8 Bd3 0-0 9 0-0 Bg4 10 Bg5 Bxc3 11 bxc3 Nbd7 12 Qd2! Bxf3 13 gxf3 Rc8 14 Kh1 Rc6 15 Rg1 Kh8 16 Rab1 Qc8 17 Qf4 Nh5?! 18 Qh4 g6 19 Bb5! Re6

If 19...Rxc3? 20 Bxd7 Qxd7 21 Qxh5! f6 22 Qh6 wins.

20 c4! Nb6?! 21 Be7! Rg8 22 c5 Nd7 23 Bd3 Re8 24 Bd6 Nhf6 25 Qg5! Qc6 26 Bb5 Qc8 27 Rgc1! Qd8 28 Bf1 Qa5?!

29 Rxb7+

I'm completely winning, but it goes bad very suddenly.

29...Qxa2 30 Bg3 Re1 31 c6??

31 Kg2 would win easily.

31...Qa6!

Now Black wins.

32 Rxe1 Rxe1 33 Rb8+ Kg7 0-1

The scales of fortune balanced out against strong Bulgarian GM Kiril Georgiev.

☐ **J.Benjamin** ■ **Kir.Georgiev**
Wijk aan Zee 1989

Black is okay with 40...Qd8; even 40...hxg3+ would have given Georgiev time to find the right move after the time control. But after **40...b5?? 41 Nf6** Black has to pitch his queen to avoid mate.

I had a more legitimate win against the "American" Tony Miles:

□ A.Miles ■ J.Benjamin

Wijk aan Zee 1989

---

1 Nf3 c5 2 c4 Nc6 3 b3 Nf6 4 Bb2 e6 5 e3 d5 6 cxd5 exd5 7 Ne5!? Nxe5 8 Bxe5 Be7 9 Bb5+ Bd7 10 Bxd7+ Qxd7 11 0-0 0-0 12 d3 Qf5 13 Bb2 Rad8 14 Qe2 Bd6 15 Nd2 Rfe8 16 Rae1 Qg6 17 Nf3 d4 18 e4 Nd5 19 Qd1! Nb4 20 a3 Nc6 21 Bc1 Qh5! 22 g3 f5?!

In hindsight I prefer 22...f6 followed by ...Qf7, ...b5, and ...c4.

23 exf5 Qxf5 24 Ng5! Bf8 25 f4 h6 26 Ne4 b5 27 Qc2?

White needed to go full speed ahead on the kingside with 27 g4! and f5, g5 to follow. Prophylaxis isn't going to work.

27...Kh8 28 Bd2 Rc8 29 Rc1?! Nb8! 30 Rfe1 Nd7 31 Qb2 Qd5 32 Re2?! c4 33 bxc4 bxc4 34 Qa2 Qh5!

35 g4 Qxg4+ 36 Rg2 Qf3 37 Rg3 Qh5 38 Rxc4 Rxc4 39 Qxc4 Qd1+ 40 Kg2 Qe2+ 0-1

Black wins a piece.

I had a +1 finish in my sights until two late losses put me in the minus column. The loss to Anand was particularly sad; Vishy mysteriously put this in his best games collection despite a multitude of errors.

□ V.Anand ■ J.Benjamin

Wijk aan Zee 1989

---

1 e4 c5 2 Nf3 d6 3 d4 cxd4 4 Nxd4 Nf6 5 Nc3 Nc6 6 Bg5 e6 7 Qd2 Be7 8 0-0-0 0-0 9 Nb3 Qb6 10 f3 Rd8 11 Kb1 d5?!

I failed to grasp the subtlety of Anand's move.

12 Bxf6 dxe4??

12...Bxf6 13 exd5 Bxc3 14 Qxc3 exd5 is better for White, but this was forced.

13 Bxe7! Rxd2 14 Nxd2!

White is already winning, because Black can't take the bishop: 14...Nxe7? 15 Nc4 Qc7 16 Nb5 wins the queen.

14...exf3 15 gxf3?!

He could have saved a lot of time with 15 Nc4! Qc7 (or 15...Qf2 16 Ne4) 16 Bd6!. But White still won in 31.

Wijk aan Zee is a quiet, isolated little town prone to harsh winter weather. The chess environment is warm, and the "B" and "C" groups add to the fun. Fedorowicz played in the B group and produced his share of stories (though he doesn't like the one where Silman had the bartender water down John's beer). I was willing to accept we would miss the Super Bowl, but Fed brought his transistor radio and was determined to listen to the game on Armed Forces radio. John wandered out into the cold in hopes of achieving reception, but had to change his plans when an unknown knife-wielding assailant chased him around.

Mississauga 1990

Canada has always been one of my favorite places to play. In the spring of 1990 I had a big result in a round-robin organized by the Croatia Club in a Toronto suburb. While Vaganian won the tournament easily, I finished a strong second by mistreating my hosts to the tune of 5½/6. I defeated Piasetski, O'Donnell, Nickoloff, LeSiege, and Vranesic, with only Hebert managing a draw. The win over the noted theoretician and author Drazen Marovic featured a memorable finish.

□ **D.Marovic** ■ **J.Benjamin**
Mississauga, Toronto 1990

With the a-pawn poised to skate home, it's clear that Black needs to look for mate. The execution is quite pleasing.

40...Rg1+ 41 Kh3 Qd7+ 42 g4 h5 43 a6 hxg4+ 44 fxg4 f5! 45 exf5 e5!!

46 Qg2 Qh7+ 47 Kg3 gxf5! 48 Qxg1 f4+ 49 Kf3 Qd3+ 50 Kg2 Qe4+ 51 Kh3 Bxg1 52 Ra3 Qh7+ 53 Kg2 Qxh2+ 54 Kf3 Qf2+ 55 Ke4 Qc2+ 56 Kf3 Qxc4 0-1

Buenos Aires 1992

I was privileged to play in the 1992 Najdorf International in Buenos Aires. Wealthy from business dealings, Miguel Najdorf celebrated his eightieth birthday three years earlier by organizing and sponsoring a round-robin grandmaster event. Najdorf was a true gentleman, a charming and generous man. He had a hands-on approach to his annual tournament, watching and discussing the games with the players every day. Beloved as he was by chessplayers and Argentinians alike, we would overlook the one eccentricity he had. To get a better view of a game, Najdorf would often sit down at the board in a player's chair. The players learned to take it in stride, whether he sat in your opponent's seat or your own. One day while playing Granda, veteran grandmaster Oscar Panno returned to the board to find Najdorf sitting in his chair. Unperturbed, Panno sat down in Granda's chair, and the two old friends had a hearty laugh.

Chesswise, it was a letdown for me. I had lots of draws, with only two wins against one loss. My win over Granda came in 19 moves when he blundered a piece. My best game (and anecdote) came against an old friend from junior days, Ivan Morovic. I had some winning chances in the adjourned position.

☐ **J.Benjamin** ■ **I.Morovic Fernandez**
Buenos Aires 1992

We went out for steaks (always a good bet in Argentina) with teen star Judit Polgar and her mother, Klara. The Polgars, I learned, were vegetarians. So Judit did not enjoy the food as much as we did, but the conversation amused her. As players often did with adjournments in the old days, we discussed the game during our meal. Morovic tried to convince me the position was a draw. Several times he appeared to be lost in space. Noticing this, Judit started laughing. "He's worried about the position," she chortled. Morovic blushed and smiled.

Later the analysis continued in my room, but Morovic still made no headway. In fact, he was playing it quite badly, though I refrained from showing him exactly why. Out of sportsmanship, I loaned him a chess set. The next morning his demeanor had changed. "You know, I could play much better," he told me, and I knew the jig was up. Before going to sleep I had ascertained the position was drawn.
61...Kd6 62 Kf1

62...Ke7

The night before Ivan had tried 62...Kc7 63 Ke1 Rb5? (63...Kd6 is correct) 64 e7 Rb1+ (64...Kd7? 65 Bc6+ wins immediately) 65 Kd2 Kd7. Here I managed to avoid suggesting 66 Kc3!, winning a critical tempo with the threat of 67 Bb3. After 66...Rb6 67 Kc4 Kxe7 68 Kc5 Rb2 69 Kc6 Kd8 70 Be4! White scoops up the h-pawn and queens something.

63 Ke1 Kd6 64 Kd1 Kc7! 65 Be4

65 Kc1 Re2 would just make matters worse.

65...Rb6!

As they say in the Informant, this move is "box". White wins nicely after 65...Kd6? 66 Kc1 Rb5 67 Bd5! Rb4 68 Kc2 Rb6 69 Kc3 Rb5 70 Kd4 Rb4+ (if 70...Rxd5+ 71 Kc4 wins) 71 Kd3 and Black is in zugzwang.

66 e7

66 Bf5 doesn't work either: 66...Kd6 67 Bxh7 Rxb7 68 Bg8 (or 68 Bf5 Ke5 69 h7 Rb8 70 Bxg4 Rh8 71 e7 Kf6) 68...Rb1+ 69 Ke2 Rh1 70 h7 Rh3! draws.

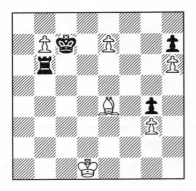

66...Kd7!

Another forced move—66...Rd6+? 67 Bd3! and 66...Re6? 67 Bxh7 Rxe7 68 Bg6! Kxb7 69 h7 Rd7+ 70 Ke2 Rd8 71 Bf7 Rh8 72 Bg8 Kc6 73 Ke3 Kd6 74 Kf4 Ke7 75 Kxg4 both win for White.

67 Ke2 Kxe7 68 Ke3 Kf6

Black also holds with 68...Rb4 69 Kd3 Kd6 70 Kc3 Rb6 71 Bxh7 Rxb7 72 Bg8 Rb5! 73 h7 Rh5 74 Kd4 Ke7 75 Ke4 Kf6 76 Kf4 Kg7.

69 Kd4 Kg5 70 Kc5 Rxb7 71 Bxb7 Kxh6 72 Be4 Kg7 73 Kd6 h5 74 Ke5 h4! 75 gxh4 ½-½

I accompanied this move with a slight j'adoube of the bishop to f4. Of course, the h-pawn is useless with a light-squared bishop.

PCA Qualifier, Groningen 1993

Today the PCA is looked upon as a mistake (even by Kasparov) which cost the chess world a unified champion for more than a decade. But the schism was hardly a calamity for most grandmasters who now had a second bite at the apple. The PCA held its own version of the Interzonals, with players invited by rating without regard to what country they were from.

The Groningen PCA Qualifier came just after my debacle in the 1993 U.S. Championship, but I was still rated at my peak, 2620. My bid for immortality—a spot in the PCA Candidates Matches—came so tantalizingly close to success before crashing down. It's a bit painful to recap those events.

The tournament started rather ironically with a match-up with Patrick Wolff, who I had just faced in Long Beach. I won and got rewarded with Kramnik in round two. Somehow I tricked him in the opening and got a clearly better position. I burned a lot of time trying to find a plan and decided to take a draw.

I went back to Black against another formidable GM, Ilya Smirin. After a 54 move struggle, I converted my extra pawn by trapping his rook on g4. Next up I battled another American, Boris Gulko, in one of many French Defense encounters. After a good opening I failed to exploit my opportunities.

☐ **J.Benjamin** ■ **B.Gulko**
Groningen 1993

After 22 Rac1! Rf8 (or 22...b6 23 b4) 23 Rxc5 Rhxf4 24 Rxf4 Rxf4 25 Nxb7! Kd7 26 Nd6 White should win, but I played **22 Rf2?** and could only draw.

It didn't matter, because the black pieces worked for me again! Evgeny Bareev would be one of the top scalps of my career.

☐ **E.Bareev** ■ **J.Benjamin**
Groningen 1993

---

1 d4 Nf6 2 c4 e6 3 Nc3 Bb4 4 Qc2 c5 5 dxc5 Na6 6 a3 Qa5 7 Bd2 Nxc5 8 b3

Bareev ambitiously invests a tempo to keep the black queen off the a4-square.

8...d5 9 Ra2 Bxc3 10 Bxc3 Qb6 11 b4

White had a worthy alternative in 11 Bxf6 gxf6 (not 11...dxc4? 12 b4! gxf6 13 bxc5 Qa5+ 14 Qd2 c3 15 Qc2) 12 b4 Nd7 13 cxd5.

11...Nce4 12 c5 Qc7 13 Ba1?!

White understandably wants to keep this bishop, but now his lack of development costs him.

13...Ng4!

14 Bxg7?!

14 Nh3 should have been preferred, since 14...Nxh2 15 Bxg7 Rg8 16 Ba1 Ng4 17 e3 is not so clear.

14...Ngxf2 15 Bxh8 Nxh1 16 Nf3 f6 17 e3 Kf7 18 g4 Bd7 19 Bxf6 Kxf6 20 Qb2+

The attempt to scoop up the errant knight with 20 Qg2 leads to a collapsed structure after 20...a5!.

20...Kf7 21 Qd4! Kg8 22 Bg2 Nhf2 23 Rxf2 Nxf2 24 Kxf2 Rf8

After all the fireworks, Black is up an exchange for a pawn but must overcome technical problems to win.

25 Kg1 Bb5 26 Ng5 Re8

The trapper gets trapped after 26...Qe7? 27 Nxe6 Qxe6 28 Bxd5 Rf1+ 29 Kg2 Bc6 30 Bxc6 and the rook hangs.

27 Nf3

Further sacrifices come up short: 27 Bxd5 exd5 28 Qxd5+ Kg7 29 Qf5 Qd7 30 Qxh7+ Kf6! 31 Qh6+ Ke7! (but not 31...Ke5? 32 Qd6+! Qxd6 33 Nf7+).

27...Qf7 28 e4 dxe4 29 Qxe4 Bc6 30 Qe3 Qf6 31 Ne5 Rf8 32 h3 Bxg2 33 Kxg2 Qf4 34 Qxf4 Rxf4 35 c6 bxc6 36 Nxc6 a6 37 Nd8 e5 38 Nc6 e4 39 Ne7+ Kf7 40 Nf5 Ke6 0-1

☐ **J.Benjamin** ■ **V.Anand**
Groningen 1993

1 e4 c5 2 Nf3 d6 3 d4 cxd4 4 Nxd4 Nf6 5 Nc3 Nc6 6 Bg5 e6 7 Qd2 Be7 8 0-0-0 0-0 9 Nb3 Qb6 10 f3 Rd8 11 Kb1 Qc7 12 Bxf6!?

Anand was kind enough to give me an "!" for this idea developed during blitz sessions with Wilder. This attempt to speed up the attack by trading White's best piece is extremely risky, though.

12...Bxf6 13 g4 g6!?

Anand makes a bold choice in return; 13...a6 14 g5 Be7 15 f4 would not provide kingside targets so easily.

14 h4 a6 15 g5! Bg7 16 h5 b5 17 hxg6 hxg6 18 f4 b4 19 Na4!

The knight is ultimately doomed here, but it slows down Black's queenside play a great deal; 19 Ne2 a5! would come at me quickly.

19...Rb8 20 Qh2 Kf8 21 Rd3 e5?!

The White attack speeds up after this error. Black's chances are no worse after 21...Bd7.

22 f5 gxf5 23 Rh3! Ne7 24 Rh8+

This was an extremely difficult decision to make over the board. I couldn't work out 24 Rh7 Ng6 25 Rxg7 Kxg7 26 Qh6+ Kg8, and only later discovered the amazing continuation (not given by Anand in his *Best Games*) 27 Bd3 f4 28 Nd4!!.

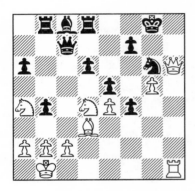

The knight threatens to jump to f5, where it—or the pawn replacing it—will crush Black's defenses. So 28...exd4 29 e5 Qc6 (forced) 30 Bxg6 Qxh1+ 31 Qxh1 fxg6 32 Qd5+ with a big advantage for White.

24...Ng8 25 Rxg8+! Kxg8 26 Qh7+ Kf8 27 exf5 Bxf5!

Black has to pitch a piece to avert 28 f6, but I can't rest easy because my knight on a4 is dropping.

28 Qxf5 Qc6 29 g6! Rb7 30 Rh7

I had to weigh the serious alternative 30 Qg5!? Rc8 31 Qg2 (if 31 Bg2!? Qxc2+ 32 Ka1 f6 33 Rf1 Ke7 seems to hold) 31...Rbc7 (not 31...e4? 32 Na5) 32 Qxc6 Rxc6 and although *Fritz* likes White a lot, I'm not convinced White's uncoordinated pieces are stronger than Black's rook and center pawns.

30...Qxa4 31 Qg5 Qe8

It seems so unfair that the black queen comes back just in time after its shopping trip. Most rook moves lose to 32 Rxg7!, while if 31...Rc8 then 32 Bg2! wins (not now 32 Rxg7? because of 32...Qc6! winning for Black).

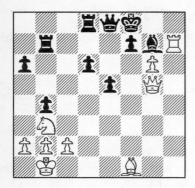

32 Bxa6?!

It seems naïve in the extreme to grab this insignificant pawn, but I vainly believed the b5-square would be important. Instead 32 Bg2 would win after 32...Rc7? 33 Rxg7 Kxg7 34 gxf7+ Kxf7 35 Bd5+ or 32...e4? 33 Rxg7 Kxg7 34 gxf7+ Kxf7 35 Qd5+, but I don't see the follow-up after 32...d5!. The forcing line 33 Qh4 Rb6 34 gxf7 Kxf7 35 Qf2+ Rf6 36 Qa7+ Qd7 37 Bxd5+ Ke8 comes up short.

32...Re7! 33 Bd3 e4 34 Bb5

My last hope was 34 Rxg7 Kxg7 35 gxf7+ Kxf7 36 Bc4+ d5 37 Bxd5+ Rxd5 38 Qxd5+ Kf8 with an uphill struggle to draw. Now Black simplifies to a winning ending.

34...Re5! 35 gxf7 Rxg5 36 fxe8Q+ Rxe8 37 Bxe8 Rg1+! 38 Nc1 Kxe8 39 a4?

I don't think White can hold after 39 c3 bxc3 40 bxc3 Bxc3 41 Kc2 Bf6! anyway.

39...bxa3 40 bxa3 Bc3! 41 Rh4 d5 0-1

Am I an idiot for playing so recklessly against the best player in the field when I stood so well in the tournament? Or just stupid for not finishing him off? Anand was proud enough of his accurate defense to include this in his best games collection, but then again he also included our dreadful game from Wijk aan Zee. I can't really regret being part of this game, but I would have liked to enjoy my +3 score a bit longer.

Over the next several rounds I failed to cash in several opportunities. Only against Topalov did I *not* have a winning position—I was only slightly better with Black. Topalov was quite young then and I didn't think he was all that special (I was wrong about that one).

I had Predrag Nikolic dead to rights but took a draw after botching most of my advantage.

□ P.Nikolic ■ J.Benjamin
Groningen 1993

Here I missed a crushing move: 31...a3!. After 32 Bxa3 Ra8 33 Rd3 (or 33 Bb2 Rxa2 34 Rb4 Ne4 and Black is well on top) 33...Ne5 34 Rb3 Nc4 35 Nc2 Rec8 White cannot hold his pieces together. Instead: **31...Rc5? 32 Rxa4 Rxb5 33 Rfb4 Rxb4 34 Rxb4 Re7 35 Nd3 Ne4 ½-½**

□ J.Benjamin ■ S.Tiviakov
Groningen 1993

Here instead of **37 Rd3?** with an eventual draw, I could have ended the game with 37 Rxe6! fxe6 38 Bxd7 Qd6 39 Rd3.

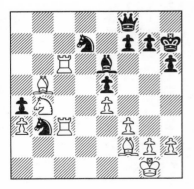

□ **J.Benjamin** ■ **J.Piket**
Groningen 1993

White has a clear pawn plus with 37 Rc5, though I'm not positive I could have won that. Instead: **37 e5+? Kg5 38 Rb7 Rxc2 39 Rxe7 Bf5 40 Kh2** (40 Rxh7 Kf4 41 Kh2 Kxe5 was better though I doubt White can win) **40...h5** with a quick draw.

I had one more chance to qualify if I could beat veteran grandmaster Oleg Romanishin. I could hardly sleep the night before and didn't continue my high level of play.

□ **O.Romanishin** ■ **J.Benjamin**
Groningen 1993

1 d4 Nf6 2 Nf3 g6 3 c4 Bg7 4 Nc3 0-0 5 g3 d5 6 cxd5 Nxd5 7 Bg2 c5 8 0-0 Nxc3 9 bxc3 Nc6 10 Be3 cxd4 11 Nxd4 Na5 12 Rb1 Nc4 13 Bc1 e5 14 Nb5 Qe7 15 Qd5 Nb6 16 Qd6 Qxd6 17 Nxd6 Be6 18 Ra1 Na4 19 Ba3! Nxc3 20 Nxb7

20...Rfb8

This move is okay, but Black has more dynamic choices:

a) 20...e4!? 21 Bxf8 Nxe2+ 22 Kh1 Bxa1 23 Rxa1 (if 23 Bc5 Bg7 24 Bxe4 Nc3 25 Bg2 Bxa2 with a solid extra pawn) 23...Rxf8 24 Nc5 Nc3 and Black has chances.

b) 20...Nxe2+ 21 Kh1 Rfb8 (21...f5!? 22 Bxf8 Rxf8 is also interesting) 22 Nc5 Bc4 and Black will have nice compensation for the exchange.

21 Nc5 Bd5 22 Bxd5 Nxd5 23 Rac1 Bf8! 24 Rfd1 Nb6 25 Rd3 Rc8?!

Black stands more comfortably with 25...Rd8! and even sets up a trap: 26 Rcd1?! Rxd3 27 Rxd3? Nc4 28 Bb4 a5 29 Rc3 axb4 30 Rxc4 Rc8 and wins.

26 Ne4 Bxa3?

Black would have at least comfortable equality with 26...Rxc1+.

27 Rxc8+ Rxc8 28 Rxa3 Rc7?

One more chance for equality—28...Rc4—goes by the way.

29 Nf6+! Kh8 30 g4! h6 31 h4 Rb7 32 Ra5

32...Re7?

I might still have survived after 32...Nd7! 33 Ne8! (33 Nxd7? Rxd7 34 Rxe5 Rd4! draws) 33...Kg8 34 Nd6 Rc7 35 Nb5 Rc2 36 Kf1! (36 Rxa7 Nf6 37 Nd6 Nxg4 38 Nxf7 Rxe2 39 f3 Ne3 40 Nxh6+ Kf8 is okay for Black) 36...Nf6 37 f3 e4! with counterplay.

33 g5 hxg5 34 hxg5 Kg7 35 Rc5 e4 36 a4! Rb7 37 Rb5! a6 38 Rb4 a5 39 Rb5 Rb8 40 e3 1-0

My tiebreaks were so good that I would have almost qualified with a draw. Only Shirov would have trumped me, and he was none too pleased to see Romanishin grab the last qualifying spot. Dropping down to +1 cost me quite a bit of prize money, too.

Munich 1994

1994 was the year of the big-time for me, with three top shelf tournament invitations. The first stop—Munich—was a difficult initiation. I still had not purchased my first laptop, but Mark Ginsburg loaned me his. I got to my room and plugged in my computer...and poof! I caused a power failure in my room! Later a dismayed electrician pointed out that the plug adapter was necessary, but definitely not the converter.

I took a beating from Beliavsky, Gelfand, Hübner, Ivanchuk, and Nikolic. I did at least enjoy my one win.

☐ **J.Benjamin** ■ **P.Van der Sterren**
Munich 1994

---

1 c4 e6 2 e4!?

Van der Sterren had a super solid classical repertoire which he never varied from. I couldn't find a hole in his Queen's Gambit Declined or Ruy Lopez, so I opted to put him in unfamiliar territory.

2...d5 3 exd5 exd5 4 cxd5 Nf6 5 Bb5+ Nbd7 6 Nc3 Be7 7 d4 0-0 8 Nf3 Nb6 9 0-0 Nbxd5 10 Re1 c6 11 Bc4

I felt comfortable in this IQP position, while van der Sterren thought my opening was pretty ridiculous. His opinion is entirely understandable when you consider that White is actually *three* tempi down in comparison with a position that could occur from a Queen's Gambit Accepted. White's position is surprisingly good under the circumstances!

11...Be6 12 Bb3 h6

It looks logical to prevent White's second bishop from developing, as well as safeguard the e6-bishop from harassment. However, there is a cost involved—Black cannot touch the g- or f-pawns without weakening his light squares.

13 Ne5 Re8 14 Qf3 Bf8 15 Bd2 Nb4?!

Sensibly aiming for simplification, but overlooking White's reply.

16 Ne4 Nbd5 17 Ng3

Now the knight is poised to join the attack.

17...Nd7 18 Rad1 Qc7 19 Nh5 f6 20 Ng6 Bd6

Suddenly the kingside is completely undefended.

21 Nxg7!

Avoiding the faulty combination (so I thought) 21 Rxe6 Rxe6 22 Bxd5 cxd5 23 Qxd5 Rae8 24 Nhf4 Qc2!, but it turns out that 22 Nhf4! gives White a huge edge as well.

21...Kxg7

22 Qh5

I don't recall if I was able to work out all the variations over the board, but they do confirm the soundness of the sacrifice.

22...Bxh2+

Black cannot keep the piece: 22...Kg8 23 Qxh6 Nf8 24 Qh8+ Kf7 25 Nxf8! Bxf8 26 Qh7+ Bg7 27 Bxd5 cxd5 (or 27...Bxd5 28 Qh5+ Kf8 29 Bb4+) 28 Bh6 Rg8 29 Bxg7 Rxg7 30 Qh5+ wins; e.g. 30...Ke7 31 Qxd5 Qd7 32 Rxe6+ Qxe6 33 Qxb7+, etc.

23 Kf1 Bf4 24 Nxf4 Nxf4 25 Bxf4 Qxf4 26 Bxe6 Re7 27 Rd3

27...Rae8 28 Rg3+

28 Rf3 is also good enough, provided White notices 28...Rxe6 29 Qxe8!.

28...Qxg3

If 28...Kh8 29 Rg6 Rh7 30 Rg7!! wins.

29 fxg3 Rxe6 30 Qxe8

This liquidation wins most easily, as the position is too spread out to defend against White's rook.

30...Rxe8 31 Rxe8 Kf7 32 Ra8 Ke6 33 Rxa7 b5 34 Ke2 f5 35 Kf3 Nf6 36 a3 Ng4 37 b3

In the time scramble, I focus on making a queen.

37...Nf6 38 a4 Ne4 39 a5 Nd2+ 40 Kf4 Nxb3 41 a6 1-0

Amsterdam 1994

The organizers of the Donner Memorial in Amsterdam expected copious consumption of alcohol from the players, but in this area I could not compete with the likes of Eric Lobron, Jan Timman, and Ivan Sokolov. I was hardly more competitive in the tournament, managing only one win over Sokolov against four losses (Yusupov, Lautier, Lobron and Timman). For a silver lining, I can only point to first place in the team blitz tournament. In fairness, it would have been difficult for a team as loaded as "Jack Daniels" (Benjamin, Adams, Lobron, and Hodgson) to finish anywhere else!

Horgen 1994

My third high-powered international brought me closest to success. I still managed just one win (Gavrikov) against three defeats (Shirov, Gelfand, and fourteen-year-old Peter Leko). I was thrilled to have an opportunity to play against Garry Kasparov. I can't be particularly proud of how I played the game, but even a lucky draw with Kasparov is one to treasure.

□ **G.Kasparov** ■ **J.Benjamin**

Horgen 1994

1 Nf3 Nf6 2 c4 e6 3 Nc3 d5 4 d4 Bb4

For some reason I added the Ragozin to my repertoire in 1994. Ironically, this was the only game I scored at all with it—I lost to Lobron in Amsterdam and Gelfand later this tournament and junked the opening.

5 Bg5 h6 6 Bxf6 Qxf6 7 e3 0-0 8 Rc1 c6 9 Bd3 Nd7 10 0-0 Bxc3 11 Rxc3 dxc4 12 Bxc4 e5 13 Bb3 exd4 14 exd4 Qd6 15 Re1 Nf6 16 Ne5 Bf5?

This is not a good line for Black to begin with, but this novelty (16...Nd5 had been played before) actually loses!

17 Rf3?

The immediate sacrifice was much stronger: 17 Nxf7! Rxf7 18 Bxf7+ Kxf7 19 Qb3+ Kf8 20 Qxb7 Rb8 21 Qxa7 Rxb2 22 Rxc6! wins, e.g. 22...Rxa2 (if 22...Qxc6 23 Qa3+) 23 Qb6! Qe7 24 Rxf6+! Qxf6 25 Qb8+ Kf7 26 Qe8 mate.

17...Bh7

Kasparov thought for more than an hour, shaking his head while he contemplated his missed opportunity. But the sac is nothing special now.

18 Nxf7!? Rxf7 19 Bxf7+ Kxf7 20 Qb3+ Kf8 21 Qxb7 Rd8 22 Qxa7 Qxd4 23 Qxd4 Rxd4 24 Rc3

If not for White's unfortunate 17th move, he could snack on the c6 pawn now.

24...Be4 25 f3 Bd5

26 Kf2 Ne8 27 b3 Rd2+ 28 Re2 Rd1 29 Rcc2 Nd6 30 Re1 Rd4 31 Ke2 Nb5 32 Ke3 Rb4 33 Rd2 Ke7 34 Kf2+ Kf7 35 Re3 Nd6 36 Ke2 Nf5 37 Re5 Nd6 38 Kd3 Nb5 39 Kc2 Na3+

I've been floundering in an essentially equal position. Such is the pressure of playing Kasparov; I played this move with but three seconds on my clock! Fortunately the check afforded me an opportunity to prepare my last move.

40 Kc3 Rb7 41 Kd4 Nb5+ 42 Kc5 Kf6 43 Re3 Nc7 44 Kd6 Nb5+ 45 Kc5 Nc7 46 a4!? Na6+ 47 Kd6 Rb8

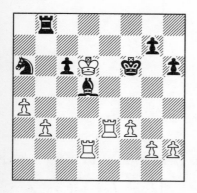

It feels good to threaten mate in one against the champ.

48 Rxd5 cxd5 49 Kxd5 Rb6 50 Kc4 Rb8 51 Kd5 Rb6 52 Kc4 Rb8 53 Re4 Nb4 54 a5 Nc6 55 a6 Rb6 56 Kc5 Rxa6 57 Kb5 Ra3

57...Nb8 58 Re8 Ra3 59 Kb4 Ra8 60 Kc4 would likely lead to a draw as well.

58 Kxc6 ½-½

Kasparov chose not to test me in three vs. two. This was the only draw he gave up with White in the tournament.

Kasparov played in Horgen without an entourage. At the sumptuous meals he comfortably engaged in deep conversation with the other players (generally offering controversial opinions). At that moment we could have been friends, but the Deep Blue experience would make that impossible.

Rilton Cup, Stockholm 1996/97

During the aforementioned Deep Blue experience I put my laboratory work to good use (without exposing trade secrets). I managed a tie for first in a strong open tournament in Sweden. I especially enjoyed the following combination:

□ **J.Benjamin** ■ **J.Hellsten**

Rilton Cup, Stockholm 1996/97

---

1 e4 c5 2 Nf3 e6 3 c3 d5 4 exd5 exd5 5 d4 Nc6 6 Bb5 Bd6 7 dxc5 Bxc5 8 0-0 Nge7 9 Nbd2 0-0 10 Nb3 Bd6 11 Bd3 Kh8 12 h3 Ng6 13 Bc2 Bc7 14 Be3 Nce7 15 Nbd4 a6 16 Qd3 Qd6 17 Rad1 Bd7 18 Rfe1 Rac8 19 Bg5 Rfe8 20 Bxe7 Rxe7 21 Rxe7 Qxe7 22 Nf5 Qf8 23 Ne3 Bc6 24 Nxd5 Rd8 25 Qf5 Bb8 26 Ng5 Kg8

27 Ne7+! Qxe7 28 Rxd8+ Qxd8 29 Qxf7+ Kh8 30 Qxg6! hxg6 31 Nf7+ Kg8 32 Nxd8 Bd5 33 Bb3 Bxb3 34 axb3 b6 35 g3 Kf8 36 Kf1 Bd6 37 Ne6+ Ke7 38 Nd4 Kf6 39 Ke2 Ke5 40 Kd3 Kd5 41 b4 1-0

Saintly Cup, Sydney 1999

In my post-Deep Blue phase I haven't played much overseas beyond Olympiads and World Championships. In January 1999 I had the trip of a lifetime—one month exploring the beaches and cities of Australia, culminating in a tournament victory.

In the Saintly Cup, a round-robin international in Sydney sponsored by the great chess patron Dato Tan, I cruised to a convincing first with a 7-2 score. Mirroring my rough treatment of the locals in Mississauga 1990, I hammered the Aussies with four wins and a draw in five games. Perennial board one Ian Rogers was one of my early victims.

□ **J.Benjamin** ■ **I.Rogers**
Saintly Cup, Sydney 1999

1 e4 c6 2 d4 d5 3 e5 Bf5 4 c3 e6 5 Be3 Nd7 6 Nd2 Ne7 7 f4 Bg6 8 Ngf3 Nf5 9 Bf2 h5 10 Be2 Be7 11 a4 a5 12 g3 f6 13 Bd3 fxe5 14 dxe5 Bc5 15 0-0 Bxf2+ 16 Rxf2 Nc5 17 Bc2 Qb6 18 Qb1 0-0 19 Ng5

19...Rad8 20 Ndf3 Ne4 21 Nxe4 dxe4 22 Bxe4 Nh4 23 Nxh4 Rd2 24 Qe1 Rxf2 25 Qxf2 Qxf2+ 26 Kxf2 Bxe4 27 Ke3 Bd5 28 Nf3 Bxf3 29 Kxf3 Kf7 30 Rd1 Ke7 31 Ke4 Rh8 32 Rd6 g6 33 Kd4 Rf8 34 h4 g5 35 hxg5 h4 36 Ke3 hxg3 37 Rd2 Kf7 38 Kf3 Kg6 39 Kxg3 Kf5 40 Rd7 b5 41 axb5 cxb5 42 Kf3 1-0

Chapter Nine

Domestic Agenda

While most American chess is and has been played on the Open circuit, international events on our shores have played a significant role in my career. In this chapter I will hit some of the highlights.

As a teenager the hunt for the International master title occupied much of my attention. In February 1980, I made my first IM norm in a New York round-robin tournament. Needing 1½ from my last two games, I pondered over which opening to use against Bob Gruchacz, a player I perceived to have stronger theoretical knowledge than I did. I asked my buddy Mike Wilder, who replied without hesitation: "Make him play 28 moves on his own." [The time control for that tournament was at move thirty.] Of course I knew he was suggesting my pet line which I later dubbed the "Brooklyn Defense" in honor of my hometown (this was analogous to Tony Miles' 1...a6, the Birmingham Defense). The plan worked like a charm.

□ **R.Gruchacz** ■ **J.Benjamin**
Philidor International, New York 1980

---

1 e4 Nf6 2 e5 Ng8

Okay, it's objectively not very good, but there is some logic behind this "undevelopment". My opponents, confused if not insulted, often reacted poorly. Occasionally they tried to take my head off, with interesting results.

3 d4 d6 4 Nf3 Bg4 5 h3 Bh5 6 g4

"Gruch" goes for it! Simple development 6 Be2 e6 7 0-0 d5 leads to a kind of French with the bishop outside the pawn chain. The same idea, in a less time-consuming form, later became quite popular: 1 d4 d6 2 Nf3 Bg4!?.

6...Bg6 7 e6

Believe it or not, this was hot theory at the time, occurring in three of my games!

7...fxe6 8 Bd3 Bxd3 9 Qxd3 Nc6!

This was my improvement on my only loss in the Brooklyn Defense: 9...Nf6 10 Ng5 Qd7 11 Qb3 Nc6 12 Nxe6 Nd8 13 Nxd8 Rxd8 14 Qxb7 with a clear advantage, F.La Rota-J.Benjamin, New York 1979.

10 Qb3

Gruchacz avoids the tempting 10 Ng5 Qd7 11 Nxh7, surprisingly refuted by 11...Nxd4!! 12 Qg6+ Kd8 13 Be3 (13 Nxf8 Qc6 is clearly better for Black, e.g. 14 Rf1 Nf6 15 Qxg7 Qc4! and wins) 13...Qc6 14 Bxd4 Qxh1+ 15 Ke2 Rxh7 16 Qxh7 Nf6 and Black went on to win, R.Kaner-J.Benjamin, Philadelphia 1980.

10...Qd7 11 Qxb7 Rb8 12 Qa6 Nf6 13 Qe2 g6 14 0-0 Bg7 15 c3 0-0

Black's weakie e6-pawn is balanced by White's holes on the f-file.

16 Ng5 Nd8

I have to avoid 16...e5 17 dxe5 Nxe5 18 f4 when White sinks a knight into e6.

17 Re1

It's tempting to cash in the e6-pawn, but White would do better to cover the f-file and complete his development. I recommend 17 f4.

17...Nd5 18 Nxe6 Nxe6 19 Qxe6+ Qxe6 20 Rxe6 Rf3 21 Kg2 Rd3!

22 Re1 e5 23 dxe5 Bxe5 24 Na3 Bf4!

Black cleans up the kingside now. The rest is easy.

25 Nc4 Bxc1 26 Raxc1 Nf4+ 27 Kg1 Nxh3+ 28 Kf1 Rf8 29 Rc2 Rg3! 30 Re7 Rg1+ 31 Ke2 Rxf2+ 32 Kd3 Nf4+ 33 Ke3 Rxc2 34 Kxf4 Rf2+ 0-1

My last two norms also came in New York City at the local clubs. The first came at the Marshall (despite my last career loss to John Fedorowicz), and the clincher occurred at the Manhattan where I beat Valvo, Bisguier, and, for the last time, Fed. On the morning of one of the rounds I took the SATs. My multi-tasking worked better for chess than academics, but the college hunt worked out in the end.

Reshevsky Memorial 1992

Peruvian grandmaster Julio Granda Zuniga won the 1992 Reshevsky Memorial, with future superstar Judit Polgar in second. My modest +1 score put me in a group of players tied for third, but did include a nice endgame against Psakhis:

☐ **J.Benjamin** ◼ **L.Psakhis**
Reshevsky Memorial, New York 1992

1 e4 e6 2 d4 d5 3 Nc3 Nf6 4 Bg5 dxe4 5 Nxe4 Nbd7 6 Nxf6+ Nxf6 7 Nf3 h6 8 Bh4 c5

9 Bb5+ Bd7 10 Bxd7+ Qxd7 11 Qe2 Be7 12 0-0-0 0-0 13 dxc5 Qa4

In the U.S. Championship five years later Christiansen tried 13...Qc6 14 Ne5 Qxc5 15 Bxf6 Bxf6 16 Nd7 Bxb2+ 17 Kxb2 Qb4+ 18 Kc1 Qa3+ and I decided to accept the perpetual rather than risk the attack.

14 Kb1 Rfd8 15 a3 Bxc5 16 Bxf6 gxf6 17 Nd2 Be7 18 Nb3 f5 19 f3 Rxd1+ 20 Rxd1 Rd8 21 Rxd8+ Bxd8 22 Qd2 Bg5 23 Qd4 Qxd4 24 Nxd4

24...Bf4 25 h3 Be3 26 Nb5 Kg7 27 Nd6 b6 28 c3 Kf6 29 Kc2 Bf4 30 Nb5 a6 31 Nd4 Bd6 32 Kd3 e5 33 Ne2 Ke6 34 c4 f4 35 Nc3 Bc5 36 b4 Bg1 37 Nd5 a5 38 Ke4 f5+ 39 Kd3 axb4 40 axb4 Kd6 41 Kc3 Bf2 42 Kb3 b5 43 Nc3 bxc4+ 44 Kxc4 Bh4 45 b5 Bd8 46 Nd5 Bg5

White uses the outside passer to engineer a win with minimal means.

47 b6 Kc6 48 Nb4+ Kxb6 49 Kd5 e4 50 fxe4 fxe4 51 Kxe4 Kc7 52 Kf5 Kd7 53 Nd3 Ke8 54 Kg6 Ke7 55 Ne5 Ke6 56 Nf7 Be7 57 Nxh6 f3 58 gxf3 Ke5 59 Nf5 Bf8 60 h4 Kf4 61 h5 Kxf3 62 Ng7! 1-0

The tournament was hosted by the law offices of Milbank, Tweed, Hadley & McCloy. New lawyer Michael Rohde had taken a job there and stimulated interest in professional chess from one of the partners, Bob Rice. A high class chess club began to meet there, with members all dressed in suits. Playing in a suit was new to me, but I got used to it. The subway ride downtown was a much greater challenge!

American Chess Challenge 1992

Rice soon put together a chess event that is virtually unknown today, except to *Chess Chow* readers. "The American Chess Challenge" pitted American players in rapid chess matches for the right to take on Garry Kasparov in a final blitz game.

Rice hired a mainstream sports announcer, Bruce Beck, for segment introductions. For game commentary he brought in the original "John Madden of chess", John Fedorowicz, and Maurice Ashley. I won three matches, the last against a surprise finalist, the promising junior Jorge Zamora (later Sammour-Hasbun). I won that and faced Kasparov in a one-game blitz match. It was pretty one-sided! I was so nervous that I burned up my time at a prodigious rate. He didn't even have to finish me off, I just ran out of time.

The "Challenge" was meant to be packaged and sold as a television show. That might well have happened, had Kasparov not attracted Rice to a different project. The Professional Chess Association (PCA) would of course change the course of chess history.

MCC/ACF International 1992

The U.S. has long lacked consistent annual round-robin tournaments. We've mixed flurries of organization with tournament droughts. While New York has hosted many round-robins, I haven't been invited to most of them. Most internationals in America are organized for the purposes of generating title norms. The rules require foreigners for title norms, so organizers generally have preferred to invest their budget on foreign GMs living in the U.S.

I did manage to play in the 1992 MCC/ACF International. The organizer and sponsor was Eric Moskow, a New York area doctor and master. Moskow had paid $10,000 to play in the Reshevsky Memorial. He was looking for opportunities to make IM norms. When I asked for a modest honorarium, he told me he didn't "believe" in appearance fees. I replied that his patients may not "believe" in paying for doctor visits but they don't have a choice about it.

I went plus against the best players, drawing with Shabalov and Fed, while beating future GMs Gennady Sagalchik and Ildar Ibragimov. Ibragimov was only visiting then, several years from becoming one of America's top players.

☐ **I.Ibragimov** ■ **J.Benjamin**
MCC/ACF International, New York 1992

1 d4 Nf6 2 c4 e6 3 Nc3 Bb4 4 e3 0-0 5 Bd3 d5 6 Nf3 b6 7 a3 Bxc3+ 8 bxc3 Ba6 9 cxd5 exd5 10 0-0 c5 11 Bb2 Bxd3 12 Qxd3 Nbd7 13 c4 cxd4 14 Qxd4 dxc4 15 Qxc4 Rc8 16 Qh4 Rc2 17 Rab1 Qc7 18 e4 Qc4 19 Rfe1 Re8 20 Bd4 Re2 21 Rxe2 Qxe2 22 Re1 Qd3

23 e5 Nd5 24 Qg4 Re7 25 h3 Nf8 26 Qc8 Qxa3 27 Rc1 Nf4 28 Kh2 N4e6 29 Be3 Qa4 30 Rc4 Qd7 31 Nh4 Re8 32 Qa6 Ng6 33 Nxg6 hxg6 34 Ra4 Qc7 35 f4 Re7 36 Rc4 Qb7 37 Rc8+ Kh7 38 Qxb7 Rxb7 39 g4 Rc7 40 Ra8 Rc3 41 f5 Rxe3 42 fxe6 fxe6 43 Rxa7 Rxe5 44 Rb7 b5 45 h4 g5 46 hxg5 Rxg5 47 Kg3 Kg6 48 Rb6 Kf6 49 Kh4 Rd5 50 Rb8 g6 51 Rf8+ Ke7 52 Rg8 g5+ 53 Kh5 Kd6 54 Rb8 Kc5 55 Re8 b4 0-1

Then I set out to beat everyone else. The rest of the field was not very strong, but the stars have to align for me to win as many as I did. My game with perennial New York opponent IM Jay Bonin illustrates the tenor of the tournament for me.

☐ **J.Bonin** ■ **J.Benjamin**
MCC/ACF International, New York 1992

1 d4 Nf6 2 c4 e6 3 Nf3 b6 4 g3 Ba6 5 b3 Bb7 6 Bg2 Bb4+ 7 Bd2 a5 8 Nc3 0-0 9 0-0 d6 10 a3 Bxc3 11 Bxc3 Nbd7 12 Bb2 Qb8 13 Rc1 Rd8 14 Bh3 Be4 15 d5 e5 16 Nh4 b5 17 Nf5 Bxf5 18 Bxf5 bxc4 19 Rxc4 Nb6 20 Rh4 Nbxd5 21 Bxh7+ Nxh7 22 Qxd5 Nf6 23 Qd3 Qb7 24 f4 Rab8 25 fxe5 dxe5 26 Qf5 Qb6+ 27 Rf2 Qxb3 28 Bxe5 Rb5

Risky decisions come easier when you're on a roll. 28...Qb1+ keeps it safe and balanced.

29 Qh3 Nh7

With Black's flag hanging Bonin eschews the solid 30 Bxc7 and goes for the kill.

30 Bxg7? Rd1+ 31 Kg2 Qb1 32 Bc3 Rg1+ 33 Kf3 Ng5+ 34 Kg4 Qe4+

Avoiding the checkmate after 34...Nxh3?? 35 Rh8, Black delivers one.

35 Rf4 Qxe2+ 0-1

The more I won, the worse I felt. I had a host of nasty symptoms. Each day I thought I could barely make it through the game, but I was on such a roll I needed to keep going. After nine wins and a diagnosis of bronchitis, I offered Soltis a quick draw in the last round. My tally of 10½-1½ reeled in a slew of Elo points. When the tournament was finally rated in late 1993, I rose to a career high of 2620.

Hudson International 1993

First time organizer Ken Ramaley, with help from IM Dan Edelman (who played in the event), put together an impressive round-robin in Westchester County, NY. Some referred to the tournament as the "Alex" International, given the high concentration of Alexanders and Alexeys (Shabalov, Wojtkiewicz, Goldin, Sherzer, and Yermolinsky) in the ten-player field. Shabalov triumphed over his namesakes, but I managed to tie for second with wins over Edelman, Sherzer, Kaidanov, and the late perennial Grand Prix champion:

☐ **A.Wojtkiewicz** ■ **J.Benjamin**
Hudson International, New York 1993

---

1 Nf3 Nf6 2 c4 g6 3 g3 Bg7 4 Bg2 c6 5 d4 d5 6 Qb3 0-0 7 Nc3 dxc4 8 Qxc4 Bf5 9 0-0 Nbd7 10 e3 Nb6 11 Qe2 Ne4 12 Rd1 Nxc3 13 bxc3 Na4 14 Bd2 Be4 15 Be1 Qc7 16

Bf1 h6 17 Rac1 c5 18 c4 b6 19 Nd2 Bb7 20 Nb1 cxd4 21 exd4 Rac8 22 Nc3?! Nxc3 23 Bxc3 e6

24 Bb2 Rfe8 25 Bg2?! Bxg2 26 Kxg2 Qb7+ 27 f3 Qa6 28 Rd3 Rc7 29 Ra3 Qb7 30 Rb3?! Rd8 31 Rd3 Qa6 32 Kh3? Qc8!

This highly unusual fork collapses White's center and decides the game.

33 Rdd1 e5+ 34 Kg2 exd4 35 Qd3 Re7 36 Re1 Re3 37 Qd2 h5 38 Rcd1 Rxe1 39 Rxe1 Qxc4 40 Re7 Qxa2 0-1

Ramaley's plans for future events fizzled due to lack of USCF support. He negotiated sponsorship with Bass, who wanted extensive coverage in *Chess Life* in return. Executive Director Al Lawrence felt an alcohol company would not be family-friendly enough for *Chess Life* and killed the deal.

PCA Rapid, New York 1994

Along with the big-time European opportunities in 1994 came a spot in the New

York PCA Grand Prix. Lots of Americans wanted to play, but as the highest rated American after Kamsky I got the honors. The luck of the draw matched me against Kramnik. Nowadays people would look upon this as a death sentence, but Kramnik was quite young and I had drawn with him in Groningen. I was actually relieved I didn't have to play Ivanchuk, who crushed me in Munich.

I was insufficiently prepared and too passive in the first game. I went all out for the win in the second game, but my piece sacrifice didn't bear dividends. With my time running out, I regained momentum. I felt I was on the verge of getting somewhere.

☐ **J.Benjamin** ◼ **V.Kramnik**
PCA (rapid), New York 1994

---

1 e4 c5 2 Nf3 Nc6 3 Bb5 g6 4 0-0 Bg7 5 Re1 Nf6 6 e5 Nd5 7 d3 0-0 8 Nbd2 d6 9 Bxc6 bxc6 10 Nc4 h6 11 h3 Be6 12 Bd2 Qd7 13 Qc1 Kh7 14 Re4 g5 15 Bxg5 hxg5 16 Qxg5 Bf5 17 Rh4+ Kg8 18 g4 Bg6 19 Re1 dxe5 20 Nfxe5 Qe6 21 Qd2 Nb6 22 Nxg6 Qxg6 23 Ne5 Qd6 24 Rh5 Nd5 25 Rg5 Qh6 26 Nf3 f6 27 Rf5 Qxd2 28 Nxd2 Rae8 29 Re6 Kf7 30 Rxc6 e6 31 Rf3 Rc8 32 Ra6 Rc7 33 c3 Rb8 34 Nc4 Ke7 35 h4 Nb6 36 Na5 Kf7 37 Re3 Nd5 38 Rexe6 Rxb2 39 Nc4 Rb1+ 40 Kh2 Rf1 41 Red6 Nxc3 42 Kg2 Ra1 43 a3 Ne2 44 Rd8 Nf4+ 45 Kf3 Ne6 46 Nd6+ Kg6 47 Re8 Nd4+ 48 Kg2 Rc6 49 h5+ Kh7 50 Rxc6 Nxc6 51 Rc8 Nd4 52 Rc7 Rxa3 53 Ne8 Ne6 54 Re7 Ra6 55 Nxf6+ Kh6 56 Ne4 Bf8 57 Rf7 Bg7 58 f4 Ra3 59 Ng3 Rxd3

And here it is! 60 Nf5+ Kh7 61 Re7 Nxf4+ 62 Kf2 gives White a big advantage. But it was so hard to think with Maurice Ashley screaming in my ear! The commentary was supposed to be confined to headphones but I could hear everything.

60 g5+?? Kh7 61 h6 Kg6 0-1

My time ran out in this hopeless position. My two losses still netted me one of the larger prizes in my career!

Chess-in-the-Schools International 1996

The successor to the ACF sponsored a round-robin at the "Home of the Heisman", the Downtown Athletic Club in New York City. CIS shelled out big bucks to entice elite grandmasters Korchnoi, Adams, I.Sokolov, and Salov. Along with a few invited Americans, the field was completed with winners from qualifying events. A message filtered down to me that I should play in a qualifier, but they were taking place during the latter stages of preparation for the first Kasparov-Deep Blue match. I didn't have the time, though I wasn't permitted to tell anyone why. To be honest, I didn't feel I should have to qualify.

In the end I received an invitation anyway. I was surprised that the American GMs did not receive appearance fees, but since the U.S. co-Champions, DeFirmian and Wolff had gone along with the plan, I was in no position to argue.

I won a nice game against Maurice Ashley, who was still working on his GM title at the time.

☐ **M.Ashley** ■ **J.Benjamin**
CIS International, New York 1996

---

1 e4 c5 2 Nf3 e6 3 d4 cxd4 4 Nxd4 Nc6 5 Nc3 Qc7 6 Be2 a6 7 0-0 Nf6 8 Be3 Bb4 9 Na4 Be7 10 Nxc6 bxc6 11 Nb6 Rb8 12 Nxc8 Qxc8 13 e5 Nd5 14 Bc1 Bc5 15 Bd3 Qc7 16 g3!? Bd4

It's tempting to sac an exchange with 16...Qxe5!? 17 c4 Nb4 18 Bf4 Qd4 19 Bxb8 19...Nxd3, but 19 Bb1! Qxb2 20 Bxb8 Qxa1 21 Bd6 wins for White.

17 c3 Bxe5 18 Bxa6 0-0 19 Bd3 f5 20 Re1 Bd6 21 Re2 Kh8 22 Qc2 c5 23 b3 Nf6 24 f4?

This attempt to block the f-file opens up critical diagonals to the white king.

24...c4! 25 Bxc4 Ng4 26 Rg2 Bc5+ 27 Kf1

Even worse is 27 Kh1 Qc6 28 h3 Nf2+ 29 Kh2 Nxh3! 30 Kxh3 Rf6 31 g4 Qf3+ with mate to follow.

27...Qc6 28 Be2 e5! 29 h3 Nf2 30 h4?!

White likely can't hold this position anyway, e.g. 30 fxe5 Rbe8 31 Bf4 Nxh3 32 Rh2 Nxf4 33 gxf4 Qg6 34 Rg2 Qh6 with imminent collapse.

30...Rbe8 31 fxe5 f4 32 gxf4 Nh3 0-1

White's extra pawns do not help defend his king.

Later I scored my only victory over the living legend Viktor Korchnoi. It was hardly a thing of beauty and only appears here because of the bizarre manner in which it unfolded.

☐ J.Benjamin ■ V.Korchnoi
CIS International, New York 1996

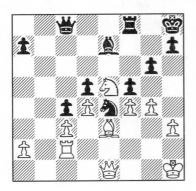

I've just played **39 Qe1**. My position is dodgy and I'm left with a single second to make the time control! I figured that my next move would be Rc2-g2, but could I make this move and swing my arm back to the left side to hit the clock in time?

Korchnoi played **39...Bf6** and I slammed down **40 Rg2**...with that second still showing on the clock. I sighed with relief until I remembered that my position was still miserable. Despite having the better part of a minute to make his last move, Korchnoi failed to do so and flagged. Two thoughts came to me as I digested this miraculous win: One, there would be no post-mortem (true) and two, Korchnoi would give me a lecture (false). Despite his well-earned reputation for post-game outbursts, Korchnoi said nothing...though no one would have blamed him in this case! Viktor the Terrible has always been very kind to me.

I finished on a high note by defeating Wolff with special Deep Blue preparation. With only a loss to Adams, my +2 finish gave me a share of second place, if not the Heisman Trophy.

Hawaii 1996

Chessplayers often have no choice but to follow the tournaments wherever they may be. Every now and then you get to play in paradise. When Eric Schiller began to organize tournaments in Hawaii in the late nineties, I took advantage. Along with the great vacation I won a tournament over Blatny and Gufeld, beating both grandmasters in the process.

☐ **J.Benjamin** ■ **E.Gufeld**
Hawaii 1996

---

1 e4 c5 2 Nf3 d6 3 c3 Nf6 4 Be2 e6 5 d3 Be7 6 Nbd2 0-0 7 0-0 Nc6 8 d4 cxd4 9 cxd4 Bd7 10 Re1 Rc8 11 a3 d5 12 e5 Ne4 13 Bd3 Nxd2 14 Bxd2 Qb6 15 Bc3 Na5 16 Nd2 Nc4 17 Nxc4 dxc4 18 Bc2 f5 19 exf6 Rxf6 20 Qg4 Rcf8 21 Re2 Rf4 22 Qh3 g6 23 Rae1 R4f7 24 Be4 Bd6 25 Qh6 Qc7

26 Bxg6!? hxg6 27 d5 e5 28 Rxe5 Rh7 29 Qxg6+ Rg7 30 Qh6 Qb6 31 R5e3 Rff7 32 Bxg7 Rxg7 33 Re4 Bc5?

After finding forced moves at 28 and 30, Gufeld misses the obligatory 33...Qc5!. After 34 Qh5 c3! White has better chances, but Black is hanging in.

34 Qxb6 axb6 35 Rxc4 Bh3 36 g3 Rf7 37 Re2 Rf5? 38 Rh4 Rxd5 39 Rxh3 Rd1+ 40 Kg2 Kg7 41 Rh4 1-0

The above game concluded without incident, but the same could not be said for the Blatny-Gufeld battle. Gufeld made a habit of recapturing pieces before Blatny hit the clock (perhaps before his hand even left the piece). When Blatny objected, Gufeld replied that this was how it was always done in Russia. Blatny reminded him that he was not in Russia anymore and should follow the rules. Gufeld then lamented that he was not in Czechoslovakia in 1968 because he would have liked to drive a tank over the Blatny family home. The two had to be put in separate rooms for the remainder of the event.

Chapter Ten

Blue Period

Sometimes the stars align to create a huge opportunity from out of the blue (no pun intended). I couldn't put a single big result on the board from all those chances in 1994. I went from the top American after Kamsky to far lower on the totem pole. In early 1995 there were two significant round-robin internationals in North America—one in Bermuda, the other in San Francisco. I didn't get an invitation to either one, leaving me wondering where to go next.

So when IBM came calling, I had nothing better to do. Deep Blue had a match with Kasparov scheduled for February 1996. The team decided to arrange practice matches with grandmasters. Murray Campbell, the best chessplayer among the programmers, checked a USCF rating list and came up with three players who lived reasonably close to the Westchester, New York IBM facility: Patrick Wolff of Boston, and Ilya Gurevich and Joel Benjamin from New York. They offered attractive conditions for a two-game match. We would each receive $500 per game, plus a $500 bonus for winning the match.

I had never encountered Deep Blue over the board. Apparently, I had taken on Blue's forerunner Deep Thought II, though I didn't know this at the time. [Well after concluding my IBM business, I came across five Benjamin-Deep Thought II games from 1993. I had no recollection of these games, but the openings were appropriate to my repertoire. Apparently they were blitz games I played on Mark Ginsburg's ("Aries") Internet Chess Server account. Ginsburg, who played a number of Internet games with DT, many published in *Chess Chow*, recalled that I had a lot of trouble with the mouse, causing (I claim) a result which might have embarrassed me, had I not repressed the memory.] Deep Blue had a new system with completely different hardware and a much more sophisticated evaluation function laying in wait for the grandmasters.

Gurevich went ½-1½ while Wolff registered a win and a loss. I don't know how seriously they took their matches; they probably didn't know the full significance of these games. I had a successful résumé against computers and I played like my honor was on the line.

* * * * *

In 1982, the people at the CBS news program *Nightwatch* came up with the idea of staging a speed chess match (five minutes per player per game) between the best collegiate chessplayer and the top computer program. Their research turned up CRAY BLITZ and yours truly. I had been in Toronto for David Levy's historic match with Chess 4.7 in 1978, and found the computer to be quite weak. I had a difficult game with BELLE in 1981, but eventually exploited some gross weaknesses. So when the *Nightwatch* anchors asked me how I expected to do, I told them quite honestly that I expected to win almost every game. "Cocky brat," they must have thought. But then programmer Bob Hyatt gave them more or less the same assessment. Even at 2 am, I made good on my prediction.

In the 90's computers began to get competitive with grandmasters, at least at fast time controls. The annual Harvard Cup pitted grandmasters against strong (often commercial) programs. When I met Deep Blue, I was the two-time defending champ of the Harvard Cup without a single loss (though the games were usually not exactly works of art).

After meeting the programmers, I was ushered into the "grandmaster room"— my future office—for the first game.

☐ **Deep Blue** ■ **J.Benjamin**
Yorktown Heights (1st matchgame) 1995

1 d4 d6 2 e4 Nf6 3 Nc3 g6 4 f4 Qa5 5 Bd3 e5 6 dxe5 dxe5 7 f5 b5 8 Bg5

This is dubious because White's dark squares will be too weak should White exchange on f6. After the game, I suggested that Deep Blue might be penalizing doubled pawns too much, or underrating the bishop pair, or not appreciating dark square weaknesses enough.

8...Nbd7 9 a3 Nc5 9 b4 Nxd3+ 10 cxd3 Qb6 12 Bxf6 gxf6 13 Nf3 Bb7 14 Qd2 c5 15 Rb1 cxb4 16 axb4 Rc8 17 Nd1 Rd8 18 Nf2 h5 19 Qe2 a5 20 bxa5 Qxa5+ 21 Qd2 Qb6 22 Qb2 Ba6 23 0-0 Bc5

White has finally managed to castle, but Black's bishops rake the board and the passed pawn is very dangerous.

24 Qc2 b4 25 Ne1 Rb8 26 Rb3 Ke7 27 Kh1 Rhc8 28 Qa2 Ra8 29 Qe2 Bb5 30 Nd1 h4 31 Nc2 Ba4 32 Rb1 Bxc2 33 Nc3

Now comes a move that computers had difficulty appreciating.

33...Bxb1!

Similarly, 33...bxc3 34 Rxb6 Bxb6 35 Qxc2 Bd4 is also quite strong.

34 Nd5+ Ke8 35 Nxb6 Bxb6 36 Rxb1 Bd4 37 g3 h3 38 Qd1 Ra2 39 Qh5 Rcc2 40 Qxh3 b3 41 Qh7 Ke7 42 Qh8 b2 43 Qb8 Ra1 44 Qb4+ Rc5 0-1

Man 1, Machine 0.

I needed only a draw in the second game to clinch the match and the $500 bonus. With the white pieces, I had the power to steer for boredom. That was part of my anti-computer strategy anyway.

□ **J.Benjamin** ■ **Deep Blue**

Yorktown Heights (2nd matchgame) 1995

---

1 Nf3 d5 2 g3 g6 3 Bg2 Bg7 4 0-0 e5 5 d3 Ne7 6 e4 0-0 7 Re1 dxe4 8 dxe4 Nbc6 9 c3 Qxd1 10 Rxd1

Not very exciting, I know.

10...f5 11 Na3 h6 12 exf5 Bxf5 13 Re1 Bd3 14 Nd2 b6 15 Nac4 Rad8 16 Ne3 Rf7 17 Ne4 a5

White has the weak e4-square to play around with, but Black's active pieces keep the balance.

18 b3 Na7 19 a4 Nf5 20 Ra2 Rfd7 21 Rd2 Nxe3 22 fxe3 Bb1 23 Red1 Rxd2 24 Rxd2 Rxd2 25 Nxd2 Bc2 26 Be4 Bxe4 27 Nxe4 Kf7 28 Kf2 Nc8 29 Ke2 Ke6 30 g4 Bf6 31 Kd3 Be7 32 Kc4 c6 33 Kd3 h5 34 h3 hxg4 35 hxg4 Nd6

Deep Blue could fight actively with 35...b5, but the bishop ending is still a clear draw.

36 Nxd6 Kxd6 37 Bd2 Bh4 38 e4 Bf2 39 Kc4 Kc7 40 b4 Bg3 41 Bg5 Bf4 42 Bh4 Kc8 43 Bf2 Kc7 44 bxa5 bxa5 45 Kd3 Bh6 46 c4 Bf4 47 c5 Kb7 48 Be1 Ka6 49 Bc3 Bh2 50 Ke2

50...Bg1??

Deep Blue finds the only way to preserve material equality, but loses the game. It calculated 50...Bf4 51 Kf3 g5 52 Kg2 would put it in zugzwang, but didn't realize 52...Kb7 53 Bxa5 Ka6 would produce an impenetrable fortress. The draw is not hard for humans to see; Murray pointed it out after the game. People can look ahead in their mind's eye and move the pieces all around the board. Computers do not understand permanent conditions; they only understand as far as their searchlight shines. No one has ever been able to address this problem satisfactorily—feed this position to your PC and see for yourself.

51 Bxe5 Bxc5 52 Bc3

Black's weak pawns at a5 and g6 prove decisive with the center opened up.

52...Bb6 53 Kd3 Kb7 54 Bd4 Bd8 55 Kc4 Kc8 56 Kc5 Kc7 57 Be5+ Kd7 58 Bf4

Zugzwang – Black has to give ground.

58...Be7+ 59 Kb6 Bb4 60 Ka6 c5 61 Kb5 Ba3 62 Bg3 Bb4 63 Bb8 Ba3 64 Ba7 c4 65 Kxc4 Kc6 66 Bd4 Be7 67 Bc3 Bd8 68 e5 Bb6 69 e6 Bd8 70 Bd2 Bc7 71 e7 Kd7 72 Kb5 Bd6 73 Kxa5 Bxe7 74 Kb6 Kc8 75 Kc6 Bf6 76 Be3 Bc3 77 Bb6 Be1 78 a5 Kb8 79 a6 Ka8 80 Kd6 1-0

I didn't know the games would serve as auditions for a potential employee. The Deep Blue guys appreciated my outperforming the competition, especially since Patrick and Ilya were both unavailable for full time work. I got the job. "You were the obvious choice," Murray told me much later. "We were especially impressed by the second game. You could have won the match with a draw, but you ground out the win."

I only had two months before the match, leaving little time to get acclimated to my colleagues and surroundings, get a sense of the program, and complete any match preparation. I did a fair amount of opening preparation (mostly in the Alapin Sicilian) which proved relevant to the match, if not highly effective. Mostly I got to know the group that I would spend the better part of the next year and a half with.

I had met two of the main architects of Deep Blue 1992 at a panel discussion on computer chess at the Harvard Cup in New York City. Another chess expert, Grandmaster Robert Byrne, and I debated with two computer experts, Murray Campbell and Feng-Hsiung Hsu. In words that may have come back to haunt me, had more people heard them, I lamented the aesthetic loss chessplayers will suffer when a computer program defeats the best player in the world.

Murray did not seem perturbed by my dismissal of his life's work. He explained his views in even tones, which showed his respect for the game and its professionals. Though modest about his abilities, Murray was an accomplished chessplayer, appearing in two Canadian Junior Championships and winning the Alberta Championship. He phased out tournament chess after high school but peaked at a level around USCF master.

Murray quit playing largely because his nervous system couldn't take it. He would be somewhat less worried about his computer program crashing or spitting out bad moves. As far and away the best chessplayer on the team, Murray took charge of "hard" chess aspects of the project like the evaluation function and opening book. His chess knowledge made watching Deep Blue and its predecessors play all the more difficult, as he knew all the mistakes a chessplayer could make!

Murray's anxiety starkly contrasted with the supreme confidence of Hsu, the father of Deep Blue. To Hsu, anything is possible. In the 1992 panel discussion, he boasted Deep Blue would be ready for Kasparov in a year or two. I thought he trivialized the process of playing chess at the grandmaster level. He had the kind of intellectual arrogance that chessplayers often find insulting in many programmers.

After getting to know Hsu by his nickname "CB", I realized he means no disrespect towards chessplayers. He just has tremendous faith in his vision, the same vision which started the ball rolling in the first place. When I asked him why he began the chess project, he said, "because I saw a way to do it." With every incarnation of Deep Blue, the team relied a great deal on CB's genius as the chip designer.

CB's confidence often produced a relaxed attitude that tried the patience of his colleagues. He frequently wandered into my "office" while I was in the middle of something. I tend to be easily distracted, and one day I really wanted to get my work done. I said, "Don't you have something to do?" "No," CB replied casually, missing my implication completely. But when crunch time approached, or an idea exploded in his brain, CB could produce a month's worth of work in a brief flurry. When he first came to work at IBM, CB neglected furnishing his house for a long time while he practically lived at the office. He never paid much attention to his physical appearance, bland clothes and Anatoly Karpov style hair being the norm. All things considered, CB fit the stereotype of a computer genius pretty well. It seems appropriate that CB stands for "Crazy Bird". [IBM understandably "changed" his name to "FH" for publicity purposes.]

While Murray and CB had been veterans of the chess project since its origins in their Carnegie Mellon days, Joe Hoane joined the chess project at IBM in 1990. By then he had accumulated good experience in parallel processing, and Murray and CB liked his understanding of search, which became his main focus.

If CB is guided by inspiration, Joe thrives on perspiration. He is a master of articulation, the process of taking a problem in the computer's behavior and formulating a solution. He might not solve the problem on the first try, but he would start the ball rolling. Murray tended to spend a long time fine-tuning his numbers. Joe would often press him to spit out a trial version. Since Deep Blue's reaction to any change was so unpredictable, this policy proved to be very effective.

Chung-Jen Tan served as manager of IBM's chess project since 1992. CJ understood well the technical capabilities of Deep Blue because he had been involved in the development of IBM's RS-6000. With the increased media attention in Deep Blue, CJ would have his hands full as the project spokesman. He had the responsibility of representing IBM with each public statement.

The members of the chess group at IBM were creatures of routine. They went down to the cafeteria for lunch at 11:30 every day. At about 2:30, they reconvened for "break", where they would grab soft drinks and sweets and discuss the day's progress. [After I brought Fed in to work on openings, he was confused by CB's thick accent. "What's a 'breck'?" he would ask.] Murray, CB, and I kept the Snapple Beverage Company in business as we drained innumerable bottles of iced tea.

The core of the team had clearly defined responsibilities—CB the chip design, Murray the evaluation, and Joe the search—but they shared insights with one another. The ultimate success in the Kasparov war effort would hinge on how well they could work together, and how well they could incorporate the observations of a computer layman in their midst. It took a while to get the process down pat.

* * * * *

February 1996 in Philadelphia, Deep Blue shocked the world by winning the first game of the match. I'm afraid I can't take much credit for that. My biggest impact came in game five; with the match tied, Kasparov (Black) offered a draw on move twenty-three.

□ Deep Blue ■ G.Kasparov
Philadelphia (5th matchgame) 1996

The Deep Blue team had a difficult decision to make. The computer's own evaluation was slightly in Black's favor. Kasparov was a bit low on time, with thirty minutes left to make seventeen moves. I didn't like our chances in the last game — Kasparov looked too strong with White. Plus I thought it would be wrong to end the game so abruptly. Playing to a finish would be more in the spirit of the match. So I recommended we decline the draw, and that's what we did.

It backfired miserably, of course. Kasparov won easily, and added a win in game six for good measure. Kasparov would later describe this as my main contribution to the first match. I didn't find it amusing.

I went back to work in August, after the Parsippany U.S. Championship. I spent the better part of the next nine months in a spacious conference room (the aforementioned grandmaster room) in the T.J. Watson facility in Yorktown Heights, NY. Playing games, testing positions, making notes and reporting my findings to my colleagues eight hours a day, five days a week, I learned what I needed to know to make the machine play more like a human.

People often ask me how I did when I played against the machine. But I rarely played it straight up — I usually forced it into certain positions for testing. I particularly focused on closed positions because I knew computers handled them poorly. I spent a lot of time working with Deep Blue on levers, pawn breaks to open up closed positions. My colleagues did a lot of further testing to try to get the numbers properly adjusted.

One particular problem I encountered involved Deep Blue exchanging pawns prematurely to open a file, often resulting in trading rooks and achieving nothing. Human players instinctively build up by doubling rooks before exchanging at the right moment. I found out, much to my surprise, that Deep Blue did not value a potential open file, only an actual one. CB (now officially "FH" for media purposes) thought it over and proclaimed a solution. "I can fix it," he said, reminding me of Jeff Spicoli in *Fast Times at Ridgemont High*. He even placed the fix directly onto the chip.

The months flew by with our work occasionally interrupted by negotiations with Kasparov. For some reason he wanted Deep Blue to decide on all draw offers by itself. The convention had been (and still is, I believe) for the operator to accept or decline draws. Since Deep Blue had no contextual knowledge of its match situation, it could easily take a draw against its interests. We resolved the dispute by explaining we would set the "contempt factor" so high that Deep Blue would never take a draw and would play out every miniscule advantage forever.

One issue remained in contention permanently. Kasparov continually demanded that we send him games played by Deep Blue. When we refused, Kasparov vented his frustrations to the media, which tended to distort the issue. While Deep Blue had access to all of Kasparov's games, they were of no use beyond opening preparation. Kasparov had all public games played in the past by Deep Blue (and its predecessor Deep Thought), though many inferred from Kasparov's claims that we had somehow held these back from him. Deep Blue was a project in constant flux. We were changing the program all the time and only playing training games. We thought it made no more sense to ask for our training games than for us to ask to see Kasparov's training games. And any game we sent Kasparov would become obsolete as soon as we changed the program. Since we actually used a completely different chip for the match, earlier games could easily be seen as disinformation. I imagine that if we had sent him games, Kasparov would have complained if Deep Blue's match play did not match his expectations.

I got time off for two tournaments, the Olympiad in Armenia and the Rilton Cup in Sweden over the Christmas and New Year's break. In snowy Stockholm I won my second European tournament, and this time I made it home with the trophy!

The last few months had me fretting over the monumental task of preparing openings to play against Kasparov. Another branch of IBM provided Miguel Illescas, who had worked with the team in the past. CJ told me I could hire two guys to help me. So I brought in Fed and Nick to help Deep Blue study.

With Fed in the office we had a few extra laughs. John liked to start the day off with a big cup of IBM's "festering" coffee. IBM officials brought in a sports psychologist to get our heads together for the match. I told them we had nothing to worry about; once the match started, we could sit back and watch while Kasparov stressed out. One day Fed showed up to the office looking out of sorts. When I asked him what was wrong, he repeated one of the buzz phrases we had learned. "I'm not emotionally prepared to compete today," he told me.

* * * * *

The second match game left the most indelible impressions. Kasparov had won the first game with apparent ease. His strategy of exploiting typical computer errors worked far less effectively the next day.

☐ Deep Blue ■ Kasparov
New York (2nd matchgame) 1997

1 e4 e5 2 Nf3 Nc6 3 Bb5 a6 4 Ba4 Nf6 5 0-0 Be7 6 Re1 b5 7 Bb3 d6 8 c3 0-0 9 h3 h6

Kasparov chooses the Smyslov variation, a solid but little-used line. He could be certain that we hadn't done any specific preparation for an opening he had never played before.

10 d4 Re8 11 Nbd2 Bf8 12 Nf1 Bd7 13 Ng3 Na5 14 Bc2 c5 15 b3 Nc6 16 d5 Ne7

Deep Blue was still playing from its general book, so these moves all occurred quite quickly. In general terms, Kasparov could have been happy with this position because of the blocked center. However, he has paid a price for this structure. White has a great deal more space, and the black pieces are rather passively placed. Kasparov would never accept this position against a human.

17 Be3 Ng6 18 Qd2 Nh7 19 a4 Nh4 20 Nxh4 Qxh4 21 Qe2 Qd8 22 b4!

This is one of the most significant moves of the match, yet it went unnoticed by all the commentators. No one thought much of this move because it is so obvious to humans—it's just the kind of move that people play in this situation. But Deep Blue didn't play this move from memory or pattern recognition. It played 22 b4 to activate its rook. By blocking the b-pawn, Deep Blue gets points for the placement of the rook on the a-file.

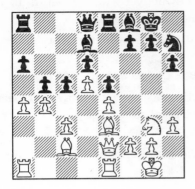

22...Qc7 23 Rec1 c4

Another move motivated by Kasparov's inhuman opposition. Against a human, Kasparov probably would have opted for 23...cxb4 23 cxb4 Qb7. Now Black's structure is rigid and his counterplay is non-existent. He must have clung to the hope that Deep Blue wouldn't understand what to do.

24 Ra3 Rec8 25 Rca1

Ordinary stuff for a human, but no computer would keep the tension (avoid axb5) for so long. Deep Blue only knows its rooks are active because of the change we made on the chip eight months earlier. The "transparent rook" leads Deep Blue in the right direction.

25...Qd8

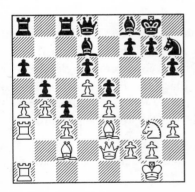

26 f4

Deep Blue seems to "understand" the maxim of stretching the defense by opening a second front. Computers generally handle levers very poorly, but the intensive work we did in the lab paid off royally. Incidentally, Karpov criticized this move, recommending 26 axb5 axb5 27 Ba7, a maneuver which he has utilized in similar positions. World Champions are not known for small egos.

Around here I appeared on stage with Ashley and Seirawan. Can you imagine a prouder moment for me?

26...Nf6 27 fxe5 dxe5 28 Qf1 Ne8 29 Qf2 Nd6 30 Bb6 Qe8 31 R3a2 Be7 32 Bc5 Bf8

Kasparov must have felt horrible about retracting his previous move, but Deep Blue was prepared to meet 32...Qf8 with 33 Nh5 to great advantage.

33 Nf5! Bxf5 34 exf5 f6 35 Bxd6 Bxd6

White has a rather obvious opportunity to win material here. Kasparov could not believe what happened in the next two moves.

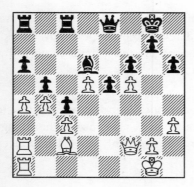

36 axb5!

Deep Blue resisted the temptation to grab material with 36 Qb6. The following lines are augmented by post-game analysis: 36...Qe7! (if 36...Rd8 37 Be4! with a clear advantage – Deep Blue) 37 axb5 Rab8 38 Qxa6 (White remains clearly better after 38 Qe3! axb5 39 Be4 – D.King) 38...e4 and Black has compensation after 39 Qa7 (or 39 Bxe4 Qe5 40 Bf3 Rd8 41 Qa3 Re8, while 39 Re1 Qe5 40 Rxe4 Qh2+ 41 Kf2 Bg3+ 42 Kf3 Bd6 43 Kf2 is just a draw) 39...Qe5 40 Qe3 Re8 (Deep Blue).

36...axb5 37 Be4!

This decision was easier: 37 Qb6 Rxa2 38 Rxa2 Ra8 39 Rxa8 Qxa8 40 Qxd6 Qa1+ 41 Kh2 Qc1 draws (Deep Blue).

37...Rxa2 38 Qxa2 Qd7 39 Qa7 Rc7 40 Qb6 Rb7 41 Ra8+ Kf7 42 Qa6 Qc7 43 Qc6 Qb6+ 44 Kf1?!

The cautious 44 Kh1! would have prevented the opportunity in the game: 44...Rb8 45 Ra6 Qe3 46 Qxd6 Re8 and now 47 Ra1! Qxe4 48 Ra7+ Kg8 49 Qd7 wins for White.

44...Rb8 45 Ra6?

White can win prosaically with 45 Qxb6 Rxb6 46 Ke2, but the text seems to end all resistance.

According to Deep Blue's readout, White's advantage bulged to +200. Kasparov could stand his miserable position no longer and resigned.

1-0

It seems that he must exchange queens here, and 45...Qxc6 46 dxc6 is clearly hopeless. It wasn't until the next day that the world awoke from this "mass hypnosis".

It turns out that Black can draw, incredible as it seems, with 45...Qe3! 46 Qxd6 Re8! and now:

a) 47 Bf3 Qc1+ (not 47...Qd3+? 48 Be2 and wins) 48 Kf2 Qd2+ 49 Be2 (or 49 Kg1 Qc1+ 50 Kh2 Qf4+) 49...Qf4+ 50 Ke1 (or 50 Kg1 Qe3+) 50...Qc1+ 51 Bd1 Qxc3+ 52 Kf1 Qc1! draws.

b) 47 Ra1 Qxe4 48 Ra7+ Kg8 49 Qd7 Qd3+ draws again.

c) 47 h4 h5!! 48 Bf3 Qc1+ 49 Kf2 Qd2+ 50 Be2 (or 50 Kg3 Qf4+ 51 Kh3 Qxf5+) 50...Qf4+ 51 Ke1 Qc1+ 52 Bd1 Qxc3+ 53 Kf1 Qc1! 54 Ke2 Qb2+ and again perpetual check is unavoidable. Even 47...Qxe4 is sufficient for a draw. Most analysts had 48 Ra7+ Kg8 49 Qd7 Qf4+ 50 Kg1 Qe3+ 51 Kh2 Qf4+ 52 Kh3 Qe3+ 53 g3 winning for White. But 52...Re7!! produces another miracle draw. After 53 Qc8+ (or 53 Qxe7 Qxf5+) 53...Kh7 54 Rxe7 h5!! White's free move offers no defense to the coming barrage of checks.

Almost immediately, the Internet was abuzz with reports that Kasparov had missed a forced draw at the end. Kasparov's handlers heard and wondered what to tell Garry. Figuring he would ultimately find out anyway, they decided to break it to him as gently as possible and let him work through his emotions before the next game.

Kasparov's second Yuri Dokhoian did the deed as he and Kasparov walked to lunch at an Italian restaurant. "Garry stopped in his tracks and grabbed his head," Friedel told Bruce Weber. "There was no shouting, no obscenities. He eventually walked on, didn't say anything." At the restaurant, I could see he was analyzing in his head—click-click, click-click-click—and after five minutes he glanced at me. And he said, "Rook e8, h4, h5. That was all? That simple? How could the computer not see that?" (*NY Times*, May 7th).

The juxtaposition of Deep Blue's savvy play on moves 36-37 and its surprising miscalculation at the end puzzled Kasparov. He could not make sense of it. At his next opportunity, he would demand answers.

After an interesting draw in game three, the audience expected a discussion of the day's game. Instead they were treated to unexpected fireworks. Kasparov shifted the topic to game two at the first opportunity. "This machine missed a—from a computer point of view—elementary draw, and I resigned a position which was probably drawn. And you know...I would try against any human being, but with computer, probably it saw it. Now I think we had an amazing game...but anybody who knows a little bit about computers understands that game one and game three are very, very different from game two."

The atmosphere strained with Kasparov's angry words. I hoped to diffuse the tension with a calm, rational explanation of Deep Blue's thought process for moves 36-37. No such luck; Garry stuck to his guns.

"It's very strange that the computer suddenly got confused. It spent so long on 37 Qb6 and I would like to know very much what was the variation. [Actually, the longer think occurred during 35 Bxd6.] By ply 25, I didn't find anything unplayable from a computer point of view. White still had a sizeable advantage. Then at the last moment it didn't calculate a much simpler line with 45...Qe3 and all these checks. It's a much easier task for a computer than to not play 37 Qb6." [Kasparov may have meant 36 Qb6, which is much more complicated than 37 Qb6.]

Maurice Ashley picked up on Kasparov's apparent insistence that Deep Blue's play in game two was unexplainable. He seemed to be insinuating something. Maurice followed his journalistic instincts and asked the most provocative possible question. "Do you think there may have been some kind of human intervention during this game?"

Kasparov replied: "It reminds me of the famous goal which Maradona scored against England in 1986. He said it was the hand of God."

He spoke a little further; I hardly heard the rest. The implication was very clear: He was accusing us of cheating! And on the basis of...well, his lack of understanding, actually. I thought of my teammates, who had worked so hard for years to produce such an outstanding achievement. They could hardly defend themselves; IBM desperately wanted to maintain amicable relations with their opponent. But I wasn't going to stand quietly. I reached for the microphone.

"I think that it is definitely a mistake for Garry to give a position to Fritz or any other computer and say, 'this is computer behavior and this is what Deep Blue must be thinking or what Deep Blue would do.' I think he's seen from the games he's played against Deep Blue that Deep Blue is no ordinary computer, that Deep Blue plays an entirely different level from any other computer he's seen. So maybe he should come to grips with the fact that Deep Blue can do a lot of things that he did not think were possible."

I felt pleased with how that came out. Kasparov, on the other hand, had steam coming out of his ears. "This is not a very fair statement. I definitely understand better than anyone else the difference between Deep Blue and any other computer—but what's most amazing is that the machine suddenly lost its intelligence and in a completely winning, strategical winning position missed the perpetual...And let me to tell you, to reject 37 Qb6 is ten times more difficult than to find 45...Qe3."

C.J. Tan tried to effect some reconciliation. "I think it is really flattering for Garry to say that Deep Blue plays so differently from other computers," he included in his remarks. CJ knows the way corporate employees are supposed to phrase their comments. But Garry wouldn't retreat. "I'm keeping my own opinion that game one and game three were typical computer games. Game two was slightly different." The gloves were off...for good.

Kasparov felt IBM should have to prove that its computer didn't cheat. Thus the "logs", the printouts of Deep Blue's screen output, became the focal point of the match. Kasparov soon demanded the programmers print out the logs immediately after each game to make sure they would not be tampered with.

For ten years I've owned printouts from all six games. IBM was slow to release them to the public, but they have been available since 2000. There is no smoking gun, just a lot of numbers that most people would find incomprehensible.

It is difficult to say exactly how Deep Blue passed on grabbing the queenside pawns in game two, even from studying the logs. The logs show the principal variation (pv), the best play continuation at various analysis depths. As it looked deeper, the computer saw more and more compensation for Black. Every facet in chess—passed pawns, king safety, mobility, etc.—is represented mathematically, just like the value of pieces. Computer decisions are made purely on points, but they aren't easily predictable, even to programmers.

For example, Deep Blue could grab a pawn (100 points) but see 60 points of compensation for the opponent, for a net of +40. Alternatively, another move which doesn't win a pawn might preserve a net of 50 points in positional advantages. Deep Blue would prefer the higher score offered by the second move. That is essentially how the decisions on move 36 and 37 were made.

When playing 35 Bxd6, Deep Blue intended to continue 36 Qb6 and rated it highly favorably. But in the brief time before Kasparov recaptured, and the early part of its calculation on move 36, Deep Blue dropped its score. After 335 seconds its score drops to +48 for 36 Qb6. The score has fallen so low that another move is able to overtake it. Just before the six-minute mark, 36 axb5 got preference, and Deep Blue played it shortly thereafter. [The extra time was generated by a "fail low". When Deep Blue's evaluation dropped substantially, it was programmed to take extra time to bring the score back up.]

On the next move, Deep Blue again leaned towards 37 Qb6, but with a much lower score than two moves earlier. At depth eleven, 37 Be4 edged into the lead, and Deep Blue played it after an ordinary three minute think.

The log explains the process by which Deep Blue made its decisions, but the chess reasons are largely absent. Still, we can see a pattern. In the first minute of its deliberations on move 35, Deep Blue recognized that the best play for Black is to sacrifice both queenside pawns to get in ...e5-e4. As Deep Blue went deeper, it evaluated the position less and less favorably for White, until it decided that White does better to take a different course. The information available indicates Deep Blue made the right decision for the right reasons.

Kasparov contrasted this brilliant phase with Deep Blue's seemingly inexplicable slip at the end of the same game. How could a computer miss an "elementary" perpetual check? If Kasparov really understood computers, he would know that perpetual check is rarely simple for computers. Lines with a lot of branches are complicated for humans, but simple for a computer's brute force approach. Deep Blue had no trouble "seeing" 46...Re8! and 47...h5!!. Very deep lines, on the other hand, can defeat a program as powerful as Deep Blue. Humans handle perpetual check much more easily than computers, because of our ability to recognize patterns. We can foresee a king unable to escape a series of checks well before a repetition draw is demonstrated. Until Deep Blue gets to the very end of the longest variation, it can only evaluate the position as highly favorable for White. Prominent computer chess programmer Ed Schroeder produced a variation 35 ply deep before a repetition occurs: 45...Qe3 46 Qxd6 Re8 47 h4 h5 48 Bf3 Qc1+ 49 Kf2 Qd2 50 Be2 Qf4 51 Kg1 Qe3+ 52 Kh2 Qf4+ 53 Kh3 Qxf5+ 54 Kh2 Qf4+ 55 Kg1 Qe3+ 56 Kf1 Qc1+ 57 Kf2 Qf4+ 58 Ke1 Qc1+ 59 Bd1 Qxc3+ 60 Kf1 Qc1! 61 Ke2 Qb2 62 Kf1 Qc1. Not so simple, Garry. In fact, as a "computer expert", Kasparov should have expected Deep Blue to muff a perpetual check!

In this case, the log offers no illumination. Deep Blue never assessed 45...Qe3 as the best move, so it doesn't appear in its output. We had to run Deep Blue from the diagram position for ten minutes to get it to recognize the draw.

After hard-fought draws in the fourth and fifth games, we went to the last game with a tied match. At the IBM meeting before the last game, I told the IBM brass that Kasparov was exhausted and might well offer a draw in game six. Would they be happy with a tied match or did they want us to go for the win? I never got a straight answer, but the question was mooted by Kasparov's surprising approach to the last game.

□ Deep Blue ■ G.Kasparov
New York (6th matchgame) 1997

---

1 e4 c6

Was this another move order trick?

2 d4 d5

No, he is really playing the Caro-Kann. Although Kasparov had favored the Caro early in his career, he had not used it in a serious contest in fifteen years! Why did he dust it off for this game?

3 Nd2 dxe4 4 Nxe4 Nd7 5 Ng5 Ngf6 6 Bd3 e6 7 N1f3 h6?!

My heart hit my throat when I saw this move. Extremely provocative, it encourages White to sacrifice a piece for an extremely dangerous attack. At the time, many computers were programmed *not* to play this sacrifice. We never dreamed of avoiding highly regarded moves. Our Caro-Kann preparation consisted of a few main lines entered by Nick DeFirmian. While he was inputting, I added a notation to answer 7...h6 with 8 Nxe6. Given no choice in the matter, Deep Blue went for the gusto in a matter of seconds.

8 Nxe6

Kasparov looked surprised by this move. His eyes opened wide and he made a gesture with his hand. But he recovered to play his next move in only thirteen seconds. If Kasparov had not foreseen this position, he certainly would have spent more time analyzing the immediate capture 8...fxe6. Many theoreticians consider that move superior on the basis of Black's win in the grandmaster game P.Wolff-J.Granda Zuniga, New York 1992.

8...Qe7 9 0-0 fxe6 10 Bg6+ Kd8

After making this move, Kasparov buried his head in his hands in apparent dejection. In the IBM booth, we observed this display with suspicion. Murray was the first to say Kasparov was acting. When all the information came in, the rest of us had to agree.

11 Bf4!

This was the first decision for Deep Blue, and a good one. I prefer it to the other popular move, 11 Re1.

11...b5?!

Kasparov plays the first new move of the game. The March 1997 issue of the International Computer Chess Association (ICCA) Journal contained a game which puts the picture in focus. Grandmaster Gennadi Timoscenko played a match against a tandem of Fritz and a mathematics professor named Ingo Althofer, won by the man/machine partnership 4½-3½. One of the games proceeded along the lines of game six, until Kasparov's ill-fated 11...b5. Timoscenko improved with 11...Nd5 12 Bg3 Qb4 and reached a playable position. The ICCA Journal article included detailed analysis promoting Black's defensive resources.

The Deep Blue team members were unaware of the article. We didn't intend to play like a computer, so we concentrated on mainstream chess journals like the *Informant* and *New In Chess* Yearbooks. But Friedel, Kasparov's computer advisor, owns Fritz. Surely he would have alerted Kasparov to the match and article, especially since Kasparov used an anti-computer strategy in the match (Kasparov's later interest in man/machine tandem chess is another giveaway).

Kasparov's 11...b5 seems hard to figure. It's not a particularly inspired move. But I tested the position against the contemporaneous version of Fritz after the match, and found that Fritz responded quite poorly. It actually played Qd1-e2, Rf1-e1, and Qe2xe6, exchanging into a losing endgame. Unfortunately for Kasparov, Deep Blue had a much more sophisticated evaluation function than Fritz did.

12 a4 Bb7 13 Re1 Nd5 14 Bg3 Kc8 15 axb5 cxb5 16 Qd3 Bc6 17 Bf5

Deep Blue's evaluation went flying over +200 when it found this move.

17...exf5 18 Rxe7 Bxe7 19 c4 1-0

Black's position is collapsing. Kasparov looked over at his mother and began to speak to her while gesturing wildly with his hands. If anyone heard them, they could not translate the conversation. It was a surreal moment to cap off a surreal game. When he was talked out, Kasparov resigned. We were almost too confused to celebrate.

We arrived late to the closing ceremony because we had to print out the log of the game. Everyone was already seated, and we had to squeeze past Kasparov's mother to get to our seats. She clapped her hands derisively a few inches from my head.

Kasparov had harsh words to say at the closing ceremonies, and for quite some time later. He was understandably upset with the confrontational approach IBM had taken, but his comments went well beyond any indignities he suffered. In post match speeches on the West Coast Kasparov described how Deep Blue's play had contradicted its "priorities". This was meant to be some kind of proof of human intervention. Kasparov didn't describe Deep Blue's operation with much accuracy, but there was no opportunity to contradict him. He issued frequent demands for IBM to show the logs from the games to the world to prove their innocence.

I find it terribly ironic that, while demanding explanations of Deep Blue's moves, Kasparov left so much mystery about his own choices. He said little about game six beyond rejecting the rather unlikely 7...h6 as *"fingerfehler"* explanation that Seirawan proposed during the game. I think Kasparov hoped to show once and for all that Deep Blue could be exploited like any other computer. His opening choice was so odd from a human perspective that he could deny the game's significance if he lost. But until Kasparov decides to show us his "logs", we will never know for sure.

The documentary *Game Over: Kasparov and the Machine* portrayed IBM's behavior during the match as mysterious, achieving this effect with several contrived scenes. [An interview with a disgruntled IBM website worker fired during the match bathed him in shadow.] Many Kasparov fans saw this film as evidence of cheating from the computer side; I think the film should be subtitled "A Study in Paranoia". Watch the scene where the Kasparov camp freaks out because they think they see a telescope in the building across from the hotel, and you will have to agree.

Despite the fact that few of Deep Blue's moves would be foreign to current computer programs, I still encounter occasional conspiracy theorists who believe human intervention occurred. I know they are wrong, but for several reasons the theory isn't even *plausible*:

1) The Deep Blue team and all the action was observed by an impartial referee, Ken Thompson. How could any cheating occur?

2) If the computer plays better than almost any human, why would you want to overrule it? Most likely you would just be making a mistake.

3) What would be IBM's motivation? The risk-reward analysis doesn't add up. The oft-repeated argument that winning the match sent IBM's stock up doesn't mean anything. The stock didn't suddenly go up; it went up consistently from the successful demonstration of IBM technology, not from winning the match. The consequences of cheating and being caught, on the other hand, would be absolutely catastrophic.

4) No one from the team has met up with an unfortunate accident. Why would IBM take a chance that someone would confess?

I'm not sure why IBM delayed so long in publishing the logs, which very few people would be able to understand. In any event, Kasparov saw them right after the match. I'm not sure how much he understood; he certainly couldn't find anything wrong. But after all this time, I don't think he will ever back off from his position.

IBM approached the match like a contest between two humans, feeling no need to make concessions. Let both sides bring their best to the table and see what happens. C.J. Tan, the manager of the Deep Blue team, decided on this strategy and followed it consistently on every issue.

Tan may have felt a hardline approach would rattle Kasparov. In some cases our team could have been more forthcoming. In the period before the match, Tan was often asked if there were extra grandmasters working for the team. He usually gave a cagey response suggesting that I had a lot of "friends" I might work with. In theory, grandmaster team members could indicate what openings Deep Blue might play. So it was reasonable to dodge that question, but once the match was about to start, why not explain the involvement of Fedorowicz and DeFirmian? When the news leaked out during the match, it appeared that team Deep Blue had things to hide.

In man vs. machine matches, the computer side is held to a higher standard. Today computers are expected to make concessions far beyond anything Kasparov would have asked for. Even then, when Deep Blue was considered the underdog the perception was the same.

Making surprising moves is not ordinarily grounds for suspicion. The Deep Blue team had every right to reject Kasparov's demand (from game three on) to see the logs. After all, you shouldn't have to tell your opponent everything you were thinking during a game.

I learned after the match that Ken Thompson, the computer referee for the match, was upset with Tan for not showing the logs. When such a respected figure of computer chess takes a position, it gives you pause. Should we have let Kasparov see the logs during the match, for the sake of good relations? A source in the Kasparov camp told me Kasparov would have been greatly placated by such a gesture.

Though the logs probably wouldn't have helped him, we were not convinced at the time. Showing him the logs after the match seemed like a sensible compromise.

Kasparov lost because he received very poor advice—that Deep Blue was no different qualitatively from any PC program. Ironically, he would have used a more effective strategy if he had listened to me. A week before the match *Newsweek* did a cover story on the two teams. In the article I told about how I had been able to eliminate typical weaknesses from Deep Blue's play. "When I play the machine now, I can no longer use an anti-computer strategy to pick apart its weaknesses," I said. "That's why I feel it has a real chance to win." I was speaking in total honesty, but Kasparov responded disdainfully—"This is crap." He still believed, after eight months of lab work that Deep Blue could be figured out in two games, and destroyed in the next four.

If Kasparov could have admitted his miscalculation, he might have had more of a chance for a rematch. As it was, IBM wouldn't have been tempted to do business again with a hostile opponent. IBM officials told us before the match that there would not be a round three. Winning the match gave the corporation little incentive to continue. Though the chess community may not have been convinced of Deep Blue's superiority after the win in 1997, the general public surely had. IBM would have nothing to gain.

After some talk about future Deep Blue participation, the project was dismantled. I received some lovely parting gifts and went back to my old job as a full-time chessplayer. Fortunately I remembered how to do it.

Chapter Eleven

Second Wind: U.S. Championships 1997-2006

1997 Chandler

Coming off a year of studying and accumulating knowledge with almost no outlets for playing, I was absolutely raring to go. The warm weather of Chandler, Arizona, pool basketball and congenial atmosphere contributed to my positive frame of mind.

In Parsippany then-USCF President Don Schultz sat down with a few of the grandmasters to discuss the future of the Championship. I proposed a new hybrid format, with two eight-man round-robins producing four semi-finalists. The champion would then be determined by match play. It seemed the best of both worlds—everyone would get a serious tournament, but the title would come down to a head-to-head finish.

Larry Christiansen set the pace in my section, but I caught him at the end with wins over A.Ivanov, Gulko, and Browne. My openings were in great shape. I had lots of ideas in the Queen's Gambit Accepted and Alapin Sicilian from my work at IBM. I had never felt so motivated before. I prepared three hours a day and still felt fresh for the games.

I drew Gregory Kaidanov for the semi-final. Greg has had enormous success in the U.S. He is always among the leaders on the USCF and FIDE rating list. He has stuck around on the Olympic team while his contemporaries have dropped off. And during all this he has been one of the most prominent coaches in the country.

But to this date he has never won a U.S. Championship, a glaring omission on a glittering résumé. Part of the reason is that he absolutely cannot play Black against me. Yeah, he has made a few comfortable draws. And he's given me problems when he's White; he just doesn't get White enough. With Black, he often equalizes but pushes too hard and loses. I've beaten him in the Alekhine, the Najdorf, the Giuoco Piano, and the Ruy Lopez. I even beat him in the '96 Championship, when I didn't beat anyone else.

I won the first game, and drew the second. In a comfortable match situation, I opted for 1 d4 and even that worked.

☐ J.Benjamin ■ G.Kaidanov
U.S. Championship, Chandler 1997

---

1 d4 d5 2 c4 e6 3 Nf3 Nf6 4 g3 dxc4 5 Qa4+ Nbd7 6 Bg2 a6 7 Qxc4 b5 8 Qc6 Ra7 9 Be3 Nd5 10 Qc1 c5 11 Nc3 Nxc3 12 Qxc3 Nb6 13 dxc5 Nd5 14 Qd2 Nxe3 15 Qxe3 Qa5+ 16 Nd2 Qb4 17 Rc1 Rc7 18 0-0 Qxb2 19 Rfd1 Be7 20 c6 0-0 21 Rb1

White can exploit his initiative much more directly with 21 Qb6! Bd8 22 Nc4 followed by Nd6.

21...Qa3 22 Nb3 Bd8 23 Rd3 Re7 24 Rbd1 Bc7 25 Nc5 Qxa2 26 Nd7 Rfe8 27 Qg5 h6

28 Nf6+! Kh8 29 Qh4 gxf6 30 Qxh6+ Kg8 31 Rd4 f5 32 Qg5+ Kf8 33 Qh6+ Kg8 34 Qg5+ Kf8 35 Qf6! Be5 36 Qxe5 f6 37 Qxf6+ Rf7 38 Qh6+

Can I miss *more* mates in U.S. Championships? 38 Qh8+ Ke7 39 Rd7+ Bxd7 40 Rxd7 mate.

38...Kg8 39 Qg6+ Kf8 40 Qh6+ Kg8 41 Rd8 Rfe7 42 Qg6+ Kf8 43 Qf6+ 1-0

This left me with a day to relax in the sun while Christiansen and Seirawan battled it out. They went well into overtime before Larry finally pulled it out. With no day off before the finals, Larry was pretty wiped out and played carelessly.

□ J.Benjamin ■ L.Christiansen
U.S. Championship final (1st matchgame), Chandler 1997

Black has a host of solid moves like 16...Ng4, but not **16...Nd7? 17 Nxc6+ Kd6 18 Na3!**. After **18...a6 19 Na5 Rab8 20 Nb3 Rxc1+ 21 Rxc1 a5? 22 Nxa5!** White had two pawns and an easy win (if 22...Rxb2? 23 N5c4+).

Larry got back to business the next day with a nice win aided by my memory lapse.

□ L.Christiansen ■ J.Benjamin
U.S. Championship final (2nd matchgame), Chandler 1997

1 d4 d5 2 c4 dxc4 3 e4 Nc6 4 Be3 Nf6 5 f3 e5 6 d5 Ne7 7 Bxc4?!

7 Nc3! is the right move.

7...a6?

7...c6! equalizes immediately. Deep Blue had found this move, but I forgot it! White won in 45 moves.

Game three was a sharp French Defense. I tried to mate with an extra exchange but had to settle for perpetual check before Larry's pawns exerted themselves. The match then turned on an unfortunate blunder in game four.

☐ **L.Christiansen** ◼ **J.Benjamin**
U.S. Championship final (4th matchgame), Chandler 1997

Black has just played **41...f4**, acquiescing to the obvious draw after 42 Rxf4 Rxb5. But Larry wasn't ready to give in: **42 Rc7+ Kf6 43 b6?? Ra5+ 44 Kb3 Rb5+** and Black won easily.

During this time I learned the drawback of the new format. With all the eliminated players gone home, the site felt like a ghost town. It's a bit weird hanging out with the guy you are trying to crush, but there wasn't any alternative. One night we were sitting in the hotel sports bar watching a game. "Buy me a drink," Larry suggested. Before I could alert the bartender, he added, "It's in your best interest."

Larry Christiansen

The perfect counterpart to the rail-thin DeFirmian, Larry's burly physique suggests the power of his attacking chess. The three-time U.S. Champion is concluding an awesome career; I think it is a joke that he is not yet in the U.S. Chess Hall of Fame. Throughout his career, Larry has been an uncom-

promising fighter over the board. As the oldest member of my chess genera-tion, I've looked up to him as a role model.

Larry is a surprisingly good cook—he and Fed have occasionally debated their respective culinary abilities. He is a fine raconteur and humorist who enjoys his own jokes with a distinctive cackle. You just have to ignore the ultra right-wing, conspiracy theory ideology.

After a draw in game five it came down to the last game. Larry threw the kitchen sink at me but I held him off.

☐ **L.Christiansen** ■ **J.Benjamin**
U.S. Championship final (6th matchgame), Chandler 1997

---

1 d4 Nf6 2 c4 e6 3 Nc3 Bb4 4 e3 0-0 5 Nge2 d5 6 a3 Be7 7 Nf4 c6 8 Bd3 dxc4 9 Bxc4 Nbd7 10 Nd3 c5 11 Ba2 b6 12 0-0 Bb7 13 Qe2 Qc7 14 Bd2 Rac8 15 Rad1 Qb8 16 f4 Ba6 17 Be1 Rfd8 18 Qf3 cxd4 19 exd4 Nf8 20 Bf2 Bxa3 21 f5 Bxd3 22 Rxd3 Bxb2 23 Ne4 Nxe4 24 Qxe4 Qd6 25 Bh4 Re8

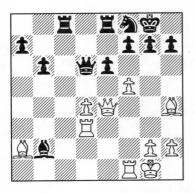

26 Bg3 Qd7 27 f6 gxf6 28 Bh4 f5 29 Qe3 Ng6 30 Bf6 f4 31 Qh3 Qd6 32 Qh6 Qf8 33 Qh5 Rc3 34 Bb1 Rxd3 35 Bxd3 Qd6 36 Bxg6 ½-½

Black is completely winning by now, but I decided it wasn't important.

Ten years after my first title, I finally had my second! The ring felt good on my finger, even though it seemed to be better sized for Larry's bear paw than my di-minutive appendage.

1998 Denver

Nick DeFirmian dominated his section, with Dmitry Gurevich taking second. My section proved to be quite a bit more complicated. I tied with three players— Gulko, Fedorowicz, and Tal Shaked at a modest +1 score. The top two would continue on to the semis, but the top three would qualify for the World Championship tournament. In the double round-robin, I broke through with a win over Gulko. Gulko beat Shaked, and Shaked beat Fed. I faced my old friend in the last game. A draw would clinch first for me and eliminate Fed. A loss would send us back to square one!

In the end I forced a perpetual check from a position of strength. There was one move where I nearly made a blunder, but pulled back in time. John likes to harp on that moment, but if it provides him some consolation, fine by me.

Shaked went on to beat Gulko and take on DeFirmian in the semis. For years, I could go to sleep dreaming about playing Gurevich in the U.S. Championship. Would I get things back to "normal"?

Dmitry Gurevich

Dmitry once said that coming to America was "like finding a million dollars in the street." He is short and slight with an facial resemblance to Garry Kasparov. Usually tense and occasionally argumentative, Dima is also honest and highly principled. He may not always be a ball of fire, but you have to respect him.

□ **J.Benjamin** ■ **D.Gurevich**

U.S. Championship, Denver 1998

---

1 e4 c5 2 Nf3 d6 3 c3 Nf6 4 Bd3

The Kopec System was part of a rotation of sidelines I employed at the time. I also placed the bishop on e2 and c4, the latter against DeFirmian in the finals.

4...Nc6 5 Bc2 Bg4 6 d3 g6 7 Nbd2 Bg7 8 h3 Bxf3 9 Nxf3 0-0 10 0-0 b5 11 a3 a5 12 d4 cxd4 13 cxd4 Nd7 14 Be3 (see following diagram) 14...a4 15 Bd3 Rb8 16 Qe2 Qb6 17 e5 Qa6 18 Bf4 dxe5 19 dxe5 Nc5 20 Rac1 Ne6 21 Bg3 Qb6 22 Bb1 Bh6 23 Rcd1 Rbd8 24 Ba2 Ncd4 25 Nxd4 Nxd4 26 Qe4 Qc5 27 Kh2 Nf5 28 e6 f6 29 Rd7 Nxg3 30 fxg3 Bg5?

Gurevich passes on 30...f5 because of 31 Qh4, but Black seems to hold after 31...Rxd7 32 exd7+ Kg7 33 Rd1 Rd8 34 Be6 Be3 35 Re1 Bf2 36 Bg8 (or 36 Re2 Bg1+ 37 Kh1 Qc1 38 Qxe7+ Kh6 39 Qh4+ Kg7 40 Rc2 Qf1) 36...Kxg8 37 Rxe7 Bxg3+ 38 Kxg3 Qd6+ with a draw.

31 h4

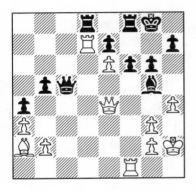

31...f5??

31...Bc1 requires accurate play to prosecute White's advantage. There could follow 32 Rfd1 Rde8 (if 32...f5 33 Qe1 Rc8 34 R1d5 Qe3 35 Qxe3 Bxe3 36 Rxe7 Rc1 37 Rb7 Bg1+ 38 Kh3 Be3 39 Rd1! wins) 33 Qe2 Rc8 (33...Be3 is relatively best, though it coughs up the b-pawn after 34 R7d5) 34 R1d5 Qc2 35 Qxc2 Rxc2 36 Rxe7 Bxb2 (or 36...Rxb2 37 Rdd7 Bh6 38 Rxh7) 37 Rb7 and wins.

32 Qd3 Bxh4 33 gxh4 Qe5+ 34 Kg1 Rc8 35 Qd4 Qxd4+ 36 Rxd4 Rc2 37 Rf2 Rc1+ 38 Kh2 Kg7 39 Rb4 Rc5 40 Rd2 f4 41 Rd7 1-0

I won game three as well to advance. Nick eliminated Shaked, and we had our second straight "All-American" final. The match turned on a misstep in the first game.

□ J.Benjamin ■ N.DeFirmian

U.S. Championship final (1st matchgame), Denver 1998

1 e4 c5 2 Nf3 d6 3 Bc4 Nf6 4 d3 Nc6 5 c3 g6 6 0-0 Bg7 7 Nbd2 0-0 8 Re1 e5 9 Bb3 h6 10 Nc4 Be6 11 h3 Kh7 12 Ne3 d5 13 Ng4 Nxg4 14 hxg4 Qd7 15 g5 h5 16 exd5 Bxd5 17 Be3 b6 18 Bxd5 Qxd5 19 Qa4 Rfd8 20 Rad1 Rac8 21 Bc1 Kg8 22 Rd2 Qe6 23 Qc4 Rd5 24 Rde2 Rcd8 25 Re3 Qd7 26 Qe4 Ne7 27 R3e2 Nf5 28 c4 Rxd3 29 Nxe5 Bxe5 30 Qxe5 Nd4 31 Re3 Nc2 32 Rxd3 Qxd3

Now I missed 33 b3! Nxe1 34 Bb2 Rd4 35 Qe8+ Kg7 36 Qxe1 more or less equalizing. But I missed something else, too...

33 Rf1?? Qxf1+! 34 Kxf1 Rd1+ 35 Ke2 Re1+ 36 Kd2 Rxe5 37 Kxc2 Re2+ 0-1

Nick carefully nursed his lead into the final game.

□ N.DeFirmian ■ J.Benjamin

U.S. Championship final (4th matchgame), Denver 1998

1 e4 g6 2 d4 Bg7 3 Nc3 d6 4 f4 Nc6 5 Be3 Nf6 6 h3 e6 7 g4 0-0 8 Bg2 Ne7 9 Qd2 b6 10 Nge2 Bb7 11 0-0 c5 12 Rad1 Qc8 13 Ng3 cxd4 14 Bxd4 Nc6 15 Bf2 Ba6 16 Rfe1 Rd8 17 Nce2 Qc7 18 Nd4 Nxd4 19 Bxd4 e5 20 Bc3 exf4 21 Qxf4 Ne8 22 Bxg7 Nxg7 23 c3 Ne6 24 Qe3 Rac8 25 Nf5 Bb7 26 Nd4 Qc5 27 Nxe6 fxe6 28 Qxc5 dxc5 29 Kf2 Kf7 30 Ke3 g5 31 Bf3 h6 32 Rxd8 Rxd8 33 Rd1 Rxd1 34 Bxd1 Kf6 35 c4 Ke5 36 Bc2 Bc6 37 a4 *(see following diagram)* 37...a6?!

Here I missed my chance. I needed to redeploy my king to the queenside. Let's consider: 37...Kd6 38 Bd1 e5 39 Kd3 Kc7 40 Bc2 Kb7 41 Kc3 Ka6 and now White has a dilemma.

a) 42 b3 Ka5 43 Bd3 a6 44 Bc2 b5 45 axb5 axb5 46 Bd3 bxc4 47 bxc4 Ka4 48 Bc2+ Ka3 49 Bb1 Ba4 and Black will likely crawl his king in behind and win.

b) 42 b4 cxb4+ 43 Kxb4 Kb7 44 a5 (otherwise Black will play 44...a5) 44...Kc7 45 c5 ba5+ 46 Kxa5 Be8 47 Kb4 h5 with excellent winning chances.

My error was really quite silly—I could simply have temporized for four moves and worked out a plan after time control.

38 b3 b5 39 a5!

With the queenside blocked, there's no more chance to win.

39...bxc4 40 bxc4 Be8 41 Bd1 Bc6 42 Bc2 Ba8 43 Bd3 Bb7 44 Bb1 Bc8 45 Bc2 Bd7 46 Bb3 Kf6 47 Bc2 Bc6 48 Bd1 ½-½

I was happy for my good friend, but when I contemplate how hard it is to win back-to-back titles, I wish I had taken him down!

1999 Salt Lake City

In Salt Lake City our biggest fears were that we wouldn't be able to get alcohol in Mormon country, but it wasn't a problem. Tennis and swimming at the hotel kept us busy in a low-key, low publicity Championship.

I lost the first round to Serper in a game that had all been played before through move nineteen. I recovered to reach +1 with wins over Finegold and Kaidanov (yes, I had White again). In a playoff with Seirawan and A.Ivanov, I managed to lose the first two games. That left me with no chance to advance but I won two games to come second and qualify for the next WCT. Gulko took the title in the final over Seirawan.

2000 Seattle

Another financial crisis jeopardized the 2000 Championship. Before the year even started, the USCF Executive Board voted to exclude the title tournament from the budget for the next year. Although the USCF by-laws only require it to hold one every other year, the Federation had managed to hold one for every one of my years, save 1982. Not so coincidentally, Tim Redman served as USCF President during both cancellations.

I don't mean to downplay the seriousness of Federation financial woes, but such actions show priorities. The Board demonstrated surprisingly little interest in holding the tournament in 2000.

Seirawan had always kept on the USCF to hold Championships with decent conditions. He recounted the sorry situation to a few wealthy and influential friends in Seattle. One of them, Erik Anderson, took the initiative in finding a solution. He asked Yasser how much money the Championship would require, and sent Yasser to ask the Board how much they were willing to contribute.

Yasser was a bit embarrassed to go back to Anderson with the Board's answer—zero dollars. The Board had, however, budgeted $10,000 to the 2000 U.S. Masters, a tournament organized by Board member Helen Warren. One could surmise a plan to make that tournament a *de facto* U.S. Championship.

Fortunately, Anderson did not get discouraged, even when two members of the Board (Warren and Doris Barry) voted against sending the Executive Director to Seattle to negotiate an agreement with Anderson. The newly formed Seattle Chess Foundation agreed to essentially take an obligation off the USCF's hands and pay them a sanctioning fee for the privilege.

The twelve-player round-robin format appealed more to Seirawan's taste. I was sad to see my round-robin/knockout hybrid go. U.S. Championships with match play worked especially well for me—in five years (90, 91, 97, 98, and 99) I had one title and two losses in the final.

The well-balanced all-GM field unsurprisingly produced no runaway scores. I wanted to "run away" after an early disaster versus Boris Gulko.

□ **J.Benjamin** ■ **B.Gulko**
U.S. Championship, Seattle 2000

---

1 e4 c5 2 Nf3 d6 3 d4 cxd4 4 Nxd4 Nf6 5 Nc3 Nc6 6 Bg5 e6 7 Qd2 Be7 8 0-0-0 0-0 9 f3 Nxd4 10 Qxd4 a6 11 h4 Qc7 12 Kb1 b5 13 Qd2 b4 14 Ne2 Rb8 15 g4 a5 16 Nd4 a4 17 Bd3 e5 18 Nf5 Bxf5 19 gxf5 a3 20 b3 d5 21 Rhg1 Kh8 22 h5 Rfd8 23 h6 g6 24 Qe1 Rb6 25 Rg2 gxf5 26 exf5 e4 27 fxe4 Qe5 28 Bc1 dxe4 29 Bc4 Rxd1 30 Qxd1 e3 31 Qg1 Rb8

In time pressure, I tried to weigh the consequences of 32 Bxf7 (unclear) and 32 Qxe3 Ne4 (probably a draw). Suddenly I had a brainstorm...

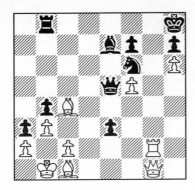

32 Bxe3?? Qb2#

There is no way to avoid a sleepless night after that. But I did something unexpected that seemed to help. I went over the game with my opponent (though I can't recall any post-mortems with Gulko in games I won). With some of the game's mysteries revealed, I felt better prepared to move on.

The next day I took on Christiansen in a Nimzovich Defense. Improving on a game I lost to A.Ivanov the year before, I quickly achieved a dominating position. It wasn't Larry's day. I was back in the running.

In the seventh round I won a gritty game from A.Ivanov to keep close to the leaderboard. In a situation reminiscent of '87, I leapfrogged Seirawan in the penultimate round with a timely sacrifice out of the opening.

□ J.Benjamin ■ Y.Seirawan

U.S. Championship, Seattle 2000

---

1 e4 e6 2 d4 d5 3 Nd2 dxe4 4 Nxe4 Nd7 5 Nf3 Ngf6 6 Nxf6+ Nxf6 7 Bg5 c5 8 Bb5+ Bd7 9 Bxd7+ Qxd7 10 Qe2 0-0-0!?

Yasser conjures up a surprising novelty. The standard 10...Be7 leads to interesting possibilities: 11 0-0-0 (or 11 dxc5 0-0 12 Ne5 Qd5 13 0-0 Bxc5 14 Rfe1 Nd7 15 Nf3 with a slight advantage, P.Leko-V.Korchnoi, Wijk aan Zee 2000) 11...0-0 12 dxc5 Qc7 (12...Qa4 is nearly my game with Psakhis—the moves ...h7-h6 and Bg5-h4 were inserted there) 13 Ne5 Qxc5 14 Bxf6 Bxf6 15 Nd7 Bxb2+ 16 Kxb2 Qb4+ 17 Kc1 Qa3+ 18 Kd2 (I accepted the perpetual against Christiansen in Chandler 1997) 18...Rfd8 19 Ke1 Rac8 with compensation for the piece.

11 Rd1

I felt my best chance for an advantage lay in putting the kings on opposite wings. Through the years, the basic formula for Yasser hasn't changed: Go for his king!

11...Qc7 12 0-0 cxd4 13 Nxd4 a6?

This prevents potential unpleasantness caused by Nb5, but White is able to exploit the unconnected rooks. Black had to try 13...Bc5, though White maintains a strong initiative with 14 Nb5 followed by 15 b4!.

14 Nxe6!

I saw the ideas within a few minutes. The variations, though deep in some places, only required ten minutes to work out.

14...fxe6 15 Qxe6+

15...Rd7

On 15...Kb8 16 Bf4 Qxf4 17 Rxd8+ Ka7 I intended 18 Qf7, though 18 Qc8 Ng4 19 g3 Qf3 20 a4 also seems to win.

16 Bxf6 gxf6 17 Rd4! Bc5 18 Rc4 Kb8

Otherwise b2-b4 will recoup the piece anyway.

19 Rxc5 Qxc5 20 Qxd7 Qxc2 21 Qd6+ Ka8 22 Qxf6

One could argue that the curtain could have been brought down here. We could have retired to watch the Mets in the first round of the playoffs. The odds of me blowing this position are pretty slim, yet he manages to create a few technical problems. Who else but Yasser could have lasted another fifty moves from here?

22...Rc8 23 h3 Rc6 24 Qd4 Rc4 25 Qh8+ Rc8 26 Qe5

The time control put thirty seconds on the clock for each move made, so naturally I'm happy to insert extra moves here and there.

26...Rc5 27 Qe3 Rc8 28 Qb3 Qe2 29 a4 h5 30 Qb4 Rc4 31 Qf8+ Ka7 32 b3 Rc3 33 Qb4 Qd3 34 Re1 Qd2 35 Rf1 Qd3 36 h4 Rxb3 37 Qc5+ Ka8 38 Qc8+ Ka7 39 Qc5+ Ka8 40 Qxh5 Qe4 41 Rd1 Rb1

Yasser takes his only chance—swap rooks and try to run his extra pawn like the wind.

42 g3 b5 43 axb5 axb5 44 Kh2 Rxd1 45 Qxd1 Kb7 46 h5 Kc6 47 h6 b4 48 Qh5

I was looking to simplify, so I don't know why I overlooked 48 Qh1.

48...Qh7 49 Kg2 Kb6 50 Qg4 Ka5 51 Qg7 Qe4+ 52 Kh2 Qf3 53 Qa7+ Kb5 54 h7 Qh5+ 55 Kg2 Qd5+ 56 Kg1

Once again, killing a few moves and stealing a few minutes.

56...Qd1+ 57 Kh2 Qh5+ 58 Kg1 Qd1+ 59 Kg2 Qd5+ 60 f3 Qd2+ 61 Qf2 Qh6 62 Qe2+ Kb6 63 Qd3 Kc5 64 g4 Qg7 65 Qf5+ Kd6 66 g5

Good enough, but as Yasser pointed out, 66 f4 b3 67 Qe5+ was cleaner.

66...b3 67 Qf6+ Qxf6 68 gxf6 b2 69 f7!

The point! Two queens for the price of one.

69...b1Q 70 f8Q+ Kc6 71 Qf6+ Kd5 72 Qg5+ Ke6

I couldn't conceive of a stalemate, so...

73 h8Q 1-0

I got home just in time to see Armando Benitez serve up a three run homer to J.T. Snow. But the Mets still won in the extra innings!

I drew with Fed in the last round (unlike in 2003, nobody minded). Only Shabalov could pass me, but he drew. Yasser rebounded to beat Gulko and create a troika at the top. A playoff decided the ring recipient, but not the title. We were considered co-champions, even though the policy since 1997 had been (and was after 2000) to determine a single champion. Naturally, with the title not at stake, I won the playoff.

2002 Seattle

The next Championship came fifteen months later, so 2001 went empty. Reflecting plans for national activities, the Seattle Chess Foundation morphed into America's Foundation for Chess, or AF4C. [They wanted to avoid confusion with the organization formerly known as the American Chess Foundation.] They had their own ideas about how to run the tournament. When the sponsors raise the prize fund (first place had more than doubled), players are reluctant to voice contrary opinions.

Erik Anderson wanted to expand the field to 56 (later 64). The Women's Championship was folded into the overall event. Only six men and six women were seeded, the other players qualifying from tournaments in the open circuit. Championship aspirants had to pay a fee (first $50, later $75) before each qualifying tournament to become eligible. Several players blew hundreds of dollars trying to get in, and many experienced grandmasters (myself included) had to bite the bullet.

The larger field added diversity and greatly increased the number of junior participants. As a veteran player, I didn't personally appreciate the changes. With a small field (ten to sixteen players), a little extra money would go a long way for each player. But with so many mouths to feed, even a $200,000 fund gets dispersed.

The Swiss system gave the Championship a peculiar feel. I pretty much muddled through with two wins and five draws until a big strike in the penultimate round. I had lost several games in a row to "Shaba", but I felt I could keep him contained with a restrained approach.

□ **J.Benjamin** ■ **A.Shabalov**
U.S. Championship, Seattle 2002

---

1 e4 e5 2 Nf3 Nc6 3 Bc4 Nf6 4 d3 Bc5 5 c3 d6 6 0-0 0-0 7 Bb3 a6 8 h3 Ba7 9 Re1 Be6 10 Nbd2 Nh5 11 Nf1 Qf6 12 Be3 Nf4 13 d4 Na5 14 Bc2 Nc4 15 Bc1 c5 16 b3 Na5 17 d5 Bd7 18 N1h2 h5 19 h4 b5 20 Ng5 c4 21 Be3 Qg6?

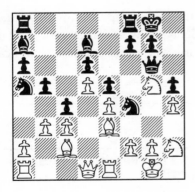

White would be held to a small advantage with 21...g6. The text is a surprising oversight for Shabalov.

22 Bxf4 exf4 23 b4 Nb7 24 e5 Bf5 25 Bxf5 Qxf5 26 Qxh5 Nd8 27 Ng4 a5 28 e6 fxe6 29 dxe6 Nc6 30 e7 Rfe8 31 Re6 Nxe7 32 Nf6+ gxf6 33 Qf7+ Kh8 34 Rxf6 Bxf2+ 35 Kh1 1-0

Alex Shabalov

I didn't understand Shabalov's chess at first. It seemed like he had a losing position in every game. Gradually I began to understand how he plays for complications where he is well equipped to outplay his opponent. He has made me rethink how I evaluate positions. I've come to admire Shaba's style and his willingness to risk all for the win—a trait that benefited all of us in 2003 and has made Shaba one of the most popular American players.

To the public he is stylish but reserved, but his humorous writings indicate his animated personality.

The final pairings were Benjamin (5½)-Christiansen (6) and DeFirmian (5½)-Yermolinsky (6). When I last faced Larry in the final in 1997, I had a ten-year thirst to quench. Now I had two titles under my belt, while Larry had not won since 1983. I felt that Larry deserved to win this year and had a hard time summoning the mental toughness to take him down. It's good to be happy for your friends, but in this case I should have been greedier.

Nick won on a late blunder and tied Larry for first. Larry won a blitz playoff that was exciting for the fans but too random to legitimately decide the Championship.

2003 Seattle

The next year's event went nearly according to the same script. I didn't do much for the first seven rounds until I again took on Shabalov who was a point clear of the field. I won a wilder game than the year before, with mind-bending complications Shaba normally excels in.

☐ **J.Benjamin** ■ **A.Shabalov**
U.S. Championship, Seattle 2003

---

1 e4 e5 2 Nf3 Nc6 3 Bb5 a6 4 Ba4 Nf6 5 0-0 Be7 6 Re1 b5 7 Bb3 d6 8 c3 0-0 9 h3 Na5 10 Bc2 c5 11 d4 Qc7 12 Nbd2 cxd4 13 cxd4 Rd8 14 d5

14 b3 is also critical, but closing the center is more my style, especially against him!

14...Bd7 15 Nf1 Rdc8 16 Re2 Nb7 17 Ng3 Nc5 18 Be3 b4

Black activates his bishop, but this compels him to defend f5 with a pawn, weakening the dark squares around his king.

19 Rc1 Bb5 20 Re1 g6 21 Bb1 Nfd7 22 Nh2 Qd8 23 Ng4 Bg5

Shabalov played this quickly and confidently, perhaps unaware of the sacrificial possibilities.

24 Qd2

This was an agonizing decision. 24 Nh6+ Kg7 25 Nhf5+ gxf5 26 Nxf5+ is extremely tempting, but I couldn't work out the complications. Shaba probably wouldn't have hesitated! I hoped to sacrifice later but didn't get the chance.

24...Bxe3 25 Rxe3 Qg5!

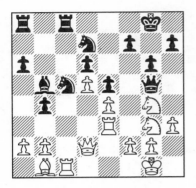

This is an easy practical decision. 25...a5 26 Rf3! (more accurate than 26 Nh6+ 26...Kf8! 27 Rf3 Nf6! staying in the game) 26...f6 27 Nh6+ Kf8 28 Nhf5 gxf5 29 Qh6+ Ke8 30 Qh5+ Kf8 31 Nxf5 and White wins.

26 Qxb4 h5 27 Nh2 h4 28 Ngf1 Nf6

White is a clear pawn ahead but must go on the defensive for a while. I didn't handle this phase very well, and Shabalov whips up an initiative pretty quickly.

29 Rce1 Nh5 30 Nf3 Qe7 31 N1h2 Nf4 32 Qd2 a5 33 Kh1 a4 34 Ng1 Rab8 35 g3

I was happy to chase away that annoying knight, but now Black develops potential on the long diagonal.

35...Nh5 36 Rc3 Ba6 37 Ree3 Rb4 38 b3

Shaba used his reserves of time to plan his big break. I knew he wouldn't let me get to the time control and consolidate at my leisure.

38...Qb7 39 Bc2 f5 40 exf5 Rd4 41 Qe1 Qxd5+

41...Nf6 may well be an improvement here, bringing about a confused situation after 42 fxg6 Nxd5 43 Nhf3 Nxc3 44 Rxc3.

42 Nhf3 gxf5 43 Kh2

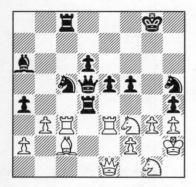

Black has managed to equalize material, but now faces counterthreats of 44 Nxd4 and 44 Bxf5. Shabalov pushes too fast when a calm move like 43...Ng7 is called for.

43...f4?! 44 Nxd4

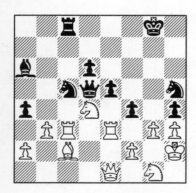

44...Qxd4

Black faces a dizzying assortment of captures. White is winning after 44...hxg3+ 45 fxg3 Qxd4 46 Ne2 fxe3 47 Nxd4 exd4 48 b4 dxc3 49 Qxe3 and 44...fxe3 45 Nf5 hxg3+ 46 fxg3 Qd2+ 47 Qxd2 exd2 48 Ne7+, but in the second line Black can improve with 45...exf2+! 46 Qxf2 Rc7 with equal chances.

45 Ne2 Bxe2

After 45...fxe3 46 Nxd4 exd4 47 Rxe3 dxe3 48 Qxe3 the queen rules, while 45...hxg3+ 46 Rxg3+ fxg3+ 47 Rxg3+ Nxg3 48 Nxd4 Nf1+ 49 Kg2 exd4 50 b4 d3 51 Bd1 d2 52 Qe7 is hopeless for Black.

46 Rxe2 hxg3+ 47 fxg3 Rf8 48 Be4

Care is still required to stamp out Black's initiative. By blocking out his queen, I threaten mayhem on the g-file.

48...d5 49 Bxd5+ Kh8 50 Rxe5

Chucking back the exchange to simplify is the surest winning method. When you are playing Shaba, it is a relief to see his attackers disappear from the board.

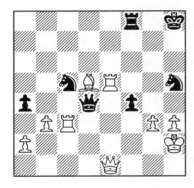

50...fxg3+ 51 Rxg3 Nxg3

51...Rf2+ concerned me until I worked out 52 Rg2 Qf4+ 53 Kg1. Black's checks are soon exhausted.

52 Qxg3 Qf2+ 53 Bg2 Qxg3+ 54 Kxg3 Rc8 55 b4

The advance of the b-pawn is decisive.

55...Nd3 56 Rh5+ Kg7 57 b5 Kg6 58 Rd5 Nb4 59 Rd6+ Kf5 60 b6 Ke5 61 Rd2 1-0

The crowded leaderboard of 5½ pointers produced the following pairings:

Shabalov-Akobian

Fedorowicz-Benjamin

A.Ivanov-Kaidanov

Stripunsky-Gulko

I was less than thrilled to see my pairing. A minor alteration—flipping Fed and Ivanov—would have averted the unpleasant aftermath.

Fed and I had always drawn against each other. Some may question this arrangement, but it's the way we always did things. I don't advocate it, but we have managed to stay good friends for 25 years.

We hadn't played a real game since 1981, excepting the playoff in the 1998 Championship. [We had a recent decisive game, in Bunratty 2007.] The situation called for us to play for a win, but a draw would be a pretty soft landing. We would each earn about ten grand, and possibly qualify for the FIDE World Championship.

So we did what we always did, figuring we would leave it to the others to fight it out for first. I had a sick feeling before we even stopped the clocks. Two other games shook on a draw before we did. As Stripunsky told me later, the qualifying spots for the FIDE WCT played a role in the last round strategy. [Ironically, several of us didn't go the tournament anyway when it was placed in Libya.] Condemnation came swiftly and unequivocally. For months I read about the "cowards" knowing that I was one of them.

Fortunately, Shabalov saved the day by going all out to beat Akobian. It was a typical Shaba game. He sacked a few pawns; maybe a computer would have defended, but Akobian didn't find the best defense.

At the closing a disappointed Erik Anderson preferred the carrot over the stick. He praised the fighting spirit of Shabalov and Akobian and gave them each a $5,000 bonus. Shaba had unquestionably earned it, but Akobian had actually hoped to clinch a GM norm with a draw!

Strangely enough, the repercussions from the drawfest led to some positive developments. In the next few years organizations devoted to combating the evil of the "grandmaster draw" would pop up and run tournaments.

I took it all as an invitation to turn over a new leaf. Since the 2003 U.S. Championship my draw percentage has gone down. I rarely offer or accept draws unless it will clearly help me win a tournament or I am very tired.

2004 San Diego

Jim Roberts offered a $5,000 prize for the player who exhibited the best fighting chess. The "Larsen Prize" became my raison d'être. In the first round I turned down an early draw offer despite the fact I knew my position was sliding downhill. I managed a lucky perpetual in the end. In the fifth round I contested one of the most entertaining games of the event:

☐ **J.Benjamin** ◼ **Y.Shulman**

U.S. Championship, San Diego 2004

1 e4 e6 2 d4 d5 3 Nd2 c5 4 Ngf3 cxd4 5 Nxd4 Nc6 6 Nxc6 bxc6 7 Bd3 Nf6 8 0-0 Be7 9 Re1 a5 10 c3 Ba6 11 Bc2 Qc7 12 Qf3 Bd6 13 Qh3 0-0 14 exd5 cxd5 15 Nf3 Bf4 16 Qh4 Bxc1 17 Raxc1 Qc4 18 Nd4 Qxa2 19 Re3 h6 20 Rg3 Kh8

21 Rxg7 Kxg7 22 Qg3+ Kh8 23 Qe5 Kg7 24 Qg3+ Kh8 25 Qe5 Kg7 26 h3

No way I'm going to take a perpetual while there's still a chance to win. I needed to make luft to be able to lift my rook, but 26 h4!? with the idea of g2-g4-g5 deserved consideration as well.

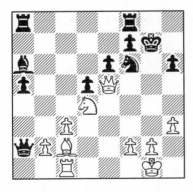

26...Qxb2

26...Bd3!? would provide an echo of later events: 27 Bxd3 Qxb2 28 Qg3+ (not 28 Rb1? Qd2 29 Rb7 Rae8 30 Bb5 Qd1+ 31 Kh2 Qh5 and Black consolidates) 28...Kh8 29 Qe3 Ng8 (or 29...Kg7) 30 Rb1 with a strong initiative.

27 Rb1 Qa3

Both 27...Qa2 28 Re1 Qc4 and 27...Qxb1+ 28 Bxb1 Rfb8 are good enough for a draw. But Shulman wants to fight, too.

28 Re1 Be2!!

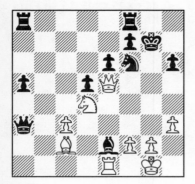

This is a brilliant conception, though it isn't necessary to draw—Black can again look to sacrifice his queen, e.g. 28...Rfb8 29 Re3 Qc1+ 30 Kh2 Qxe3 31 fxe3 Rb2.

29 Nxe2

Not 29 Rxe2 Qc1+ 30 Kh2 Qg5.

29...Qb2

Black can try for a win with 29...Rfc8, but White can keep the balance: 30 Qg3+ Kf8 31 Qf4 Ng8 32 Nd4 Qxc3 33 Re3! (not 33 Nxe6+? Ke7 and wins; but now in view of the threatened 34 Nxe6+ Black has to give the queen) 33...Qxd4 34 Qxd4 Rxc2 35 Rc3 and a draw is likely.

30 Nf4 Qxc2 31 Nh5+ Kh7 32 Nxf6+ Kh8 33 Nd7+ Kh7 34 Nf6+ Kh8 35 Nd7+ ½-½

Almost all my draws came by perpetual, repetition, or bare kings. But you can't win a fighting prize with six draws. Fishbein won the Larsen Prize with a whopping eight decisive games. Ironically, Fishbein had once written an article about the art of the strategic draw offer.

I enjoyed the challenge of a rematch with a blast from the past, Gata Kamsky. In his first serious tournament since a decade-long exile, Kamsky was not sharp. But he was always dangerous in technical positions, and I needed all my wits to hold a draw. Then he asked me if I wanted to analyze the game. This had been unthinkable in the Rustam era. I had heard that the new Gata was a nice guy. Indeed it was true; he very politely demonstrated he had a much better grasp of the endgame than I did!

I finished strong by beating Perelshteyn in the last round. He came at me hard, and I counterattacked successfully. But I was hurt by an after-effect of the previous tournament. The top five places were now divided by tiebreak. I tied for 3rd-9th and came 6th. The tied players below me received the same prize, but the ones above me earned much more. Kaidanov, in third place, took home $8,000 more than I did.

2006 San Diego

My spirit was just as strong for my 23rd Championship in 2006. I started fine against defending Women's Champion Rusa Goletiani. But then my technique totally deserted me. I drew game after game against opponents contemplating resignation. The worst of it might have been the third round debacle.

□ **J.Benjamin** ■ **J.Friedel**
U.S. Championship, San Diego 2006

Here 53 Rd7 leads to a simple win, e.g. 53...Rh1+ 54 Kg3 Ne4+ 55 Kg2. Instead I inexplicably "chimneyed" my king with **53 Kg5??** and had to settle for a draw after **53...Rf1 54 Kh5 Rh1+ 55 Kg5 Rf1 56 gxf7+ Nxf7+ 57 Kh4 Rh1+ 58 Kg3 Ra1 59 Re8+ Kh7 60 Re7 Kg8 61 Re8+ ½-½**

I couldn't keep my confidence up after seven straight draws. Playing on my birthday again proved unlucky for me, as Ben Finegold dropped me to fifty percent. It's not the way I would choose to go out, but I think it may be my U.S. Championship swan song.

Chapter Twelve

The World Championship is not Enough

Despite debuting in the Interzonal at 23, I didn't participate in the World Championship cycle again in my prime. But a good run in my "post-Blue" U.S. Championships put me in the thick of the World Championship Tournaments that replaced the traditional Interzonals.

Qualifying turned out to be a lot easier than getting through the first round. Year after year I had my chances. But somehow I always managed to stumble at the doorstep of victory. I've never really been able to explain it; my success in the U.S. knockout Championships just didn't translate overseas.

Groningen 1997

The 1994 U.S. Championship got me a slot in the Groningen WCT in '97. The draw brought me Vadim Zvjaginsev, a young protégé of Mark Dvoretsky, in the first round. On paper I was a 55-point underdog, but I hung with him well. While so many modern players are "ironbutts", running their computers twenty moves deep into the Najdorf or Marshall Attack, Zvjaginsev likes to explore unorthodox opening territory much as I do. After two draws, our rapid playoff games went way out there.

□ **V.Zvjaginsev** ■ **J.Benjamin**
FIDE World Ch. KO, Groningen 1997

---

1 c4 Nf6 2 Nf3 e6 3 Nc3 Bb4 4 g4!?

I had never dreamed of this move before. Ironically, Krasenkow had the same idea and played the same way against Garcia. Rarely do you see such an unusual double debut. I managed to get a good position, but couldn't turn the game in my favor.

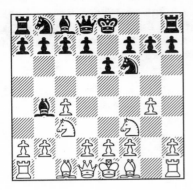

4...h6 5 Rg1 d6 6 h4 e5 7 g5 hxg5 8 hxg5 Ng4 9 Nd5 Bc5 10 d4 Bb6 11 Nxb6 axb6 12 Qd3 Nc6 13 Qe4 f5 14 gxf6 Qxf6 15 dxe5 dxe5 16 Rxg4 Bf5 17 Rh4 Bxe4 18 Rxh8+ Ke7 19 Bg5 Rxh8 20 Bxf6+ gxf6

21 Bg2 Nd4 22 Nxd4 Bxg2 23 Nf5+ Ke6 24 Ng3 f5 25 f3 f4 26 Kf2 fxg3+ 27 Kxg2 Rh2+ 28 Kxg3 Rxe2 29 b3 c5 30 Rh1 Kd6 31 Rh6+ Kc7 32 Re6 Rxa2 33 Rxe5 Rb2 34 Re3 b5 35 cxb5 Kb6 36 f4 Kxb5 37 f5 Rd2 38 f6 Rd8 39 Re7 b6 40 Re4 Rf8 41 Rf4 Kc6 42 Kg4 Kd5 43 Kf5 b5 44 Kg6 c4 45 Rf5+ Ke6 46 f7 cxb3 47 Rxb5 Rxf7 48 Rb6+ Kd5 49 Kxf7 Kc4 50 Ke6 Kc3 51 Kd5 b2 52 Ke4 Kc2 53 Rxb2+ ½-½

He repeated an offbeat Sicilian line that worked well for him in game one, but I had prepared something for the next encounter.

☐ **J.Benjamin** ■ **V.Zvjaginsev**
FIDE World Ch. KO, Groningen 1997

1 e4 c5 2 Nf3 d6 3 d4 cxd4 4 Nxd4 Nf6 5 Nc3 Bd7 6 Bg5 e6 7 Ndb5 Bxb5 8 Bxb5+ Nc6 9 Qf3 h6 10 Bh4 Be7 11 e5 Nd5 12 Bxc6+ bxc6 13 Bxe7 Qxe7 14 Qg3 dxe5 15 Qxg7 Qf6 16 Qxf6 Nxf6 17 0-0-0 Nd5 18 Ne4 Ke7 19 Rhe1 Rad8 20 g3 h5 21 Rd3 f5 22 Nc5 e4 23 Ra3 Ra8 24 f3 Kd6 25 fxe4 Kxc5 26 exd5 exd5 27 Re6 Rac8

I win a pawn, but it proves insufficient for victory. Perhaps 28 Ra5+ was stronger.

28 Rxa7 h4 29 Rg7 Rhg8 30 Rgg6 Rxg6 31 Rxg6 hxg3 32 hxg3 Rf8 33 c3 f4 34 gxf4 Rxf4 35 Kc2 d4 36 b4+ Kb6 37 c4 Rf3 38 Kd2 Rc3 39 b5 Rxc4 40 Rxc6+ Rxc6 41 bxc6 Kxc6 42 Kd3 Kd5 ½-½

We moved on to a blitz playoff, where my quest ended with a whimper. As crushed as I felt, I appreciated my young opponent's approach to the game.

I had a few days before my flight home, which I planned to spend watching the matches. Christiansen, who lost an equally excruciating match to Ulf Andersson, told me about a big money rapid tournament in Cologne. Larry invited me back to his Bundesliga-provided apartment in nearby Porz. It would be an opportunity to visit with Mourka, who I took care of as a kitten seven years earlier. Plus I could see if Natasha took up the astroturf in the living room.

I'm no specialist in rapid chess, but it was worth a shot. When half the Elo list made their way from Groningen, I figured I would have some fun and maybe take down a top GM or two. But sometimes the best results are the ones you never anticipate. If it had been a FIDE rated tournament, Cologne would have been the greatest result of my career!

I won a whole bunch of games; though I can't remember all my victims, I know Wojtkiewicz, Chernin, Levin, Rotstein were among them. The following game was the only one I could dig up.

□ **J.Benjamin** ■ **F.Levin**
Cologne (rapid) 1997

1 e4 e6 2 d4 d5 3 e5 c5 4 c3 Nc6 5 Nf3 Qb6 6 Be2 Nh6 7 Bd3!?

This was a specialty of mine for a while.

7...cxd4 8 cxd4 Nf5 9 Bxf5 exf5 10 Nc3 Be6 11 Ne2 Be7 12 h4 h6 13 Kf1 0-0-0 14 h5 Kb8 15 Kg1 Rc8 16 Rb1 Qa6 17 a3 Na5 18 b3 Rc7 19 Nf4 Rhc8 20 Bd2 b6 21 a4 Nc6 22 Rh3 Nb4 23 Rg3

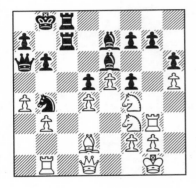

23...Bf8 24 Bxb4 Bxb4 25 Rxg7 Ba3 26 Qe2 Qxe2 27 Nxe2 Rc2 28 Nf4 Rc1+ 29 Rxc1 Bxc1 30 Nxe6 fxe6 31 Rg6 Rc6 32 b4 b5 33 axb5 Rb6 34 Kf1 Rxb5 35 Rxe6 Rxb4 36 Rd6 Rb5 37 e6 Kc7 38 Rd7+ Kc8 39 Ne5 Bg5 40 e7 Bxe7 41 Rxe7 a5 42 Nc6 a4 43 Na7+ 1-0

There was a computer program in the field, but we were given the right to refuse to play it. This was a no-brainer for me. Computers were not yet superior to humans in rapid chess, but they certainly didn't feel the pressure of losing and blowing the big money. Instead of a silicon monster I faced Peter Leko in the last round, who played it safe and accepted the draw that clinched a share of first place for me.

Las Vegas 1999

They say what happens in Vegas, stays in Vegas. But I'll still tell you about the heartbreak that was my match with Danish GM Peter Heine Nielsen. I was a decided Elo favorite when the pairings were announced, but the rising young Dane had closed the gap by match time. I should have chalked with my first White. Despite an overwhelming opening, I nearly lost!

☐ J.Benjamin ◼ P.H.Nielsen
FIDE World Ch. KO, Las Vegas 1999

1 e4 e5 2 Bc4 Nf6 3 d3 c6 4 Nf3 d5 5 Bb3 Bd6 6 exd5 cxd5 7 Bg5 d4 8 Nbd2 0-0 9 0-0 Nc6 10 Re1 a6 11 h3 h6 12 Bh4 Re8 13 Nc4 Bc7 14 Bg3 Nd7 15 a4 Qf6 16 c3 dxc3 17 bxc3 Nc5 18 Bc2 Bf5 19 d4 Bxc2 20 Qxc2 Nd7

Black is totally tied up, and the e5-pawn is on life support. 21 Qe4! would have accentuated my advantage.

21 Re2?! Qe6 22 Ncxe5 Ndxe5 23 dxe5 Rad8 24 Rb1 b6 25 Rbe1 b5 26 axb5 axb5 27 Re4 Rd5 28 Qe2 Ba5 29 Rc1 f5 30 Re3 g5 31 Bh2 Bb6 32 Rd3 f4 33 Re1? Nxe5 34 Nxe5 Qxe5 35 Qxe5 Rexe5 36 Rxe5 Rxd3 37 Kf1

37...Rxc3?

Missing 37...Bc7! 38 Rxb5 (38 Re1 Rxc3 is also depressing) 38...f3! winning.
38 Rxb5 Rc1+ 39 Ke2 Bd4 40 Rd5 Bc5 41 h4 Be7 42 hxg5 hxg5 43 Rd1 Rxd1 ½-½

I finally cashed in on the first g/25 +10 game. I sacrificed a piece for a mess of pawns which I took into the endgame. Eventually the pawns overwhelmed his bishop, the game ending on move 87 in the Lucena position.

I had finally broken through for the elusive win! Drawing had not been a problem for me, and I needed just one to advance to round two. For the third time, I defended a King's Indian, but I made some poor decisions and got my queen in trouble. I had to sacrifice her, but my active pieces offered some chances.

□ **P.H.Nielsen** ■ **J.Benjamin**
FIDE World Ch. KO, Las Vegas 1999

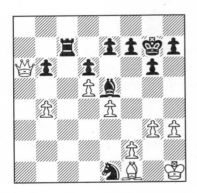

After the natural 36...Rc2! 37 f4 (37 Qxb6 Bxg3! 38 fxg3 Nf3 39 Bg2 Rc1+ 40 Bf1 Rc2! draws immediately) 37...Bd4 38 Be2 h5 39 h4 Kh7 I don't see how White is going to make progress.

Unfortunately I played **36...Bd4?** and resigned after **37 Qe2 Bc3? 38 Qe3 b5 39 Qb6 Rc8 40 Qc6! 1-0**

I nearly won—and then nearly lost—a wild Petroff in the first g/15 +10, and drew the second as well. The sudden death blitz provided a bigger disaster than the last time. I consoled myself with a few extra days in Caesar's Palace (my room had a Jacuzzi!) before heading off to Reno for the U.S. Open. But I would have rather played Judit Polgar in round two.

New Delhi 2000

My memories of the 2000 WCT start with my father driving me to the airport, something he had done many times before but would not do again. The long, arduous trip to India required a few extra days to acclimate. I figured I might not get another chance to explore the rich history of India, so I took a taxi ride with Jennifer Shahade to explore the city. We did more shopping than sightseeing, though monkeys fornicating in the park was quite a sight! It was enough to drive me back to the hermetically sealed environment of our four-star Western hotel.

Safe from the demoralizing poverty and pollution outside the door, I concentrated on my little-known opponent, an Argentinian rated 2415 named Fiorito. For some reason, FIDE had decided to use Swiss system pairings for the first round. I was ranked just above the middle, so I got one of the lowest rated players in the field. The database didn't provide all that much information, so I used a newfangled method to prepare.

John Fernandez sent me some games played on the ICC by my opponent under the handle "Fioro". I play very rarely on the ICC, so there isn't much on me. But a lot of strong players try things out online, so there is often gold to be mined there.

Fiorito opened particularly passively (1 Nf3 c5 2 e3) and I countered aggressively. I eventually traded into an opposite-colored bishops ending where my connected passers on the kingside won the game. My first decisive game in regulation time! Again I needed a draw to clinch a match, but this time against a much lower-rated player in a slow game.

Fiorito surprised me with Petroff's Defense, hardly the indicated choice in a must-win situation. Under the circumstances, safe mode seemed an appropriate reaction.

☐ **J.Benjamin** ■ **F.Fiorito**
FIDE World Ch. KO, New Delhi 2000

---

1 e4 e5 2 Nf3 Nf6 3 Nxe5 d6 4 Nf3 Nxe4 5 Qe2 Qe7 6 d3 Nf6 7 Bg5 Qxe2+ 8 Bxe2 Be7 9 Nc3 c6 10 0-0-0 Na6 11 Ne4

My opponent was coughing and wheezing as he had been the day before. I deduced that he wanted to end his suffering and leave India with a few cheap Elo points. But he turned down my draw.

11...Nxe4 12 dxe4 Nc5 13 Bxe7 Kxe7 14 Rd4 Ne6 15 Rd2 Nf4 16 Bf1 Bg4 17 Nd4 Rad8 18 h3 Bc8 19 g3 Ng6 20 f4 Nf8 21 Bg2 g6 22 Rhd1 Ne6 23 Nb3 Ng7 24 Na5 h5 25 Nc4 Ne8 26 Rd4 f6 27 R4d3 Be6 28 Ne3 f5 29 h4 Nf6 30 exf5 gxf5 31 Ra3 Rhg8 32 Re1 Kf7 33 Rxa7 Rd7 34 Nf1 d5 35 Ra3 d4 36 Nd2 d3 37 Re3 dxc2 38 Nf3 Ng4 39 Ng5+ Rxg5 40 hxg5 Rd1+ 41 Kxc2 Rg1 42 Re2 Bc4 43 Rd2 Re1

Fiorito did a pretty good job of keeping the game going, but he really pushed it when he didn't take back the exchange. Now he offered a draw. It's one thing to give a friend a break, like Larry C. in the '97 Championship, but not for a stranger 160 points lower than me! After I convinced myself I could not possibly lose, I gave him the bad news.

44 Ra7 Ke6 45 b3 Ba6 46 Bxc6 1-0

Although my match had not been too taxing, I wasn't quite ready for the second round. I faced Brazilian GM Rafael Leitao who had upset my namesake, Joel Lautier. I was used to my matches going to overtime, but this one didn't. I didn't press hard enough with White in the first game, and got ground down in 97 moves in the second.

Moscow 2001

I almost declined to go the next WCT. 2001 had been the worst year of my life. My parents and I planned a trip to the Bermuda Open in February. After buying the tickets I found a cheaper fare, so my father came to Manhattan to give me their tickets to trade in. On his way home, my father suffered a fatal heart attack. I have not been back to Bermuda since.

In September, a terrorist attack drove me from my home. Yes, that one. My apartment was about three blocks from the World Trade Center. While I could not see the planes crash, I *heard* them. I looked out my window to catch a scene reminiscent of a Japanese monster movie—people were running around screaming. I turned on the TV and found out the cause of the commotion. Soon that would go out—along with my phone, lights, and toilet. I hopped a police boat and rode across the river to Jersey City. After a few hours at an army base, I was transported into town and caught the PATH train back to mid-town Manhattan. I rode the subway to Brooklyn and arrived at my mother's house by the evening.

I was still living out of a suitcase in my mother's house while making arrangements to go to Moscow. I made two fruitless trips to the Russian Consulate in New York trying to get a business visa arranged through FIDE. "I have nothing here for you," the clerk told me. "You better go to a travel agent and get a tourist visa." That's what I did. Nice going, FIDE.

Everyone knows it's cold in Moscow in November, but I've never known cold like that before. Christiansen's wife, Natasha, a fluent Russian speaker, found us a hotel within walking distance. I still felt like an ice cube when I got to the hall.

Under the circumstances, I wasn't able to focus on my preparation. My junk-ball openings worked surprisingly well (at least with Black) as my young Ukrainian opponent seemed baffled by my retro Cozio Defense.

☐ **V.Baklan** ■ **J.Benjamin**

FIDE World Ch. KO, Moscow 2001

1 e4 e5 2 Nf3 Nc6 3 Bb5 Nge7 4 c3 d6 5 d4 Bd7 6 Bc4 Na5 7 Be2 Nac6 8 dxe5 dxe5 9 Bc4 Nc8 10 0-0 Be7 11 Nbd2 0-0 12 Bd5 Nd6 13 Qe2 Bf6 14 Rd1 Ne7 15 Bb3 Ng6 16 Nf1 Qe7 17 Bc2 Rad8 18 Ng3 Rfe8 19 Nf5 Bxf5 20 exf5 Nf4 21 Qf1 c6 22 c4 e4 23 Ne1 Qe5 24 g3 Nh5 25 Qh3 g6 26 fxg6 hxg6 27 Bb3 Bg5 28 c5 Bxc1 29 Rxd6 Rxd6 30 cxd6 Bxb2 31 Rd1 Rd8 32 d7 Kg7 33 Ng2 Nf6

This position cannot be *more* winning for me. All I have to do is scoop up his d-pawn and enjoy my material bonanza. But somehow, I just didn't take that pawn...until it was too late!

34 Nf4 Ba3 35 Qf1 b5 36 h4 Be7 37 Qh3 c5 38 h5 c4 39 Bc2 gxh5 40 Re1 Bc5 41 Kg2 e3 42 Bf5 Kf8 43 fxe3 b4 44 Re2 b3 45 axb3 cxb3 46 Nxh5 Nd5 47 Nf4 Nxe3+ 48

Rxe3 Bxe3 49 Qh6+ Ke7 50 Qg5+ f6 51 Ng6+ Kd6 52 Nxe5 Bxg5 53 Nf7+ Kc7 54 Nxd8 Kxd8 55 Be6 b2 56 Bf5 a5 57 Kf3 a4 58 g4 a3 59 Bb1 Kxd7 60 Ke4 Ke6 61 Kd4 Bc1 62 Ba2+ Ke7 63 Kd3 Kd6 64 Kc2 Ke5 65 Kb1 Kf4 66 Be6 Kg5 67 Bf5 Kf4 ½-½

Aargh! Despite this blown opportunity, I rolled to an easy win in the first playoff game.

□ **V.Baklan** ■ **J.Benjamin**

FIDE World Ch. KO, Moscow 2001

1 e4 e5 2 Nf3 Nc6 3 Bb5 Nge7 4 0-0 g6 5 c3 a6 6 Ba4 Bg7 7 d4 exd4 8 cxd4 b5 9 Bb3 d6 10 h3 0-0 11 Nc3 Bb7 12 Bg5 h6 13 Bh4 Na5 14 Bc2 Qd7 15 e5 Nf5 16 Bxf5 Qxf5 17 exd6 cxd6 18 Be7 Rfe8 19 Bxd6 Nc4 20 Be5 Bxf3 21 Qxf3 Qxf3 22 gxf3 Bxe5 23 dxe5 Rxe5

24 f4 Rf5 25 b3 Nd2 26 Rfd1 Rd8 27 Ne4 Nf3+ 28 Kf1 Rxd1+ 29 Rxd1 Rxf4 30 Nc5 a5 31 Rd8+ Kg7 32 Ra8 Rf5 33 Nd3 b4 34 Rd8 Nd2+ 35 Ke2 Ne4 36 Rd4 Nc3+ 37 Ke3 Nxa2 38 Rd7 Nc3 39 Kd4 Ne2+ 40 Ke3 Ng1 41 h4 Nf3 42 Nf4 Nxh4 43 Ne6+ Kf6 44 Nd8 Re5+ 45 Kf4 Re7 46 Rxe7 Kxe7 47 Nc6+ Kd6 48 Nxa5 h5 49 Nc4+ Kd5 50 Ke3 Ng2+ 51 Kd3 Nf4+ 52 Ke3 Ne6 53 Nb6+ Kc6 54 Nc4 g5 55 Ne5+ Kd5 56 Nd3 f5 57 Kd2 Nc5 58 Nxb4+ Ke4 59 Ke2 f4 60 Kf1 Nxb3 61 Nc6 Nd4 62 Ne7 0-1

As in 1999, I needed one draw to advance to the second round, but now I needed to do it with White. But I couldn't manage that! Once again, I went down to defeat in blitz. This was the worst loss for me of all the WCTs. I missed chances in the other matches, but quite frankly, Baklan did not play well at all and still managed to knock me out.

The next time I qualified for a World Championship the event was eventually held in Libya. I decided to sit that one out. I think the World Championship is another closed chapter for me.

Chapter Thirteen

Feed Your Mind

I've always enjoyed writing. I had two monthly columns in *Chess Life*, first "Theoretically Speaking", and later "Unorthodox Openings". Currently my "Ask GM Joel" column appears online at www.uschess.org. I've written articles in many major chess publications and periodically contribute to *New In Chess*. But nothing compares to my days at *Chess Chow*.

Soon after moving into my first apartment in New York City, my roommate, IM Mark Ginsburg, pitched the idea of putting out our own chess magazine. In a brainstorming session in Sea Girt, New Jersey, I produced the distinctive title "Chess Chow", with the subheading, "Feed Your Mind". The emerging desktop publishing technology enabled us to run a Mom and Pop business with a small but avid following.

Chow specialized in humor, but we were proud of our coverage of events (generally ones that Mark or I attended). We built a cadre of contributors, mostly our friends who supplied articles in exchange for subscriptions and/or stays on the infamous blue couch at W. 75th St. Our tone was so inside that our subscribers often did not follow us—few people could answer our trivia quiz, though they eagerly attempted to do so.

We innovated in delightful ways. "Talk like a Grandmaster" provided chessplayer lingo. "Top Ten Lists" (borrowed from David Letterman) covered ground such as "Most Unfortunate Chess Names" and "Best Nicknames at the Olympiad" (e.g. Anatoly "Bud" Vaisser). We used hilarious diagram captions. My favorite: In a diagram depicting a blow I delivered to Lev Alburt, the caption read, "We're so sorry, Uncle Alburt."

The Trivia Quiz was particularly trivial. I'll give a little taste with my favorite question (answer at chapter's end):

Why did IM Alex Sherzer stand like a statue for ten minutes near the Gurevich-Benjamin game from the Reshevsky Memorial?

    a) He was fascinated by all the complications and tried to calculate them all.

    b) He ripped his trousers and was afraid to turn around and expose himself.

    c) He was asked by the arbiter to stand in front of the window.

    d) He was hoping Zsofia Polgar would notice his sporty new tie.

Michael Wilder's "Agony" column always had me in stitches. Smashing a bug into his pizza would remind him of a painful game. He would try to distract Matthew Sadler by changing his socks—which meant exchanging the left one for the right.

Though Mike killed every time, he would constantly insist he had exhausted his supply of jokes. Ferd Hellers picked up the slack with a steady stream of dry humor. Even Fed pitched in with an occasional installment from the "Lucky Pen" saga.

I wrote most of the articles. One of my favorite pieces came very early in the saga, a parody of a piece from *Inside Chess*. Yasser's "Seirawan on Seirawan: State of the Yaz" became "Benjamin on Benjamin: State of the Yoel". While Yasser wrote about becoming an uncle, I wrote about becoming an uncle. But we diverged from there. Yasser wrote about the glamorous life of traveling to first class European events, while I described 4:30 in the morning bus trips to Hartford with Fed for a small rapid tournament.

In hindsight, I would have done some things a bit differently. We often sought out controversy and confrontation. In "Swill" we criticized works of other writers. The chess world is really pretty small, and making enemies takes a lot more energy than making friends.

I don't know if we ever had more than a thousand subscribers. There may have been lots of potential "Chowhounds" out there, but to reach them, we would have had to become a real business. It was always a sideline for us, and we weren't prepared to hire staff and invest a lot of capital.

Chow had always been on top of the Internet. We were the first to cover Internet chess, back when the ICC was still the ICS. We knew print magazines were in for heavy competition, and that didn't bode well for the future.

By 1994, Mark had gone through changes in his life, getting married and starting a family. I was embarking on a series of major tournaments. We didn't have the heart to continue, and so suspended operations after nineteen issues over four years. Over the years we considered reprising *Chess Chow* in some fashion. Our old material is not conveniently accessible; we lost our files years ago to a computer virus. Chess Chow online may be viable, but I'm not anxious to be a businessman again.

The *Chow* era covered an especially prolific and successful period in my career. Did the magazine distract me from my studies? Or did the work I did keep me focused on chess? They were fun days, and I have no regrets. Writing will likely be a large part of my future, and nothing could prepare me more than being the publisher and editor of my own magazine.

Trivia answer: C—The future GM shielded the players from the sun's glare.

Chapter Fourteen

Searching for a Film Career

In the spring of 1992 I visited a Soho building which housed Avy Kaufman Casting. After a brief wait I was ushered into the office to meet the big shots, producer Scott Rudin and director Steve Zaillian. We chatted for a bit and I read the line in the script attributed to me. The scene was an old Bar Point tournament where I had just been asked how I did. My response:

"Not bad. Two wins, two draws. Tied for third place. After expenses, I only lost a little."

When the little group burst out laughing, I wondered what I had done wrong. But the line is kind of funny, and obviously my reading was perfectly authentic.

In the end I didn't get my line. New actors need to join the Screen Actors' Guild (SAG), and films can save the membership fees if the actor doesn't have a speaking part. That's why Kamran Shirazi stared mutely in his scene. But I did get to make an appearance in the major motion picture *Searching for Bobby Fischer*, the adaptation of Fred Waitzkin's book about (among other things) the early chess experiences of his son, Josh. They selected three grandmasters for cameos in a certain scene: Dzindzichashvili, Fedorowicz, and myself. When they announced the shooting schedule, Fed bowed out to play in the U.S. Open, and Pal Benko took his place (sadly, Benko's scene ended up on the cutting room floor).

Most of the film is set in New York City, and the scenes from Washington Square Park were shot on location there. The stage sets were built in Toronto, however, to take advantage of cheaper production costs. So the three amigos flew north for a new experience.

When the van driver met us at the Toronto airport we realized a fourth cast member, the veteran character actor Austin Pendleton, had flown in with us. We were curious who he would play in the movie, and when he told us, we just cracked up. After all, we knew the real Asa Hoffmann and couldn't believe a Hollywood actor would portray him! And they paid Asa for the right to use his name in the film.

The producers put the chessplayers up in a good hotel and gave us a trailer to share on the set. We had a lot of free time to watch them film other scenes. Zaillian had already won an Oscar for his script of Schindler's List, but had not directed a film before. He shot an unusually high number of takes, which gave me the opportunity to watch Pendleton's overly manic Hoffmann *ad infinitum*. For a long time I could not rid my mind of the line, "I think I got him. I think I got him. Maybe I'll win a pawn."

My scene did not require much preparation. After a visit to wardrobe and make-up, I sat down at a table in a set that eerily captured the feel of the seedy old Bar Point club. Ben Kingsley, as Bruce Pandolfini, takes Joe Mantegna, as Fred Waitzkin, to an adult tournament to show him a slice of the future for Josh if he actively pursues chess. Kingsley points to me, speaks my name, and describes my status in the chess world. The camera hits me for four or five seconds. I think I move a piece, but mostly just look intently in front of me. It's tricky to evaluate one's own performance, but I think I really nailed it.

I only briefly met Kingsley, who played Pandolfini with a bizarre kind of Irish accent. Joe Mantegna proved to be quite friendly—a regular guy, really—during lunches on the set. [He also ensures I cannot be beaten in "Six Degrees of Kevin Bacon"...except if you actually know Kevin Bacon.]

I met a young actor who had been assigned my line from the book. It felt a bit surreal hearing him read it; I didn't know if I should make any suggestions. In the end they cut the line and the actor out entirely.

The movie came out in 1993, a year after my shoot, with all the principals of the film going to the premiere. I liked the film, though I could tell it took a fair amount of artistic license. Since then I've always thought twice when I see a movie "based on a true story".

Though I later got a lot more face time in a Kasparov documentary, I was never offered another dramatic role. I don't know why; perhaps I've been typecast?

Chapter Fifteen

Teach Your Children Well

There's an old saying, "those who can't do, teach." In the chess world, teaching offers stable income that the playing arena cannot match, even for many grandmasters. With so many opportunities provided by scholastic chess, American grandmasters are becoming increasingly reliant on coaching and teaching. There was no one moment when I decided to give teaching priority over playing, but over time the transition became inevitable.

During my playing career I gave occasional lessons, but teaching was a sideline I didn't aggressively pursue. Around the turn of the century things started to change when I took a job with Fed coaching the U.S. contingent at the World Youth in Oropesa del Mar, Spain. I had accompanied Ilya Gurevich and Alex Sherzer to the World Cadet Championship way back in 1986, but didn't see myself as a coach. In 1999, U.S. coaches were poorly paid and overworked. It's no wonder that grandmasters rarely applied for the job.

We found a great group of talented but ill-prepared kids. Most of them didn't study enough or were misled by weak private coaches. Fed and I felt like we had to reprogram a lot of kids. I remember asking eleven-year-old Laura Ross what she played against the Sicilian. She showed me a line in the Grand Prix her coach had given her, but felt (correctly) that it was unsound. That's a rather big fix to make in a short time. [I ended up coaching Laura off and on for six years.]

Fed and I both realized that we could really make a difference in this job. Since our trip to Oropesa del Mar in 1999, we have coached at the Pan-American and World Youth several times, under great conditions (three times in Greece) and abysmal (Belfort, France). Joined by the extremely capable coach FM Aviv Friedman, we have had success that cannot be measured in medals. I learned in that first year that the prize from the blitz tournament on the free day would equal a month's

239

salary in Azerbaijan. There is no way to match that kind of motivation for our American kids. Many things would have to change for us to be truly competitive.

Today the team is better funded, the coaches are better paid and grandmasters are readily applying for the jobs. Despite the windfall of Alex Lenderman's gold medal in the 2006 Under-16, we still have to remember that our part-time players are going up against kids embarking on a professional career.

In 2001 I entered another forum of instruction, the chess camp. The Castle Camp, operated by Dr. Robert Ferguson, invited me to join the staff in 2001. I didn't know what to expect, but the camp seemed to hit the right notes on instruction, camaraderie, and relaxation. Many other camps have followed in Castle's footsteps, and I've done a couple other sleep away camps, but Bradford is the best. Unfortunately, Dr. Ferguson decided to retire from running the Camp in 2005, and it will likely not be resurrected (a spin-off camp in Atlanta is now the official Castle camp).

Camps, Youth Championships, and private students are important sources of teaching income, but my main business now is in the school system. My mother arranged for my first experience teaching a class in a program administered by Brooklyn College. To be honest, I wasn't good at all. It's a long way from lecturing to a group of experienced chessplayers to teaching novice schoolchildren. I was teaching over their heads.

Sophia Rohde invited me to teach a class at a girls school in Manhattan. I started to get the hang of it, so she invited me to teach at the flagship school in her Kids Chess Network program, Columbia Grammar. Currently I teach after-school classes four days a week, three days at Columbia.

Teaching in schools has its pleasures and frustrations. To illustrate, let me take you through "a week in the life" (as of spring 2007):

Mondays: two classes at Collegiate, a private school on New York's Upper East Side. The teaching roster is pretty impressive, including three grandmasters (Fedorowicz, Michael Rohde, and myself) and one international master (David Goodman). We start off with a challenging kindergarten group. They enjoy their snack and water as much as the chess. In fact, the highlight of the class comes when Fed goes to fetch pitchers of ice water. With great joy the kids mob him, the highest paid waterboy since Adam Sandler.

In the next hour we teach the other grades; I usually work with the first graders. Though just last year *they* were in kindergarten, they are particularly enthusiastic about chess. You never know what kind of group you're going to get. Probably the general passion level would be higher if the school had chess in its curriculum.

Tuesdays: first and second graders at Columbia Grammar. Last semester I had the privilege of teaching this class with Fedorowicz. The kids seem to love Fed, who has a quirky technique of talking to the kids as if they were adults. They laugh when I ask the class a question and Fed raises his hand.

Wednesdays: hump day is free for me. I use it for private lessons, ICC work, writing my column, and running errands. It's nice not to have to go into the city for a day, and I'm not giving up this delightful respite!

Thursdays: usually I have more Columbian first and second graders with John MacArthur, though this semester I had another free day (more time to write my book).

Fridays: advanced class at Columbia Grammar. The kids range from second grade to sixth, but they are all serious tournament players. Most of the best players are rated between 1100 and 1300. They all have a fair amount of talent, but they repeat a lot of mistakes. But when they turn a corner and make an advance, it is extremely rewarding to watch.

My partner in crime Fridays, John MacArthur, is the hardest working man in the teaching business. He has developed a number of innovative techniques for the class (I'm not going to give them away) and does a fine job teaching curriculum to the second grade. But he does so much beyond what he gets paid for. He puts all his students' games in a database on his computer. He convenes a special extra early morning class—"chess dojo"—for any students ready to commit the time.

John has also become one of my best friends. I invited him to serve as my best man for the third wedding after my brother embarrassed me too much with his speeches in the first two [three weddings, one wife]. Over the last decade we have formed mixed doubles teams for the U.S. Amateur Team East. We haven't won yet, but it's been a blast.

The school and parents at Columbia (no connection to the University) are strongly committed to the chess program, which makes the job a lot more pleasant. The Grammar School Principal, Dr. Stanley Seidman, was my elementary school principal in P.S. 222! He was there when my mother started her seminal program and later oversaw successful chess programs at Dalton and Hunter before settling in at Columbia. He certainly knows the value of the game as much as any educator.

Kindergarten and first grade also learn chess during the day. There was a time I thought that just wouldn't work. Sophia Rohde has an incredible rapport with children and has developed an impressive repertoire of chess phrases for kids. Whether it be "opening the front doors", attacking the "tickle spot", or moving the knights to the "comfy chairs", the kids remember the point.

Sophia is a terrific boss, by the way. She pays a good wage and doesn't argue when I want to take time off. As detail oriented as she was as a teenager in England, Sophia has developed warmer qualities over the years.

While teaching important lessons, I've learned a few of my own:

1) The kids are very young. Most of my students are in kindergarten, first, and second grade. Though often talented, they are undisciplined and will often not absorb information the first time around.

2) Even the top kids are weaker than I'm accustomed to from private lessons, camps, and youth championships. At their level they need to learn different things.

3) Teaching is so political! What you can accomplish depends so much on the commitment of the school. Parents also play a huge role. Most of them are nice, some of them are incredibly nice, and some of them cause problems. Dealing with them is a big part of the job.

I was hesitant to immerse myself in the scholastic milieu because the competition can become cut-throat. I know that our program always keeps the best interest of the children at heart. The level of instruction is extremely good. Sophia and Michael have the hardest job in running the program. Competition for schools, especially in New York, can be intense and not always above board. Many teachers use their schools as a springboard to recruiting students for lucrative private lessons. I have actually taught very few students from the program privately. Since moving to New Jersey in 2005, I have mainly taught older children at home rather than hustle around Manhattan in the evening. I've had the privilege of working with some of New Jersey's finest youth – Evan Ju and Victor Shen. Unfortunately, school and other activities place a great demand on their time. They don't have so much time for taking lessons and studying. It illustrates to me the difficulties our high schoolers have in competing with juniors internationally.

We run tournaments at Columbia Grammar that offer kids around the city excellent opportunities to hone their skills. Directing them, particularly in the K-2 room, requires an adjustment in thinking. The kids are often so raw that they have trouble recognizing checkmate, or even understanding stalemate. When they think they have a checkmate, they raise their hands and summon a director.

We are supposed to let the players agree on a result, even if it might be the wrong one. Sometimes these scenes can be quite surreal. I remember one Friday afternoon looking around and noticing that these situations were resolved by three grandmasters – Rohde, DeFirmian, and myself!

There are three traits I hope to find in kids. In a school program, you don't expect to see many children possess all three attributes in abundance, but if they excel at one I feel that I've made a difference:

Talent—This is of course, a relative term; some have the talent to be among the best at the grade level, others to be competitive.

Passion—Many kids enjoy playing, but I like to see kids who follow chess events on the ICC and pay attention to current events and chess history. They have an appreciation of chess that extends beyond wins and losses, and are more likely to maintain the hobby when they no longer have a school program to participate in.

Effort—Talented kids are not always fun to coach; I've seen a lot of them who didn't make much effort to learn or work on their weaknesses. On the other hand, I've been very proud of marginally talented kids who hung in there and worked their way up a level or two. Chess is in some ways a microcosm of the challenges kids face in real life, and this latter group has prepared themselves through their chess experiences.

If my kids learn anything from me, it will be good sportsmanship. I constantly harp on being honest about touching a piece, making sure not to say anything about someone else's game, and other issues. Unfortunately, sportsmanship is not always valued by other coaches, as indicated by the following story.

At a Columbia Grammar tournament, a boy and a girl were struggling through a game when the boy, raised his hand. "My opponent isn't moving," he said (there was no clock on the game). "I moved a long time ago," the girl replied. "I castled," she said, and physically pointed to her king and rook. At which point the boy told me: "My teacher says you're not allowed to tell your opponent your move."

Apparently his coach thought this information would be too critical to pass on, and delivered the instruction with the force of a USCF regulation. When kids complain that their opponents are using good sportsmanship, we've gone wrong somewhere.

Twice a year I go on the road to coach Columbia Grammar in National Championships—the Grade Championships in the fall, and the National Elementary in the spring. I endure long weekends of harried plane travel, long working days, and analysis of frustrating games. And I love it. I have no ego tied up in the individual or team results. I don't need for them to win to make myself important or further my career. And I know that coaches have very limited control over what goes on in the giant playing hall anyway. I just want the kids to succeed. The school has just the right level of success that we know we will win trophies but we always have room for improvement.

Chapter Sixteen

Chess in Retirement

Most people in the chess community would consider me an "active" player, but I'm not sure I can justify that designation. In the first half of 2007, I played in only five tournaments. Two of them were memorial tournaments for friends; another, a local rapid event. I played in the U.S. Amateur Team East with my wife and John MacArthur. I went to one overseas event, the Bunratty Masters. While Bunratty is arguably the biggest tournament in Ireland, it has a fast time control and isn't FIDE rated. The social scene at the bar is taken nearly as seriously as the chess games. I played a few grandmasters, but I would hardly suggest I played any "serious" chess this year. I don't have a lot of plans for serious tournaments in the near future.

A few years ago, Yasser Seirawan announced his retirement from competitive chess. The move had the virtue of focusing attention on the totality of Yasser's tremendous accomplishments. [The U.S. Chess Hall of Fame finally enshrined Yasser after his announcement.] Everyone understood what it meant when Yasser, or for that matter, Kasparov retired, but I'm not sure what it would mean for me. I've always played in a variety of tournaments, big and small. I may slow to a crawl, but I'm never going to completely stop playing chess. While I most likely won't be training for serious tournaments, I would never say never. I wouldn't hesitate to play on the American team in the Olympiad again, as unlikely as that opportunity seems.

I find myself in this state of semi-retirement not because of an inability to compete with other grandmasters. I consider only a handful of players in the U.S. to be stronger than me, plus several who are my equals. While I have talked about getting old, at 43 I am still younger (sad to say) than many of my American competitors. But competing on a consistent basis requires things I am no longer prepared to do—constant studying, grueling "two-a-day" open tournaments, and surviving FIDE hellholes.

You can compare me to a baseball player who can still pitch but has no stomach for staying in shape, spring training, and constant traveling. [If you're Roger Clemens the rules are a bit different.] The baseball player collects a fat contract for going through some discomfort. But the grandmaster has no such guarantee. It's difficult to stay motivated in the absence of good playing opportunities. The longer you wait, the harder it is to recover. As you take on other commitments to your time, you become more prepared to move on.

My friends and colleagues are going through a similar process. Christiansen makes much of his living off the ICC. DeFirmian teaches in six schools a week in New York. Fedorowicz trains half of America's youth over the telephone. The Fischer-boom generation has essentially concluded its run. [At least we lasted a decade longer than Soltis predicted.]

For a lot of players, marriage boosts their careers by stabilizing home life and freeing them to concentrate on chess. For me, marriage opened up a whole new set of future challenges and adventures. I would rather spend my weekends with my wife than Mr. Goichberg.

I go to most tournaments with Debbie, and they tend to have a fun/vacation aspect to them—the 2005 Phoenix U.S. Open, the Bunratty Festival (three times), the 2007 Curacao International. I'm not interested in suffering for my craft at dubious locales. There are always nice places to go to and we will explore them in the future.

Professional challenges come in many forms. I'm keeping things fresh by branching out in my chess endeavors. I enjoy entertaining and educating the masses with my column on Chess Life Online, "Ask GM Joel," and my weekly show on ICC, "Game of the Week." I'm proud to join the U.S. Chess League as top gun for the New Jersey Knockouts. Whether it be playing, teaching, writing, or Internet commentary, I know I'll keep busy for a long time..

Chapter Seventeen

How I see it: The Current State of Chess in America

Made in America?

You cannot assess American chess without addressing, as Jennifer Shahade put it to me once, the "800 pound gorilla in the room"—the domination of foreign born players. Just from reading through this book you can see the huge role played by Russian immigrants. The numbers are more lopsided than ever; Hikaru Naka-mura was the only homegrown title competitor in the 2007 U.S. Championship.

America is proud of its reputation as a melting pot. We hesitate to make rules to protect native players, and welcome new imports with open arms. I personally hate to frame the issue as "American born" versus "foreign born". Players like Seirawan and Nakamura were not born here but certainly don't belong in the for-eign category. Players like Dlugy, Ilya Gurevich, and Irina Krush came from Rus-sia but developed in the U.S. I prefer to place value in developing homegrown talent versus importing developed products.

USCF policy has wavered a bit over the years. A key marker is the eligibility requirements for the U.S. Championship and Olympic team. For a while we had a three-year residency requirement that was more in line with international stan-dards (we have never required citizenship, as many countries do). The three-year policy protects not only homegrown players but immigrants who have estab-lished themselves in the American community (e.g. Shabalov, Kaidanov). It gives younger players a better shot for the Olympic team as well.

A one-year policy appeals to two possibly overlapping groups. One feels that players who are strong enough and desire to represent the U.S. should not be dis-criminated against. Another values expedience and just wants the U.S. to have the strongest possible team right now, regardless of what ties they have to our coun-try.

The current one-year requirement went into effect in 2003. When the Executive Board debated the issue, USCF President John McCrary failed to inform his colleagues that several prominent American players had urged him to maintain the three-year rule. Mr. McCrary had his own agenda. He felt that every new player in America creates a net gain for the community. But the math is not so simple.

Chess is in large part a zero-sum game. Every time a new player wins an open tournament or qualifies for the FIDE World Cup, that is one plum that does not go to a player already established in our community. When Tony Miles represented the U.S. in the 1990 Interzonal, that was one opportunity taken from a homegrown 26-year-old player.

When Russian chessplayers first began to arrive on our shores they provided competition necessary to stimulate American talent. But the numbers have gotten so out of whack that any young player would be discouraged from a career as a professional player. My Fischer-boom generation encountered few immigrants in our early years and hung around for thirty years. Young stars of later eras—Wolff, Rachels, Gurevich, Sherzer, and Shaked—moved on to new chapters in their lives. Competition is healthy, but so is the opportunity for success. The market has not grown to support the huge number of grandmasters we have now. [The rest of the world also has a problem with a market overloaded with players.]

In 1989, amid the euphoria of the changes in the Soviet Union, I was asked for my opinion on *glasnost*. I replied that it was "the greatest disaster in the history of American chess." A lot of good people have come over and made their mark in America, and I am happy for them. On the personality level, it's hard to see the objection to most of these additions to the U.S. community. When you look at American tournaments today, you see more strong players and high level chess than ever. But if you are a young, up-and-coming player, you do not see opportunity. It saddens me that it is harder than ever for an American to have the kind of career that I had.

Professional Chess Keeps Losing to Scholastic Chess

1. R.I.P. ACF

I've seen organizations devoted to professional chess flourish for a while but ultimately morph into organizers of school programs. I'll recount some of the checkered history of the American Chess Foundation (ACF), with an emphasis on my personal experience (hey, it's my book). Founded by wealthy members of the Manhattan Chess Club (MCC), the Foundation completely focused on professional matters like the U.S. Championship. [Some say it was created to support

Reshevsky.] It was still an important presence when I came on the scene in the late seventies and eighties.

In my time, the ACF often found itself embroiled in controversy. There was a general perception that the Foundation preferred Soviet émigrés to American born players (we felt ACF President James Sherwin didn't like us). That seemed to manifest in 1984, when the ACF, sponsors of the U.S. Olympic team, decided the team should be chosen by a committee with ACF representation. The selected team managed a solid third place, but the selections were a bit odd. They chose Dzindzichashvili for board one, slighting our clearly strongest player, Seirawan. When Seirawan left the team in protest, they replaced him on board two with Lubosh Kavalek, who wasn't even in the original six (a great gentleman, Kavalek was noticeably a bit past his prime by then). The committee dropped young players rated in the top six, Benjamin and Fedorowicz. They added the veteran Alburt on the strength of his U.S. Championship victory, but kept Browne despite his poor result.

In 1987 the ACF received the duty of administering the Samford Fellowship. Frank P. Samford Jr. created a two-year fellowship worth $60,000 in cash and expense money to be awarded to the top American player under 26. At first the ACF had high hopes for molding a champion with the Samford (there were no twelve-year-old grandmasters from Azerbaijan, China, or India then). ACF Executive Director Allen Kaufman came to Brooklyn to meet with me. Upon request, I provided a list of people I would like to work with, Korchnoi on top. Kaufman told me world renowned trainer Mark Dvoretsky was available for coaching. I knew Dvoretsky had not accomplished much as a player, and I wanted someone who could share with me the experience of being a world-class grandmaster. Right or wrong, I had every right to say no.

Dvoretsky retaliated years later with a libelous interview in the short-lived *American Chess Journal*. He uttered head-scratchers like "Benjamin is not a strong player in the European sense" (I was in my prime racking up wins against Europeans in 1993) and factual errors like "Benjamin did not use the Samford for training" (apparently sessions with Korchnoi, Dorfman, Seirawan, and Christiansen, plus a six-month training camp with Fedorowicz and Wilder fall into some other category). Even worse, the magazine did not publish for a year after that article, and then the editors cut most of my reply. Many players are enthralled with his books, but in my book, Dvoretsky has no class.

Korchnoi, on the other hand, was a joy to work with. No player was more intense in his work ethic, and I gained valuable lessons from a week in Switzerland.

The ACF administered the Samford with a counter-productive bottom line atti-tude. When I tried to carry over $5,000 remaining from the first year, I got a shock-ing refusal. At the National Open, I took a call from Kaufman regarding an ex-pense sheet I submitted for $300 from a tournament in Allentown, Pa. "We have a board member who says he was at that tournament and you weren't there," he told me. "Really?" I replied. "Then why did they give me the first prize when I won all my games?" [The Board member confused the years.]

When my fellowship concluded, I made what I thought were constructive criticisms. For instance, many young people don't have credit cards and laying out large sums for expenses before reimbursement could be quite cumbersome. Why not issue a credit card billed to the ACF? I was never asked to serve on the Samford Committee, so I suppose my suggestions were not well taken. Though I had a bad experience with the ACF, I am grateful to Frank P. Samford Jr. for his generosity and his son Frank Samford III for continuing the legacy.

When the 1990 Interzonal went on without me, I felt a double-whammy from the ACF. I lost a qualifying spot to the ACF import Tony Miles, and watched in amazement when they secured a spot for virtually fresh off the boat Gata Kamsky.

So why do I miss this organization? Despite their strange reluctance to em-brace a player they should have actively promoted, the ACF used to do a lot of good for chess. They had a policy of paying half airfares for Americans traveling to tournaments abroad. They sponsored professional chess, even if strings were occasionally attached. They had an extensive program of sponsored lessons for promising juniors. This policy not only developed young talent (I had my lessons covered for a few years), but gave teachers an opportunity to make money while working with players who could benefit from their wisdom.

Fan Adams became President and unwittingly led the ACF to self-destruction. With a desire to help children and an understanding of the realities of fund-raising, Adams changed the organization to Chess in the Schools. CIS would focus on a program of bringing chess programs to disadvantaged children in New York's inner city.

We did not feel the full impact of the change at first. CIS sponsored an Interna-tional tournament in March 1996 (see Chapter 9) which brought opportunities to professional players. It's true that showing off star attraction Josh Waitzkin to their students meant more to CIS than anything else, but we still got a good tour-nament out of it. And promoting an accomplished junior player is a good thing. *Searching for Bobby Fischer* had arguably made Waitzkin the most famous and marketable player in America. In hindsight, he may not have been the most talented and deserving young player. He didn't garner a single GM norm in any of the many tournaments organized on his behalf in the mid-eighties, but these tournaments nevertheless benefited professional chess. [After his retirement from chess, Waitzkin took up the martial art *tai chi chuan* and achieved even greater success than he did in chess!]

With the tragic death of Fan Adams in 1999, the ideals of the ACF died for good. The ACF had been run by a chess master, Allen Kaufman, but the Director of CIS, Marly Kaplan, was a professional fund-raiser with no interest in chess whatsoever. CIS pursued a consistent agenda of discontinuing any policies unrelated to the core business of inner city chess. They tried unsuccessfully to redirect the Samford funds, despite the specific bequest from Frank P. Samford Jr. They terminated their association with the previously prestigious fellowship, now administered by the U.S. Chess Trust. They also made a play for other ACF bequests like the Cramer Awards and Thomas Emery's Armed Forces.

The demise of the Manhattan Chess Club is a particularly sorry chapter in the CIS story. The club had rented quarters throughout its long history and found paying New York rents increasingly challenging. The ACF and the MCC jointly purchased a four storey building in midtown for about one million dollars. Both boards were well intertwined, including Fan Adams, who engineered the purchase. The MCC struggled to produce revenue to pay its share of the mortgage, and soon found itself dependent on the ACF.

The MCC continued on the benevolence of the ACF for a while, but after Adams died, CIS evicted them. Adams left funds in his will to the MCC, but only after the death of his wife (who was much younger and no chess fan). The MCC rented rooms in the New Yorker Hotel, but could not turn its fortunes around. After operating continuously since 1877, the club ceased operations in 2001. When you consider that the MCC had created the forerunner of the CIS in the first place, CIS is guilty in this case of matricide.

2. The Rise and Fall of AF4C

The metamorphosis of AF4C (America's Foundation for Chess) shares similarities with its near namesake, the ACF. AF4C began as the Seattle Chess Foundation for the purpose of organizing the 2000 U.S. Championship. With a name change to reflect its new national focus, and a ten-year contract to sponsor and run the Championship, AF4C looked to be the force for professional chess we had always dreamt about.

Erik Anderson had his own ideas about the event, but his tinkering with the format never brought about the desired consequences. His first move folded the Women's Championship into the overall event. While the fairer sex offered increased chances for marketability, the field had to be expanded. 32 would have been manageable, but an increase to 56 and later 64 left the Championship bursting at its seams.

The problems caused by a 64-player tournament outweigh the convenience of having all squares signed on commemorative boards. While the large field can produce oddities for promotion (e.g. thirteen-year-old Hana Itkis in 2002), so many players below the usual standard dilute the field. You can't brag about having the best players in the country competing the way you can with a twelve or sixteen player all grandmaster field.

More players also means more egos and potential complainers. While none of the eccentric personalities caused any real messes, the staff had to contend with the possibility. Most importantly, having 64 mouths to feed puts a strain on the prize fund. One or two hundred thousand dollars goes a long way in a short field. With so many prizes to give out, Anderson could not raise them to the levels he had intimated to the players.

As a top player for many years, the changes were a bit depressing. With the new format I had to compete with players who didn't belong, instead of testing my mettle against the elite players. Like others, I held my tongue; as long as Anderson came up with big prizes, I went with the flow.

After three years in Seattle, AF4C moved the Championship to a new "permanent" base in San Diego. The move grew out of a desire to find a free playing site, eliminating the $20,000 price tag for the Seattle Center. It seemed a strange decision; headquartered in Seattle, the AF4C had staff available to handle organization and promotion. Anderson could not come to terms with Yvette Seirawan for a full-time position. Yvette, an experienced chess event planner, pulled up stakes and moved back to her native Netherlands with her famous husband. Yasser announced his retirement from competitive chess and the U.S. Championship had lost two valuable resources.

As part of a significant construction project, the Naval Training Center (NTC) in San Diego erected a building which would house the Championship. It wasn't built yet in November 2004, so we played at the beautiful Hilton Torrey Pines in nearby La Jolla. It turned out to be a much better site than the intended one.

The NTC promised to have the building ready for February 2006. After AF4C scheduled the tournament, they found out NTC's timetable had been optimistic. AF4C had no choice but to push the start into March, which caused a conflict with the Women's World Championship. Irina Krush acrimoniously pulled out of the field, but there was really nothing the AF4C could have done.

The finished building fell far short of expectations. The promised special lighting did not materialize. The building had not been soundproofed, a major liability in an area so close to the San Diego airport. While the hall was sizeable enough, the building had few other rooms and no impressive facilities whatsoever.

NTC personnel handled logistics and publicity, but not very well. AF4C's John Henderson had to do much of the organization, and the NTC did little to attract national media. [They were mostly concerned with promoting the building for other future events.]

Though intended to host for ten years, San Diego proved such a bust that Anderson decided to evacuate. After keeping the U.S. chess community in suspense for months, a proposed tournament began to take shape at the end of 2006. A 32-player tournament would be contested in a knockout format. The first two rounds (at least) would be played over the Internet, with players making their moves in three regional sites. Anderson hoped to bring the final eight together in New York, with Merrill Lynch sponsoring. The final two would play a match, hopefully for big money, in Las Vegas.

Though many of the details were tentative, Anderson guaranteed a prize fund of $100,000, much higher if the expected sponsorship came through. After quietly accepting the changes made by AF4C since 2002, the USCF Executive Board questioned the AF4C plans this time. The USCF delayed making any official announcement through the end of 2006.

Premier players like Alexander Onischuk and Hikaru Nakamura protested the proposed tournament. I thought they were very short-sighted; the format wasn't perfect, but it wasn't any worse than the year before. I wrote a letter of recommendation to the USCF board.

As the new year dawned, the USCF made a surprise announcement that the AF4C would not organize and sponsor the 2007 U.S. Championship. There were several reports that the Merrill Lynch funding fell through when they did a little investigation. Googling Erik Anderson led them to Sam Sloan; the more they read, the more they realized they did not want to be associated with the USCF.

Perhaps Anderson and AF4C will return to the Championship, but it looks like the seven-year, five-tournament association will end without the pot of gold pro players had hoped for. The first prize rose to $25,000—an improvement, but no quantum leap. Below that, the payoffs from an increased prize fund were balanced by so many players in the field. Grandmasters did not benefit nearly as much as women, juniors, and second-tier players.

Meanwhile, the USCF went back to organizing their own Championship. They hastily put together a tournament in Stillwater, Oklahoma, with a generous donation of $50,000 from Frank Berry. Unfortunately, the Federation did not feel equipped to match that largesse. Pledging $15,000 into the prize fund, the USCF claimed they could improve the prize fund with a radical measure. Spots in the field were made available for princely "patron fees", ranging from $3,000 for grandmasters to $50,000 for low rated players.

The USCF announced they would reclaim the first $15,000 raised by patron fees to pay for their contribution. The next $20,000 would be split between the USCF and the prize fund. These financial details don't speak well for the Federation's financial health and their ability to support future Championships. If they do not find a corporate sponsor, the U.S. Championship will go back to darker days. Allowing people to buy their way into the event jeopardizes the Championship's elite status, and might make the tournament less attractive to potential sponsors.

For me, the 2007 U.S. Championship did not seem worth my while. The modest prize fund, starting with a $12,000 first prize and rapidly dropping off, did not promise any profit (factoring in expenses and lost income). I could look past the money if I found the competition more intriguing. A Swiss system event with a number of weaker players seems more like a World Open than a U.S. Championship. I decided to decline my invitation for the first time. All streaks have to come to an end at some point. With teaching and writing occupying most of my time, it might be time for me to move on.

For some time, AF4C had been moving away from professional chess. At the outset, the Executive Director Michelle Anderson (no relation to Erik) worked on several grandmaster projects. AF4C organized two U.S. v. China matches, planned a pro-am event with celebrities which never took place, and flew grandmasters out to retreats to meet with sponsors and donors. The current Executive Director, Rourke O'Brien, is totally focused on scholastic programs. AF4C trains schoolteachers to teach chess, which isn't necessarily a positive development. Teachers who are unsophisticated in chess will be limited, even with training. Chessplayers who support themselves teaching classes may see their jobs disappear. AF4C is in danger of becoming a West Coast version of CIS. Hopefully, Anderson and AF4C will get beyond their frustration with the USCF and help professional chess again in the future. At this point, it is difficult to predict.

Why Has Chess Become a *Little* Kids Game?

The USCF has become dependent on scholastic members. Adult membership is generally around 30,000. Scholastic members account for another 50,000. Despite the enormous popularity of school chess programs, scholastic membership isn't increasing. Tremendous numbers of children join the USCF but most of them don't stay very long. America does a good job of introducing children to chess, but a poor job of nurturing and maintaining their interest.

The USCF can hardly afford to ignore this enormous fickle membership base, but retaining these youngsters is proving elusive. Most American children who learn chess are almost completely unaware of professional chess. Imagine a young basketball enthusiast who has never heard of the New York Knicks or LeBron James or Kobe Bryant. Yet we have loads of kids who are not at all chess fans — they just compete against other kids. When they start losing, or their friends drop out, there is nothing to hold them. The USCF has never made a concerted effort to link scholastic and professional chess. AF4C tried for a while, but now seems focused mainly on schools. The policies of the schools often don't do all they can to promote USCF growth.

The chess community has worked hard to popularize chess by infiltrating the school system. Educators have been convinced by studies indicating students exposed to chess show improvement in scholastic performance. To reap this benefit as early as possible, schools typically provide chess in the curriculum to the youngest students. In Columbia Grammar, one of the finest programs in the country, first and second graders get in-school chess classes. Not surprisingly, two of the three after school classes are composed completely of kids second grade and below.

When kids move into higher grades, they often lose incentive to stick with chess. Schools reinforce the notion of chess as a little kids game. Even at Columbia Grammar, several of the older, experienced tournament players decide that they could spend their time with "cooler" activities. Many elementary schools have no programs for the older kids. The problem only worsens into junior high/middle school and high school — fewer programs, fewer teams, and fewer USCF members.

When I learned chess at eight, it was young for the day. My school chess club was for fourth graders — I was too young for it. Now the standards for this complex game of strategy have been turned on its head. I wouldn't argue that 5-7 year-olds shouldn't learn chess, but they aren't equipped to benefit the most from instruction. The casting aside of older children not only harms the chess community, but deprives children of many of the benefits of chess.

I don't know if any discipline truly makes one "smart", but chess has the potential to teach many valuable skills. These include:

1. concentration
2. patience
3. planning, coordination of ideas
4. logical thought process
5. empathy: seeing a situation from an opponent's view point.
6. sportsmanship
7. ability to deal with ups and downs of competition

In my work with grades K-2, I have seen many kids improve their level of play, but they struggle to show proficiency in the first five categories. Dealing with competition, a vital quality in the real world, can be difficult for young children. Parents and educators often look to make chess less competitive for them. In a game with a winner and a loser, it's hard to take away that element, and self-defeating anyway.

In May 2006, I attended a USCF strategic retreat in Boca Raton, Florida. We discussed the problem of scholastic member attrition at great length without finding a solution. We need to push the schools in the right direction. Let's get more schools to establish chess in the curriculum for older students. Encourage junior highs and high schools to offer chess as a credited elective (like typing or music). Make our kids chess fans by emphasizing the link between scholastic and professional chess. The Federation will grow and chess will expand its market.

Participation is Great, but What about Talent and Excellence?

In 1985 Fan Adams approached Bruce Pandolfini, then working as the manager of the Manhattan Chess Club, and told him of his plans to use his personal fortune to help improve chess in America. Pandolfini steered him towards scholastic chess, with the bold ambition to teach everyone in America how to play chess. Their efforts led to a program that grew into Chess-in-the-Schools, reaching 38,000 students by 1999.

The CIS programs have given many students an improved quality of life. These noble accomplishments compensate for the darker associations mentioned earlier. But there is a sad side to this organization: They don't actually care if the kids *get good* at chess.

It is a natural process that some school programs will produce talent and strive to become winners. In any other sport this process would be universally applauded, but the experience of I.S. 318 shows CIS' unusual approach to winning. According to *The Kings of New York* author, Michael Weinreb, "CIS would like to think of itself as a purely altruistic organization, as a refuge for inner-city children, concerned more with long-term than short-term results." CIS eventually stopped issuing press releases or contacting newspapers or the Board of Education when 318 would win another Championship. [The freshman team won the 2007 K-6 Championship without their coach, Elizabeth Vicary.] Despite much larger participation than any other school, CIS cut the 318 budget. Weinreb felt CIS president Marley Kaplan seemed embarrassed by 318's domination. "Some teams become dynasties," she told him. "But eventually that dynasty is going to die. We don't want dynasties. It's not really what we are looking for. Our program isn't really about what chess can do for the kids. We aren't trying to create champions."

CIS antipathy towards winning has apparently been extended towards individual champions. A few years ago, CIS sent one of their star students, Medina Parilla, to the World Youth Championships. CIS not only paid for Medina and her mother to travel, but also provided her with two coaches. In 2006, CIS cut her loose and she could not afford to go.

Chess seems to make for good social engineering, but talent has to matter, too. Right now, middle class kids often fall between the cracks. Private schools can afford great programs, whether funded by the school or affluent parents or both. Poorer schools can qualify for funding as in CIS. But if you are middle class and go to an ordinary school you are under pressure to keep up. While my scholastic career turned a profit, parents now have to shell out big bucks to win one of those giant trophies.

In 2004 Tom Braunlich wrote "Scholastics and the Soul of Chess", a paper deeply critical of the scholastic chess community in America. While many of his assertions are overstated, he made a lot of good points. Braunlich distinguished between "scholastic chess", which is driven by educators recruiting kids for their school programs, and "junior chess", unaffiliated young adults who came to chess on their own who possess long-term ambitions in chess. The two are less distinct than he asserts. A lot of schools have experienced chess coaches who enlighten students about the chess world beyond scholastics. A lot of kids come out of school programs to be star juniors, like Marc Arnold of Columbia Grammar.

Scholastic chess has boomed in America for many years now, but junior chess is not faring as well. I'm part of a generation that put their stamp on U.S. Championships and Olympic teams for decades. In the twenty-one years since my grand-master title, we've seen a slow trickle of homegrown players make it to that level. There is no question that it is harder for Americans to be successful as professional players today than in the 80's and 90's. While databases and the Internet enable players to progress faster, the market is too crowded with grandmasters both in the U.S. and abroad. To have any opportunity or inclination to "be all they can be" American juniors are going to need all the help they can get.

We have to be smarter with the allocation of funds. The shabby treatment of the U.S. Junior Championship is a pet peeve of mine. The 2007 U.S. Junior saw an impressive win for 14-year-old Marc Arnold and second place for 12-year-old Ray Robson. Despite their youth, they were actually the favorites! The field lacked most of the highest rated American juniors, including defending champion Robert Hess, Hikaru Nakamura, Lev Milman, Sal Bercys, and Alex Lenderman. It's true that the great prize of winning the Junior, entry to the World Junior Champion-ship, has lost most of its appeal (most teenagers now prefer to go to the World Youth Championships and hang out with their friends). But the USCF does noth-ing to increase the incentive of participating. Participants got low-end accommo-dations, had to pay travel expenses, and played without a prize fund. Moreover, the June dates conflicted with finals for some of the players who were still in school at the time.

The best juniors in the country should not dip into their pockets to play in the national championship—they should be receiving prize money! I know, some of you will say they are just kids and not "professionals". But they are potentially the future leaders of American chess. Their ability to earn prizes may be crucial to their continued commitment to chess. In contrast, the field of the U.S. Women's Championship played for a $7,000 first prize. Outside of Irina Krush and Anna Zatonskih, no one in that field could be considered a strong player independent of gender. A full strength U.S. Junior would present a much stronger field. If the goal is to promote women's chess, a financially self-sufficient open championship (with conditions given to a few elite players) would do a better job.

The women have benefited from exceptionally generous treatment from AF4C, which established a precedent for a big money Women's Championship. But there really isn't any logic to it. Frank Berry, the sponsor of the 2007 tournament, could have donated his money to a more worthy cause, the U.S. Junior Championship.

While women's chess has a committee in the USCF and a powerful spokesper-son in Susan Polgar, no one speaks for the juniors. We have a scholastic committee which does fight for World Youth funding but has not otherwise supported our juniors much (hopefully that will change).

Chess-in-the-Schools and AF4C have helped introduce philanthropists and corporations to chess. I hope that in the future more sponsorship will be talent based. AF4C will hopefully do a lot in this area. Sponsored lessons, funds for travel, and training camps will help our young players and keep our current pros involved in the community. There are positive developments. The Kasparov Chess Foundation has brought American juniors together with the best chessplayer in the world. The U.S. Chess School has provided several training camps taught by Greg Kaidanov. Jim Roberts, a major player in AF4C, provided sponsorship (I pitched the idea of junior training camps to Roberts six years ago, but kudos to Greg Shahade for making it happen). As we go to press, it appears that I will participate in this program in 2008.

Chess has to be seen as something more than an educational tool. Whether you appreciate it as sport, science, or art, it has intrinsic value. While the money may be easier to find for introducing children to chess, we still have to look for funding for professional chess. It's the right thing to do.

Future Chess Promotion

How do we position chess to expand funding and participation? For one approach we have to acknowledge the value of chess as an art, one of the ultimate exercises of the intellect. Chess can appeal to private patrons and corporate sponsors who wish to support culture. [Mig Greengard has been making this point on his "Daily Dirt" website.] Of course, this approach will require improved contacts with business and philanthropists, as well as putting forward a positive image.

The sporting model offers another approach. Chess seems unlikely to generate mass appeal as a spectator sport, but there is some potential. A match between Kasparov and X3D Fritz ran on ESPN and produced promising ratings.

Chessplayers are especially interested in the recent poker explosion. It seems that every day we hear about how hundreds of poker players earn more than the very best chessplayers. Indeed, chessplayers are increasingly tapping poker as a major income source. It has been suggested that Grischuk and Bacrot, two FIDE Candidates, were spending as much time on poker as on chess. Several chess teachers in the New York area quit their jobs to win big prizes on the poker circuit. The big news out of the Las Vegas National Open this year was Walter Browne, who didn't play a single round. He had to skip the event because he made almost $200,000 from nearby poker tournaments.

Chess does not have the telegenic appeal of poker. It is too slow and requires far more specialized knowledge to follow. But if chess could have a fraction of the television success of poker, that would still be a lot more revenue than we are used to. Standard chess tournaments would not work as well as made-for-television events. Celebrities and poker has already proven a profitable mix. Many celebrities are known to have a fascination with chess, too. Getting them involved in public events can potentially open up new markets for chess. AF4C once had plans for celebrity events; Don Schultz is currently working on such a project.

Death to Draws!?

Periodically people complain about draws and propose artificial point-scoring systems to try to eliminate them. There is nothing wrong with a game resulting in a draw. A lot of excellent games end in draws. Draws are part of our established endgame theory, and there is no reason to throw out years of accumulated knowledge in that regard.

The reasonable objection is to draws without fights, whether they be pre-arranged or not. [I have always felt that the objection towards pre-arranged draws is misplaced. A draw is a naturally agreed upon result; it is not immoral if done before the game, and should not even be illegal.] "Grandmaster draws" have a long history and made sense in the context of old tournaments. But in the Internet age few tournament games take place without an audience. A draw without a fight always disappoints the crowd. Such draws have no place in the movement to grow chess as a spectator sport with healthy sponsorship.

After the 2003 U.S. Championship, organizers began to take steps to prevent short draws from harming their tournaments. Generation Chess organized an international round-robin with a fifty move minimum before draws could be agreed on. The U.S. Championship instituted a thirty move minimum, and the notorious "Sofia rules" ban draw offers altogether, unless approved late in games by a tournament official.

There is nothing wrong with such regulations. Some fans speculate about players circumventing the rules, but I don't think players will try to do so very often. The very employment of such rules show the players that the organizers are serious about the issue. Chessplayers like to be invited back to nice tournaments.

I think move minimums will work very well and eliminate the need for more drastic measures like adjusted scoring systems. The so-called BAP system developed by Clint Ballard favors scoring with Black; most players would probably want an extra Black under that system. It can lead to apparently unjust results, like a lower-rated player getting no points for drawing with a grandmaster. No points for a White draw may convince players to throw in the towel when they would ordinarily struggle for a draw, a factor that can distort results.

But fans shouldn't expect short draws to completely disappear from play. Move minimums work because the players are receiving conditions to play and are obligated to give something back. In America, players participate in most tournaments on their own dime. If a grandmaster pays for his own hotel, food, and travel in hopes of winning prize money, he should be allowed to pursue that prize however he sees fit (as long as it's legal). Fans may not like to see two players draw in the World Open, but they are not disappointing any sponsors or paying customers.

The Class System

Michael Aigner had the tournament of his life at the 2006 U.S. Open, tying for second with a host of grandmasters. Yet he wasn't interested in the $800 share of second place because his class prize (under 2400) netted him considerably more money. In fact, several other class prize winners took home more money than every grandmaster except the first prize winner, Yury Shulman.

In my first two World Opens, I played in the Booster section (under 1800). Tournaments then had only two or three sections, with limited prize money in all of them (though it has to be said, prizes were much lower than in open sections as well).

Today the biggest tournaments have sections for every rating class. The prize money available to club level players is staggering. While open sections offer larger prizes, ties at the top are quite frequent. In practice, the biggest money winners tend to come from class sections. There are probably dozens of amateurs in America who have made more money in a single tournament than I have in any single event. That just seems wrong on a fundamental level.

The class system developed out of the practices of America's biggest entrepreneur, Bill Goichberg. Over the course of forty years, outside sponsorship has played little role in Goichberg's events. He funds his prizes entirely from entry fees; by offering large prizes to lower-rated players, Goichberg was able to draw record-setting numbers of entrants. Chessplayers by nature are somewhat compulsive. The introduction of the controversial re-entry option fed off players' gambling instincts. Players could pay more money to start over with a clean slate or half point byes to replace their losses.

To be fair, all those entry fees enable Goichberg to offer large prizes to the professionals as well. I don't think anyone is making a living purely by playing in open tournaments, but these events offer significantly more than anything else here. He can't be blamed for hitting on a successful formula. If other organizers choose to imitate rather than innovate, that isn't his fault.

Yet it seems the Goichberg model of high entry fee, high class prizes has become so entrenched that you have to wonder if alternatives can develop. Are we locked into the class system, and can it survive?

Tournament play is the biggest perk of USCF membership. With the growing popularity of Internet play, tournaments have to meet a higher standard than ever.

Though highly under reported, cheating has always plagued big open tournaments. The concentration of prizes at the top encourages arranged results ("dumps"). In the lower sections, players would occasionally get advice from stronger confederates on the premises.

Casual players who would rather play smaller entry fees for less prize money are already concerned they may not be on a level playing field. Incidents at the 2006 World Open showed that technological cheating has arrived. With today's technology—cell phones, powerful miniature chessplaying programs, sophisticated transmitters and receivers—cheating may become an epidemic.

Widespread discussion of the threat will surely lead to various security measures at tournaments. Honest players will feel they are treated like criminals, mirroring the frustration many people feel with air travel today. Even if cheating is curtailed, the atmosphere may drive players away.

American tournaments will not dramatically change overnight but there are a few things that organizers can consider for the future:

1. Trim Excesses

The rules of Kilkenny, one of the top Irish tournaments, stipulate that prizes will be altered if a class prize becomes greater than the top prizes. Perhaps we can work towards the same sensibility with American prizes, so that the top scores in the top section give out the most money.

2. Redistribute Prizes

Bolster the middle prizes in open sections so that the second group of players (those not tied for first) have a decent payday. Step down the prizes gradually in the class sections so more people have a chance for a good prize. Players will have less incentive to cheat if the prize differential is not as great.

3. Experiment with New Formats

Swiss system tournaments could be held in one section with lower-rated players receiving handicaps from higher-rated players (Goichberg used to use time handicaps nearly thirty years ago with 30 minute tournaments; material handicaps could be used as well). By leveling the playing field, class prizes would become completely unnecessary.

4. Replace Prizes with Perks

The 2005 HB Global Foundation Open in Minneapolis proved a one-shot deal, but it did provide innovative ideas, like opportunities for lessons with the grandmaster participants. Services could be substituted for big prizes to class players.

5. Better Sites

The site of the 2006 U.S. Open in Oak Park, Illinois, offered easy access to a nearby shopping mall and little else. Even with one game per day, I question how many players made it into Chicago. Cherry Hill, New Jersey, is an even more boring U.S. Open site. It's true that it isn't easy to find vacation spots (like the 2005 U.S. Open's Biltmore Hotel in Phoenix) at reasonable costs, but let's try (and not just at casinos). One hopeful sign: The Chicago Open will move from Oak Park to a Westin hotel in Chicago in 2008.

Transforming tournaments from gambling expeditions to vacations will require fundamental changes. We need lower entry fees and greater sponsorship. Let's strive to go in that direction.

The USCF: Handicapped By its Own Structure

Like most professional players, I've had a love-hate relationship with the USCF. I've taken a fair share of prize money and writing fees from them over the years, but I've often been frustrated by their poor decisions and dubious policies. As the largest American chess body, I would like them to do well, but sometimes they make it difficult to believe in them.

The USCF is a contradiction; a multi-million dollar organization run like a club. Its major decisions are made by the Executive Board (formerly Policy Board), an elected group drawn from the USCF membership. Pretty much anyone can run if they can get a small number of signatures on a nominating petition. In the past a few hundred "voting members" selected from state associations elected the Board. Candidates focused more on strategic phone calls than cogent policies. The vote was given to all adult members a few years ago, to no discernible improvement. Few members vote and the ones that do are uninformed or misinformed by attacks and innuendo posted on the Internet.

Charges of conflict of interest are frequently lobbed at candidates (most often Goichberg), but few of these organizers, directors, and politicians could be expected to be disinterested in all the issues they deal with.

Sovereignty rests in state delegates who are elected by members within each state. [In the past they were often simply appointed by state officials.] The delegates convene at the annual congress during the U.S. Open and vote on a variety of policy issues. In practice, several non-elected persons replace delegates who don't travel to the meeting. The delegates are as fractured as any group as you can imagine, divided along lines of regions and special interests.

Day to day operations are handled by the full-time employees of the USCF office. From executive director on down, turnover is high, with frequent loss of corporate memory. Job security is lousy, with the Executive Board micro-managing operations with increasing frequency.

For as long as I can remember, USCF affairs have been dominated by a group of hardcore organizers, directors, directors, and regional power brokers. They revel in the "democracy" afforded by the USCF structure, but essentially take turns wresting power from each other.

Periodically, true believers will say, "if we just get the right guys elected, we can turn things around." It never works. The "right guys" do not always show wisdom in office, and the "wrong guys" do whatever they can to regain power, even if it means sabotaging the organization.

The mudslinging and scandals are more destructive than ever. The Internet assures that the Federation's dirty laundry can no longer be kept in house. The USCF will repel corporate sponsors until it runs a clean shop.

The USCF may continue to exist as it is, but it will never thrive without a proper business structure. It needs a strong, capable office that can do more than carry out directives. It needs a Board of Directors drawn from professional, well-connected businessmen. The delegates have to decide if they want to maintain their power or if they want to get the right people running the Federation. Otherwise the USCF will continue to struggle, while other organizations may try to fill the void.

* * * * *

On the whole my outlook for chess may seem pessimistic. It can be hard to stay positive after seeing so many missed opportunities and divisive politics over the years. But I would love to see future generations of chessplayers thrive and prosper. I'll be watching.

Index of Opponents

(Numbers in bold indicate that I had White.)

Other games

(Numbers in bold indicate that the player had White.)